REBEL WOMEN
Feminism, Modernism and the Edwardian Novel

Jane Eldridge Miller

The University of Chicago Press

To Mac and Emma

The University of Chicago Press, Chicago 60637
Copyright © Jane Eldridge Miller 1994
All rights reserved. Originally published in England by
VIRAGO PRESS Limited.
University of Chicago Press Edition 1997
Printed in the United States of America
03 02 01 00 99 98 97   6 5 4 3 2 1

Library of Congress Cataloging-in-Publication Data

Miller, Jane Eldridge, 1954–
   Rebel women : feminism, modernism, and the
Edwardian novel / Jane Eldridge Miller.
       p.   cm.
   Includes bibliographical references (p.) and index.
   ISBN 0-226-52677-1 (alk. paper)
   1. English fiction—20th century—History and criticism.
2. Feminism and literature—Great Britain—History—
20th century.   3. Women and literature—Great
Britain—History—20th century.   4. English fiction—
Women authors—History and criticism.   5. Great
Britain—History—Edward VII, 1901–1910.
6. Modernism (Literature)—Great Britain.   7. Sex role
in literature.   8. Realism in literature.   I. Title.
PR888.F45M55   1997
823'.91209352042—dc20   96-38641
                                                  CIP

⊚ The paper used in this publication meets the minimum
requirements of the American National Standard for
Information Sciences—Permanence of Paper for Printed
Library Materials, ANSI Z39.48—1984.

CONTENTS

Acknowledgements

I have been helped by many people while writing this book, and I would like to express my gratitude here: to Samuel Hynes, who provided careful guidance and wise criticism as this book was taking shape, and who encouraged me to be an historian as well as a literary scholar; to Elaine Showalter, whose pioneering work on women and fiction made my own work possible, and whose interest, advice and enthusiasm have been invaluable; to Kitty Bancroft, a true friend and a good writer, who read the manuscript with astonishing sympathy and perception, and whose many suggestions have enriched this book; to Robert Warde, who was my first mentor, and whose love of literature continues to inspire me; to Allan Hepburn and Natania Rosenfeld, who contributed an abundance of information as well as friendly encouragement; to U.C. Knoepflmacher and A. Walton Litz, whose wonderful seminars on the Victorians and the modernists (respectively) set me thinking about the space in between; to Maria DiBattista, Jay Dickson, and Richard Kaye, who shared insights from their own work on modernism; and to my editor, Lynn Knight, who has been unfailingly gracious and supportive, especially during the long hard winter of '94. My research was greatly facilitated by the staffs of Interlibrary Loan and the Department of Rare Books and Special Collections, Firestone Library, Princeton University. Finally, I would like to thank my family and friends for their forbearance and support during the years it took to complete this book. In particular, I want to express my deep gratitude to my husband Mac and my daughter Emma. They have sustained me with humor and patience and love, and it is to them that I dedicate this work.

Introduction

That women should refuse to be any longer servants to men, before God, or in the eyes of Nature; that they should affirm their energies must be devoted first of all to the development of their own personalities and the advancement of their personal aims; that they should, taking into account only their own need for a new freedom of self-expression, not only not regard society, but should set deliberately about the task of changing it to lessen friction upon and opposition to their new demands – all this tends toward the actual creating of 'something new in the world' that cannot be left unrecognized and that is to be analysed indifferently, very badly, and now and then excellently well for years to come.

(EDNA KENTON, 'A Study of the Old "New Women"' [1913])

Many different narratives have been constructed to chart the development of the British novel from 1890 to 1914, but Edwardian novels about women and feminism have been left out of almost all of them.[1] Studies of fiction at the turn of the century focus on the 1890s rather than the years immediately following the 'turn', and usually assume that women ceased to be a dominant force in fiction after the decline of the New Woman novel.[2] Accounts of the genesis of modernism also exclude Edwardian novels about women and feminism, in part because they give the Edwardian age itself little credence as a significant literary period; it is usually annexed as part of the late-Victorian age, or dismissed as a kind of literary drought which preceded the flowering of modernism. Those

1

studies which do consider the Edwardian age as a distinct period in literary history have tended to pay little attention to women, feminism, and the suffrage movement as concerns of or influences upon the fiction of the age; they have also almost completely disregarded the existence of female Edwardian novelists.[3]

My purpose in this study is a dual one: to introduce Edwardian novels about women and feminism into the literary history of the period from 1890 to 1914 and, in so doing, to make a claim for the importance of feminism in the development of the modern novel. The new narrative I construct is not intended to be an exclusionary one but, rather, one which works to enrich and complicate and broaden our understanding of what modernist fiction is, and how it came to be. As recent feminist analyses have emphasized, no single definition of modernism can encompass the variety of modernism's concerns and expressions; those who attempt to create a monolithic modernism inevitably do so at the expense of women, by privileging male writers, male experience, and aesthetic criteria based upon the dominant attributes of male modernist writing.[4] This tendency is exemplified by the fact that while developments in political theory, psychology, biology, physics and philosophy have been frequently discussed as important factors in the development of modernism, feminism has been largely ignored. It is my intention to redress this imbalance as I examine Edwardian fiction about women and feminism, and explore the intimate link that exists between feminist challenges to traditional social organization and the artistic challenges to formal conventions which characterize literary modernism.

I have selected the novels for this study based upon the degree to which they are informed by and comment upon the concerns of modern women and contemporary feminist issues. Some of these novels do call for particular social or legal changes, but it was not one of my criteria that a novel have an explicit political agenda. Instead, I have chosen novels, written by both women and men, which attempt to depict modern women and their struggle for equality with honesty and sympathy and, in so doing, make purposeful breaks with nineteenth-century novelistic conventions regarding female characters and female narratives. These novels are not necessarily 'feminist' novels; rather, they are novels *about* feminism, and about the ways feminism was changing British society and the lives of individual women and men.

I begin my study in the early 1890s, when a demand for greater realism in fiction resulted not in the anticipated development of an elite and serious masculine literature, but in an unprecedented and immensely popular outpouring of sexually frank fiction about (and often written by) women. Although I consider briefly New Woman novels by Mona Caird and Sarah Grand, new realism by George Moore, George Gissing and Thomas Hardy, and the short stories of George Egerton, my particular emphasis in Chapter 1 is on the numerous and vehement critical denunciations of this new fiction. Conservative critics warned repeatedly that British fiction was being 'feminized', and pointed to the publication of Hardy's *Jude the Obscure* in 1895 as a confirmation of their worst fears. But even though their literary criticism was based on their conservative and reactionary responses to social changes, these critics saw clearly – where twentieth-century critics have not – the dominant place of women and feminist issues in British fiction, and the important connection between changes in women's lives and changes in the novel. By the early twentieth century, it was obvious that both had changed irretrievably.

There was a brief reactionary period in the late 1890s in which realism was replaced by idealism, and feminist topics were consciously avoided. But the woman-centered fiction of the early 1890s had opened up new areas for fictional exploration which could not be closed, and women and feminism began to dominate fiction once again during the Edwardian years. The changing status of women in British society at the time constituted nothing less than a social revolution, and it served as a major energizing and complicating force in Edwardian fiction. Expanded opportunities for higher education and employment not only led to a greater number of women living independent lives, but also contributed to critical scrutiny of the institution of marriage, renewed efforts to improve women's legal and political status, and reevaluations of traditional gender definitions. All these issues fell under the rubric of 'the Woman Question', and its predominance in the public mind is evident not only in the novels of the period, but in plays, non-fiction works, magazines, journals and newspapers as well.

At the time, it was generally accepted that women and feminism were making a significant impact on the course of British fiction. In discussing 'the future of the novel' in 1900, Henry James declared that 'nothing is more salient in English life today, to fresh eyes, than the revolution taking place in the position and outlook of women'.[5] Numerous critical essays discussed how Edwardian fiction was suffused with what one critic called 'the prevailing spirit of feminine unrest'.[6] The most obvious indication of the influence of feminism upon fiction during the Edwardian years is the large number of novels by women and men which place modern women and their particular concerns at the center of their narratives. The increasing acceptance of sexual candor in fiction, the Edwardian vogue for social problems novels, and what H.G. Wells called 'that extra-ordinary discontent of women with a woman's lot' all made the modern woman an irresistible subject for Edwardian novelists.[7] Following in the mode of the new realists of the 1890s, Edwardian novelists were eager to discard what Wells termed 'the sawdust doll' – the conventional heroine who, although presented in a variety of guises, basically served as an

3

embodiment of British society's stereotypes of femininity, and tended to be insipid and unrealistic – and write about modern women realistically, with psychological complexity and sexual frankness.

One of the most popular heroines in Edwardian fiction is the rebellious woman, and one of her main functions is to blatantly contradict conventional ideas about femininity and female behavior. But interestingly, there is no single type of woman who is the rebellious woman, which indicates how widely feminist ideas had spread into British society. In Edwardian novels, rebellion is not the exclusive purview of unmarried, middle-class, young New Women, but is something longed for and sometimes accomplished by middle-aged wives, elderly spinsters, mothers, adolescent girls and, in a few novels, working women. Some want independence, some want a career, some want to redefine marriage, and some want the vote. But what all these various rebel women have in common is a dissatisfaction with the circumstances of their lives, and a recognition that those circumstances are dictated in large part by the fact of their being women.

Having created new characters, Edwardian novelists were then confronted with the formidable problem of constructing new narratives for them to occupy. The principal difficulty they faced was the centrality of marriage to the novel, both as a subject and as a structuring principle; tradition dictated that the dominant narrative desire of female characters be romance, and that the achievement of marriage signify their ultimate fulfillment. Edwardian novelists created modern heroines who refused to accept marriage and motherhood as their only destiny, and defied gender definitions in their 'unfeminine' desires for independence and sexual fulfillment and vocation. But they had to place these women within a form which was grounded – not only thematically but structurally – in the 'naturalness' of gender opposition and the inviolability of the institution of marriage, a form in which a heroine's worth was determined by her attractiveness as a romantic object, a form in which female quest narratives were traditionally transformed into narratives of romance, or resulted in failure or death. The rebellious women in Edwardian novels fight against the binary oppositions that reinforce gender polarization and limit women's choices – oppositions between marriage and vocation, private and public, feminine and masculine; yet traditionally, the novel form relied upon those oppositions in its construction of narrative desire, conflict and closure. Edwardian novelists writing about feminists found that the principal forms of nineteenth-century British fiction were, at the most basic level of narrative dynamics, inimical to the representation of feminist rebellion, for they inevitably moved toward or endorsed stasis, the status quo, and social integration through marriage, and thus ran contrary to the heroine's desire for independence, rebellion and social change.

4

But it was not simply novelistic conventions which limited the narrative possibilities for female characters; those narrative limitations were reenactments of social expectations and limitations. Edwardian novels about women illustrate the interrelations between formal conventions and social conventions in particularly illuminating ways; they demonstrate how a society's values, beliefs and institutions are constructed, expressed and perpetuated in fiction – not only through characterizations, themes, and explicit authorial statements, but also through novelistic conventions and narrative structures. As Rachel Blau DuPlessis states in *Writing Beyond the Ending*, 'any literary convention – plots, narrative sequences, characters in bit parts – as an instrument that claims to depict experience, also interprets it. No convention is neutral, purely mimetic, or purely aesthetic.'[8] I am indebted to DuPlessis's study, and to Joseph Allen Boone's related work in *Tradition Counter Tradition*, for they prompted me to scrutinize the ideological implications of the narrative structures, particularly the endings, of Edwardian novels about women.[9] Both DuPlessis and Boone cite as a basis for their analysis Louis Althusser's theories of ideology, which are especially useful for understanding how narrative, like ideology, privileges unity, coherence and resolution, while eliding or disguising contradictions. But my interest in ideology is generic rather than Marxist. What I want to emphasize is simply that form makes meaning, and that challenges to social and political forms cannot be expressed within traditional narrative forms without some degree of disruption, subversion or contradiction. My focus in this study is on what happens to the form of the novel in the Edwardian age, when novelists begin to express and depict feminist rebellion against nineteenth-century ideals of gender and marriage.

Jefferson Hunter characterizes 'the two most salient facts about Edwardian fiction' as 'thematic adventurousness and formal conservatism', and in general, this is an accurate assessment.[10] In the case of fiction about women and feminism, however, feminist characters and themes served to exert significant pressure upon the novel form, and novelists who wrote about rebellious women were forced to confront and respond to the implications of the formal conventions they had at their disposal. As a result, rebellion is not only thematized but often formalized, as the novelists themselves struggle with the constraints of tradition. Edwardian novels about women and feminism exhibit a marked self-consciousness about their form. There are obvious manipulations of traditional plots and purposeful disappointments of readerly expectations; conventions and stereotypes are exposed and ironized; the discrepancies between traditional narratives and the actual lives of modern women are frequently commented upon, by characters as well as narrators. Not only do these novels place marriage early in the novel so as to subvert its association with closure; they also tend to employ indeterminate endings or circular narrative patterns so that the social criticism they have articulated will not be diminished through satisfying resolutions. In some instances it is the content which yields to formal pressures, resulting in narrative contradictions, ambiguities and instabilities. But all the novels about women and feminism that I examine in this study reveal what Frank Kermode has discussed as 'the pressure of the times' upon fiction, 'a genuine though obscure relation between techniques and the times, the condition of fiction and the Condition of England'.[11]

In Chapters 2 through 5 I consider the representations of modern women and feminist issues in different Edwardian novel genres, and examine the ways in which these representations forced Edwardian novelists to confront the ideologies of the narrative structures they had inherited, and to challenge the formal traditions of the novel. Chapter 2 discusses the popular genre of the marriage problem novel, considering novels by E.M. Forster, Ada Leverson, John Galsworthy, Arnold Bennett and Elizabeth von Arnim, and looks at the difficulties these authors encountered in their attempts to scrutinize and criticize the institution of marriage within a form predicated in large part upon that institution and its assumptions about gender roles. Novels in which the narrative dominance of courtship and marriage is explicitly resisted are discussed in Chapter 3. Forster, D.H. Lawrence, Violet Hunt, F.M. Mayor, and others wrote novels about spinsters, unwed mothers, and independent-minded young women which enact, both thematically and formally, women's struggle to create a life apart from romantic love and marriage. Chapter 4 considers fiction inspired by the women's suffrage campaign, in which personal desire is supplanted by political yearnings, and the domestic sphere gives way to a public arena. The peculiar demands of documentary realism and polemical fiction – the two genres most often adopted by proponents of the movement – are examined in works by Elizabeth Robins, Evelyn Sharp and Gertrude Colmore, among others. Chapter 5 focuses on H.G. Wells and May Sinclair, and their Edwardian novels about women, marriage and feminism. Nowhere in Edwardian fiction are the pressures which modern content and feminist ideology exerted on traditional fictional forms, and the concomitant restrictions imposed on fictional content by formal conventions, more evident than in their work.

In all my chapters, but perhaps most obviously in Chapter 5, I argue that the innovations I trace should be seen as part of the development of literary modernism. I realize that the struggle against traditional forms and conventions in Edwardian novels about women and feminism is obviously different from the formal experiments of the modernists; the mode of representation employed in most of these novels is basically that of nineteenth-century realism, and they pay little attention to the issues of language, perception, and narrative point of view that would be so important to modernist fiction. Edwardian novelists derived momentum from the content of their fiction, not from any desire to alter its form. They clearly wanted to be perceived as *modern* writers, yet as participants in an extremely competitive literary market, they did not consciously choose to be *experimental* writers. It was their need to write about women in new ways, and to challenge ideas about gender and marriage, that forced them to attend to and subsequently reshape narrative form. But as a result, many Edwardian novels about women and feminism mark a significant movement away from the traditions of the nineteenth-century novel; thus I argue that these works of fiction should be considered examples of the modernism of content, an antecedent stage to the more familiar, canonized modernism of form.

In categorizing Edwardian novels about women and feminism as such, I do not mean to indicate that their modernity is located solely in their content. Although there have been recent attempts to reject the criteria of formal experimentation, that is not my intention here.[12] By modernism of content I mean that because of the exigencies of their content, many of these novels were forced to be formally innovative. They exemplify, in important and usually overlooked ways, the *process* by which modernist fiction evolved. I contend that only *after* traditional forms and conventions have been revealed to be inadequate can formal innovation and experimentation occur. It was during that stage of experimentation that the fiction which has been canonized as modernist was produced – fiction in which considerations of form are equal to, if not emphasized over, considerations of content, fiction which I have termed the modernism of form. But I am primarily interested in the process which leads to experimentation, for it not only reveals how non-traditional content exerted pressure on traditional forms and conventions, but also demonstrates how feminism functioned as a significant source of pressure in the development of modernism.[13]

In general, modernism constitutes a break with tradition; it involves the questioning of the most basic certainties which provide the foundation for social organization, morality, and concepts of self, among other things. This is unquestionably what Edwardian novels about women and feminism were doing. To write about women with sexual frankness and psychological realism instead of sentiment and prudery, to challenge ideals of femininity and maternity, to depict women as active participants in the public sphere, to write about women's desires for power and autonomy, entailed a radical break with social and cultural traditions. In *Adultery and the Novel*, Tony Tanner contends that marriage is 'the structure that maintains the Structure, or System', and that 'in confronting the problems of marriage and adultery, the bourgeois novel finally has to confront not only the provisionality of social laws and rules and structures but the provisionality of its own procedures and assumptions'.[14] While I agree with this contention, I want to use it to make a different but related claim: that in revealing the constructed nature of society's essential concepts of gender, the feminist novel also reveals not only the provisionality of its own procedures and assumptions but also the provisionality of social organization, the family and, ultimately, essential concepts of identity and self. It seems illogical to dismiss the radical social critique expressed by the novels in this study simply because they lack the kind of explicit formal experimentation privileged by critics and theorists as the primary indication of modernism. A tremendously important shift in consciousness was initiated by feminism at the turn of the century, but it has yet to be accorded the degree of significance it deserves, by either social historians or literary critics.

In her essay 'Mr. Bennett and Mrs. Brown', Virginia Woolf wrote about the transition from the modernism of content to the modernism of form, but she described it in terms of a shift from the Edwardians to the Georgians. Edwardian novelists, she explained, relied upon established tools and conventions to write their novels, but for Georgians such as herself, 'those conventions are ruin, those tools are death'.[15] She argued that Lawrence and Forster spoiled their early work because 'instead of throwing away those tools, they tried to use them. They tried to compromise.'[16] Her intuitions about the transition from Edwardian fiction to modernist fiction were right, but she erred in trying to make a clear-cut division between them. The movement from complete trust in tools and conventions to an attempt to modify them to what Woolf calls 'the smashing and the crashing' of those tools and conventions was a gradual process, one in which not only Forster and Lawrence, but Woolf herself and James Joyce and many other writers participated, though not at the same time (and surely not 'on or about December, 1910') and not at the same pace.

Edwardian novels about women and feminism – into which category fall those 'spoilt' early novels of Forster and Lawrence – are valuable illustrations of the first stage of modernism, of the compromises and adjustments and maneuverings necessitated by the modernism of content. These novels are neither weak Victorian novels nor failed modernist ones, but unique expressions of a particular moment in history that need to be understood on their own terms. Their authors thought of themselves as modern, and they strove to write fiction that was new; in their basic intentions they were not so different from the modernists, despite Woolf's dismissal of them. These novels remind us that modernism, contrary to one of its key myths, did not suddenly burst forth but was part of a line of development that had its roots in the convergence of feminism and realism in the new fiction of the 1890s. If we are to better understand the achievement of the modernists, we need to see them in relation to other novelists who were trying to 'make it new', who were struggling against the limitations of novelistic conventions. Forster, Lawrence, Joyce, Woolf and Dorothy Richardson all wrote their first novels during the period from 1901 to 1914: their novels, like those of their fellow Edwardians, were shaped by the profound social changes that feminism was effecting; their novels, like those of Bennett, Galsworthy, Sinclair and Wells, strain against the limitations of traditional narrative forms. Thus it follows that if we are to understand British modernist fiction in all its richness and complexity and variety, we need to add feminism and Edwardian fiction to existing genealogies of modernism.

CHAPTER ONE

The Crisis of 1895:
Realism and the Feminization
of Fiction

And that the nineteenth century should possess a literature characteristic of its
nervous, passionate life, I hold is as desirable, and would be as far-reaching in
its effects, as the biggest franchise bill ever framed.

(GEORGE MOORE, *Literature at Nurse* [1885])

Set the maiden fancies wallowing in the troughs of
    Zolaism –
Forward, forward, ay and backward, downward too
    into abysm.

(ALFRED, LORD TENNYSON,
'Locksley Hall Sixty Years After' [1886])

In the early 1880s, translations of new foreign literature such as the fiction
of Zola and other French naturalists, the novels of Tolstoy and
Dostoevsky, and the dramas of Ibsen, were introduced into England, and
the innovations of this literature in terms of subject matter, social
criticism, psychological insight and sexual frankness had a profound
impact upon British writers. In particular, naturalism – or realism, as it
came to be called in England – with its candid presentations of social
inequities and sexual relations, held a strong appeal for writers who had
begun to chafe against the restrictions imposed by circulating libraries
and the periodicals which serialized their work.[1] Censorship became the

major literary issue of the 1880s, and writers who wished to benefit from the force of 'Zolaesque honesty' joined in a campaign for artistic freedom of expression, portraying themselves as sophisticated and sensitive intellectuals who were being held back by ignorant Philistines. But the opponents of realism were shocked by the sexual frankness and ignoble subject matter of the new realists, and they reminded British writers that novels were sources of knowledge, and powerful moral influences, particularly upon their impressionable female and lower-class readerships. These critics insisted that the 'Real' must be tempered by the 'Ideal', the latter being aesthetically as well as morally necessary for a work of literature: 'the visible when it rests not upon the invisible becomes the bestial'.[2] Zola became synonymous with amorality and licentiousness (especially to those who had never read him), and was considered such a threat to the morals of the nation that Henry Vizetelly, the English publisher of translations of his novels, was imprisoned in 1889.[3]

Four years earlier, George Moore had published a pamphlet entitled *Literature at Nurse, or Circulating Morals*, in which he severely criticized the circulating library system, and in particular the proprietor of the largest one, Charles Edward Mudie, for acting as the public's moral arbiter and banning books that he felt to be 'immoral'. Moore complained that 'the character for strength, virility, and purpose, which our literature has always held . . . is being gradually obliterated to suit the commercial views of a narrow-minded tradesman'. Mudie had refused to carry Moore's novel *A Modern Lover* in 1883, so Moore published his next book in an affordable edition which could be purchased by individuals at their own discretion. Moore reproached Mudie's for characterizing the majority of novel readers as 'young unmarried women who are supposed to know but one side of life', and circulating only those novels deemed suitable for them; as a result, he declared, 'men have ceased to read novels in England'.[4] The rhetoric of virility and masculinity that Moore and others employed in its defense underscores the fact that the trend towards realism in the late 1880s and early 1890s was not just an attempt to free the novel from censorship, but also a movement to reclaim it for male readers and writers, and free it from literary conventions and restrictions that had come to be identified as feminine: realism was to masculinize the British novel.

Throughout the nineteenth century, male writers had demonstrated their discomfort with what were considered the romantic and feminine aspects of the novel, and the increasing popularity of the novel among the newly (and considered by many imperfectly) educated women and working classes seemed to be a confirmation that the novel was an inferior literary form. Realizing the impossibility of wresting the novel from the hands of women, many writers, critics and publishers worked to promote a new kind of novel that would be perceived as serious literature, not entertainment, and which, by its very nature, could be written only by male writers.[5] With its focus upon the brutal economic and sexual realities of modern life, the new realism was presumed to be out of the reach of women writers, who specialized in the genteel domestic world of romance and marriage. Flaubert had declared that the unadorned precision of the realist style could be achieved only with 'masculine, not feminine phrases'; the formal requirements of realism – objectivity, lack of sentiment, sexual frankness, breadth of experience – were all considered constitutionally impossible for women novelists.[6] And the alliance of realism with scientific theories of biology and sociology gave the novel an intellectual respectability and high purpose which it was felt hitherto to have lacked. Many writers saw realism as a chance to develop an elite, 'masculine' novel that would aim for literary greatness and social significance instead of mere popular success. The resultant hierarchical system of masculine and feminine fiction would also do the double duty of keeping dangerous sexual knowledge, taxing intellectual ideas, and unpleasant truths away from women. Although Moore flippantly said he was not interested in reconciling 'those two unreconcilable things – art and young girls', he did go on to point out that young girls would actually be better served by reading realist fiction, because the current popular novels gave girls 'erroneous and superficial notions of the value of life and love'.[7] But most proponents of the new realism accepted that the prudery and sentimentality that were hampering the novel were 'naturally' feminine; few saw the irony in blaming young girls and women for adhering to the values their society and the male literary establishment had imposed on them.

In a forum entitled 'Candour in English Fiction', published in 1890, the odd trio of Walter Besant, Mrs Eliza Lynn Linton, and Thomas Hardy all agreed that the constrictions placed upon fiction by censorship were detrimental to the development of great literature. Hardy, the most liberal of the three writers, was blunt about what English fiction lacked: 'Life being a physiological fact, its honest portrayal must be largely concerned with, for one thing, the relations of the sexes ... to this expansion English society opposes a well-nigh insuperable bar.' But apart from a few critical asides about 'parental anxiety' and 'conventions concerning budding womanhood', Hardy declined to challenge the ideals of female ignorance and innocence that censorship was based upon. The anti-feminist novelist and essayist Mrs Linton called for honest, 'virile work', which would be appropriate for 'a strong-headed and masculine nation', and complained about England's 'schoolgirl standard' which allowed for only 'feeble, futile, milk-and-water literature'. But she accepted without question the existence of the 'Young

Person' who, although responsible for 'the emasculation of all fictitious literature', must nevertheless be absolutely protected from all references to sex.[8] Both Linton and Besant (who was a novelist as well as a literary critic) presumed the existence of an intimate chain of moral influence reaching from the novel to women to the family to society; thus the actual topic of the forum was how to achieve greater freedom and honesty in fiction, without allowing concomitant freedom and honesty in women's lives. All three authors proposed various solutions for keeping 'candid' literature away from young women, ranging from locked cabinets in Father's library (Mrs Linton) to the development of periodicals written exclusively for adults (Hardy). But the respondents never confronted the fact that women's increasing independence and mobility made any plan for the segregation of fiction unrealistic and outmoded, and that greater frankness in fiction would inevitably have an impact on all of society.

This same trio of authors, along with other novelists and notables, continued to wrestle with the problem of women, novels, and sexual frankness in a 1894 symposium entitled 'The Tree of Knowledge'. It is indicative of the public's anxiety about the novel as a powerful source of information for girls and women that novelists were here elevated as figures of moral authority; no one seemed to think it odd that the advice of fiction writers was sought on such issues as how much a girl should be told about the 'great mysteries of life' before marriage, or whether her future husband should inform her of his sexual history. But the novelist Israel Zangwill gave the lie to the whole enterprise:

> . . . your symposium is too late; it is like discussing, after the steed is stolen,
> whether the stable door should be shut or left open. Owing to the circulation of
> the woman-novel (much greater than mine, alas!) and of the modern
> newspaper, nine out of ten girls must know as much as their parents, and the
> tenth a great deal more . . .[9]

The symposium was indeed an anachronism. An astonishing new frankness had emerged in British fiction, but Mrs Linton's locked cabinets had proved ineffective, and the new novels were not, as she had predicted, obviously 'virile'. In the four years between these two forums, developments in literature and changes in women's lives had coincided with a tremendous impact, and women as well as men had chosen to 'revolt against insincerity in the art of fiction'.[10] The circulating library system was quickly waning, and its role as censor was greatly diminished as the Victorian three-decker was replaced by inexpensive single-volume novels which could be purchased by individuals.[11] By 1893, censorship had been eased to such an extent that Zola received an enthusiastic welcome on a visit to England. At the same time, what was generally known as the Woman Question was becoming one of the most popularly discussed and volatile issues of the decade; increased opportunities for education and employment for women, and feminist challenges to conventional gender roles and the sexual double standard, prompted an ongoing debate, in newspapers, magazines, and journals, about the nature and status of women. Given permission, in a sense, by proponents of realism, male and female novelists carried this debate into fiction; purposely breaking taboos and discarding stereotypes, they began to write about women with unprecedented social, psychological and sexual frankness. The call for candour and masculinity in fiction had backfired into an explosion of creative activity which derived its momentum from women and feminism. In the first half of the 1890s there was an extraordinary outpouring of fiction about women, much of it written by women and intended for women – what Zangwill called 'the woman-novel'.

Many appellations were devised by reviewers to characterize the new kind of fiction being published in the early 1890s. Although the fiction itself was quite varied, any novel which exhibited a certain latitude in its depiction of women or relations between the sexes, or offered critical analysis of contemporary society, fell under the general rubric of the 'new realism' or the 'new fiction'. Terms such as the 'marriage problem' or 'sex problem' novel, the 'fiction of sex', or the 'woman novel' indicated the dominant themes of this fiction more specifically. Another of these almost interchangeable labels was the 'New Woman novel', which was applied rather indiscriminately by the popular press to any novel which featured a heroine who was frankly 'advanced' in her views about women and marriage.[12] But the label 'New Woman novel' is most accurately applied to the works written by a particular group of women authors who used the new realism as a vehicle for feminist expression. Some of the most popular of these novels were *The Heavenly Twins* (1893) and *The Beth Book* (1897) by Sarah Grand, *A Superfluous Woman* (1894) by Emma Frances Brooke, *The Story of a Modern Woman* (1894) by Ella Hepworth Dixon, *The Daughters of Danaus* (1894) by Mona Caird, *Gallia* (1895) by Ménie Muriel Dowie, and *Nobody's Fault* (1896) by Netta Syrett.[13]

What was most new about New Woman novels were their heroines, and despite differences in subject matter and feminist philosophy in these novels, it is possible to sketch a typical New Woman character from their heroines. The New Woman – independent, outspoken and creative – is antithetical to the Victorian stereotypes of the proper lady and the angel in the house. Almost always from a middle-class background, she is well read, learning the facts of life from French novels and medical textbooks, and deriving her feminist principles from Herbert Spencer and John Stuart Mill. Although a few of the New Woman heroines are feminist reformers (as in the novels of Sarah Grand), most are not politically active; the New Woman's rebellion, though purposeful and based on principle, is mainly personal. She challenges social norms and conventional morality in order to achieve her own fulfillment – sexual, artistic, intellectual, or otherwise.[14] The New Woman is frequently characterized as being exceptional in her intelligence and artistic abilities, even to the point of having artistic 'genius', despite her lack of formal education. But to counter the stereotype of the mannish 'Wild Woman' that was perpetuated by anti-feminists such as Mrs Lynn Linton and Mrs Humphry Ward, the New Woman character is also usually beautiful and traditionally 'feminine' in appearance and manner.[15] The New Woman novelists, like most women of their time, feared a blurring of gender distinctions as much as men did; while feminists demanded the rights and opportunities that men enjoyed, they did not want to lose their female identity and become like men. But the New Woman novelists did try to create a new kind of feminine ideal, one which allowed for women's intellectual abilities and sexuality, and privileged sexual knowledge, not sexual ignorance.

Its candid treatment of sex was the most innovative, as well as the most notorious and misunderstood, aspect of the New Woman novel. Victorian women were taught to be reticent about their personal experiences and physical sensations, and this repression in turn tended to hamper self-scrutiny or any fictional representations of female introspection. In order to tell the truth about women's lives, and explore women's emotions and motivations with psychological honesty, this long tradition of silence had to be broken, and female sexuality acknowledged – by the novelists and by the New Woman heroines themselves. But most New Woman novelists (and most feminists at the time) did not equate women's liberation with sexual liberation.[16] With their conservative views on sexual continence and monogamy, they were hardly the 'erotomaniacs' the press would make them out to be. They sought to improve or redefine rather than abolish the institution of marriage, for they realized that it afforded essential legal and economic protection for women and children. And while the New Woman novelists were critical of conventional sexual morality (particularly the sexual double standard), and wanted to show that women could be both sexual and 'pure' (following the lead of Hardy's novel *Tess of the d'Urbervilles*), they did not endorse 'free love' or promiscuity. Sex in the New Woman novel mainly takes the form of the heroine's frank sexual discussions, which serve to symbolize her new-found sense of self and freedom; sexual relations, both good and bad, are handled with great seriousness and discretion. Grand, among others, stressed that love and sexual relations should be only one aspect of a healthy and varied life; she was disdainful of popular novelists like Ouida, whose romance novels were 'inflated with sexuality', to the exclusion of all else.[17] But in order to portray women realistically, to examine the relations between men and women, and to criticize what they saw as the destructive effects of unrestrained male sexuality – sexual abuse, prostitution and venereal disease – New Woman novelists had to be sexually frank.

Predictably, conservative critics who had opposed the movement for realism were appalled by its unexpectedly powerful influence on women writers. But most proponents of realism (the majority of whom were male) also opposed the popular New Woman novels. A few critics noted with appreciation the importance of feminism for the new realism – such as the reviewer of *Gallia* who praised New Woman novelists for the 'unveiling and exposure of the deformed image of Priapus in the innermost recesses of the Temple of Marriage': 'Thanks to the courage and dash of the lady novelists who have led the vanguard, the citadel of convention is taken, and the most proper male novelist may now call a spade a spade without expecting prompt vengeance at the hands of Messrs. Mudie and Smith.'[18] But most critics who advocated realism, such as Edmund Gosse, Hubert Crackanthorpe and D.F. Hannigan, resented the ways in which the new realism was being associated with feminism, and they refused to acknowledge the similarities between New Woman novels and novels by male realists such as Moore and George Gissing. Instead, they sought to redefine realism, to draw clear divisions between the novels of men and women, and to stress the differences between serious literature and popular or polemical fiction.

An exchange on 'Reticence in Literature' in the first two issues of *The Yellow Book* (published in 1894) illustrates how New Woman novels were targeted for criticism by both opponents and proponents of the new realism. In the first article, Arthur Waugh, a prominent editor and publisher, argued that literature of idealism and romance was far superior to the current trend of realism. He explained that British literature was in decline at the moment, due to the absence of stimulation from 'some vast movement of emancipation' of which, curiously, he was unable to see any evidence in his own age. Literature, like women in general, had come to live on its own 'sensations', and had degenerated into 'effeminacy', which Waugh saw as characteristic of all literary realism, by men or women. But 'the revolt of women' and the work of 'our women-writers' had led to a particularly loathsome type of realism which combined effeminacy with 'brutality', and 'infects its heroines with acquired diseases of names unmentionable, and has debased the beauty of maternity by analysis of the process of gestation'. Waugh was shocked that a woman would think it artistically permissible to describe the sensations of childbirth in a novel, and asked indignantly: 'what has she told us that we did not all know?' Presumably a great deal, but the point was that Waugh did not want to hear 'her unpalatable details'.[19] He evidently found it intolerable to be reminded that women are physical, sexual beings, and he demanded a resurgence of reticence in literature to put women back in the realm of the ideal where they belong.

In contrast, Hubert Crackanthorpe, in his response to Waugh, revelled in the new possibilities of the modern age and its variety of fictions – but the works he cited are all by male authors. A short-story writer and an admirer of Maupassant, Crackanthorpe had no objection to the subject matter or candor of realism in the hands of men, but he saw a great danger in the female usurpers who had the temerity to think that they too could be realists. He warned the reader to beware 'the society lady, dazzled by the brilliancy of her own conversation, and the serious-minded spinster, bitten by some sociological theory', who, through writing fiction, will try 'to astonish or improve the world'; it is 'the intelligent amateur', not 'the British Philistine', who is now 'the deadliest of Art's enemies'.[20]

It is curious that although the shortcomings of British fiction had previously been blamed upon women and the restrictions required by their 'schoolgirl standards', when women eschewed those standards they were still held responsible for what was wrong with British fiction. In his disdain for women writers, Crackanthorpe supported Waugh's contention that a woman is incapable of producing serious literature unless perhaps she 'throws off the habit of her sex' and writes like a man – meaning that she must stop writing about things like childbirth.[21] Both Waugh and Crackanthorpe, despite their aesthetic differences, were anxious to define a male literary enclave that could not be annexed by women, and such a reaction was not uncommon: throughout the nineteenth century, every time women advanced into traditionally male areas, men usually sought new ways in which to distinguish themselves in opposition to women. But the irony in this case was that the novel had become even more 'feminized' as the result of a literary movement that was supposed to have made British literature distinctly masculine.

Many critics were dismayed by the sheer number of women realists, and they refused to consider them as professionals, discrediting them as dilettantes; noting that not long ago Moore had been 'attacked on all sides' for promoting realism, a critic for the *Athenaeum* sneered, 'Now every literary lady is "realistic", and everybody says, "How clever! How charming!".'[22] Gosse denigrated the New Woman novels for being bestsellers, and attributed their popularity solely to the power of publicity, novelty and sex. He blamed the education of the lower classes and women for a general levelling of literary taste, and complained that large sales figures were replacing traditional literary standards of value.[23] D.F. Hannigan, in several essays, carefully made distinctions between the 'virile and rational' realist novels of men and those currently being written by women; he maintained that realist novels by women erred in being too polemical, for their authors followed in the tradition of George Eliot in 'that tendency towards pedantry which appears to beset all women of profound learning and fixed intellectual habits'.[24] Gissing also insisted that since fiction about the New Woman 'cries aloud as the mouthpiece of social reform', it did not have the requisite narratorial objectivity to be considered true realism.[25]

New Woman novels were indeed polemical, but the New Woman novelists were unconcerned whether critics perceived them as *bona fide* realists or not, for they saw themselves as disciples of a social, not a literary, movement. Although their sexual frankness, their almost scientific scrutiny of psychological responses and physical sensations, and their efforts to confront the hidden and sometimes sordid aspects of life were all influenced by the new realism, New Woman novels were first and foremost purpose novels. Most of the New Woman novelists were committed feminists, and their dominant concern was that their purpose be clearly articulated and their novels widely read. Sarah Grand, the first, most influential and most popular of the New Woman novelists, was an outspoken feminist and supporter of women's rights, marriage reform, and Rational Dress; she was known for exhorting fellow feminists to look feminine and pretty, so as not to alienate potential supporters.[26] Her fictional strategy was similar: she presented radical new causes, discussions of sexual relationships, and social criticisms in a familiar and readable form, in hopes of achieving a broad dissemination of her ideas. Grand's strategy worked: *The Heavenly Twins*, an old-fashioned three-decker filled with enough characters and plot twists to rival Dickens, was a sensational bestseller, and writers scrambled to follow in Grand's footsteps and capitalize on her success.

Grand, speaking through the autobiographical heroine of *The Beth Book*, insisted that incorporating polemic into fiction presented no difficulties: 'Manner has always been less to me than matter. When I think of all the preventable sin and misery there is in the world, I pray God give us books of good intention – never mind the style!' (460). And Beth's friend Ideala agrees: 'If you have the matter, the manner will come . . . it will be good, too, as you are conscientious, and as beautiful as you are good' (461). Grand denigrated any conscious stylistic efforts as idle game-playing, and associated them with decadent French literature and 'art for art's sake'. As a result, her well-intentioned novels are unwieldy and rambling, and often tiresome in their accumulation of detail. Venereal disease, Lock hospitals, vivisection, suffrage, the sexual double standard, education for girls, women's fashions, the benefits of physical exercise, and the abuse of caffeine, alcohol and tobacco are just a few of the topics she offers her opinions on in the course of *The Beth Book*. The majority of New Woman novels have similarly proselytizing narrators and heroines who never stop talking; it is as if these women writers, finally given a voice and an audience after decades of silence and isolation, felt it imperative to speak out – about anything and everything.[27]

One of the most significant innovations of New Woman novels was the use of women's consciousness as the center of the novel; women characters are invariably the dominant subjects rather than the objects of a male-orientated narrative. This tactic allowed the authors to place a great deal of their feminist argument in the mouths of their heroines, and New Woman novels are characteristically filled with either lengthy private speculations or long discussions about the inequities of women's position in society. But this central female consciousness is rarely translated into active agency in the novel; New Woman novels are also marked by the psychological pain of their heroines, their agonized revelations of the unfairness of their lot in life, and their frustration at being excluded from education and careers. It is part of the realism and social criticism of these novels, of course, that their heroines are for the most part thwarted in their rebellion – late-Victorian society did not easily accommodate new ways of life for women. But neither did the late-Victorian novel, and the fictional efforts of the New Woman novelists were hampered by the conservative ideologies of gender, love and sexuality inherent in its conventions and traditional narrative structures. There was little precedence in fiction for portraying women outside their social and domestic sphere, and the patterns of romance, courtship and marriage were closely intertwined with conventions of plot and narrative resolution: romantic desire was the principal narrative impetus for women, and marriage was the ultimate expression of feminine success and social integration. Like their counterparts in real life, the New Woman heroines – educated, eager to work, and desiring equitable relationships with men – soon found that there were no new narratives awaiting them which could accommodate their desire for autonomy; they either had to conform to the ways of society in order to achieve a modicum of happiness, or live as outcasts on society's fringes.

The innovations of the New Woman novelists in terms of characterization and sexual frankness coexisted uneasily with the narrative traditions they had inherited and attempted to work within. The Marriage Question was the central issue in 1890s feminism, and as a result, marriage retained its traditional centrality in the New Woman novel, even while novelists were striving to challenge it. Some New Woman novelists, most notably Grand, tried to make strategic use of novelistic conventions of courtship and marriage for their own purposes. In her novels *The Heavenly Twins* and *The Beth Book*, Grand used marriage as a bad beginning rather than the traditional happy ending; having no other options, the heroine marries, but instead of settling into her new marital and social role, she proceeds to go through a process of disenchantment and feminist radicalization. Grand's heroines reject the sexual double standard and, applying society's standards of female purity to their husbands, are shocked to discover their moral laxity. Beth in *The Beth Book*, and Evadne, Angelica and Edith in *The Heavenly Twins*, all realize in various ways that the narrative pattern of 'they lived happily ever after' is not only unrealistic but, in their own case, impossible.

But although Beth eventually leaves her husband for London and a career as a writer, Evadne's dissolute husband finally dies, and Angelica, dressed in her brother's clothes, finds happiness in a secret friendship with a young man, these are all merely temporary narrative detours, not final escapes from convention. Grand was obviously concerned that her exceptional and rebellious heroines should not be considered unnatural or unfeminine; thus she emphasized their stereotypically 'feminine' qualities, such as self-renunciation and a need for romantic love. In *The Heavenly Twins*, Evadne, though suicidal as a result of the pressures of her first marriage, can be released from her severe depression only by a second marriage, this time to the capable and comforting Dr Galbraith. In *The Beth Book*, after Beth is finally established as a writer, she suddenly finds she cannot live without romance; the novel ends not with her achievement of literary success, but when the man of her dreams literally rides into her life. To achieve these romantic happy endings, Grand had to polish off all the rough and realistic edges she had created; for example, Beth's marriage conveniently never produces any children to tie her down, and the sticky problem of her divorce is avoided entirely. Beth's characteristic anger and need for independence disappear abruptly, and by the end of the novel she jumps at any chance for self-sacrifice, be it for her lover or for the suffrage movement. Though she was highly critical of the inequities of women's position in society, Grand ultimately did not reject or even significantly alter social and novelistic conventions concerning love and marriage. In part, this can be seen as a concession on Grand's part to her reading audience. It is also indicative of the conservative nature of feminism at the turn of the century: Grand criticized bad marriages in order to posit an ideal of marriage, the achievement of which she saw as one of the goals of feminism. But the final effect of her novels is one of stasis and narrative satisfaction; her heroines' rebellious energies are made to conform to the more dominant needs of the novel, such as social integration and closure.

Other New Woman novelists attempted to subvert the conventional role of marriage in the novel by making marriage indicative of defeat, or even tragedy. Hadria, the New Woman heroine of Mona Caird's *The Daughters of Danaus*, spends much of the novel speaking against the idealization of marriage and motherhood, but she is never able to live out the implications of her theories and place her desires over those of her husband and her family. Forced to give up her dream of being a composer, Hadria quietly capitulates to the traditional narrative of feminine self-sacrifice that she despises.

But it was not easy for New Woman novelists to change the signification of strongly rooted conventions which associated marriage with feminine success and the suffering or death of the heroine with some kind of moral retribution. Novels like *The Daughters of Danaus*, in which the heroine does not suffer from blatant evils but merely succumbs to a traditional marriage, were often read as supportive of the status quo, despite all rhetoric to the contrary.[28] New Woman novelists such as Emma Frances Brooke and Ménie Muriel Dowie tried to make their heroines' failure an indictment of society, not an indictment of their heroines' ideals, but they found it difficult to create a heroine out of a woman who rejects the social order, particularly when the defeat she suffers is of a personal and physical nature. For many readers the nervous breakdown, illness, madness and suicide that were characteristic of New Woman novels did not connote high tragedy but, rather, confirmed that the heroine had gone too far outside her sphere, and suffered because she tried to do things for which she was unsuited; the social order triumphs by the very fact that it has endured and the woman has not. The narrative strategy of making the heroine a martyr also came perilously close to reinforcing female stereotypes which romanticized self-sacrifice and failure; some reviewers intuited this when they faulted the New Woman novelists for glorifying and encouraging their heroines' psychic disorders.[29]

Male authors of the new realism – those whom their proponents worked to distinguish from the New Woman novelists – were in fact also struggling with the same kinds of tensions between the feminist content of their fiction and traditional narrative forms. With their reputations already established, novelists such as Hardy, Moore, Gissing, and George Meredith were not categorized as New Woman novelists, yet they saw the current debate on women as integral to the development of modern fiction. Drawn by the opportunity to explore aspects of women's lives that had previously been elided in fiction, they turned their attention to the inequities in women's social and economic status, and did so with a particular emphasis on women's psychology and sexuality. These writers had always shown an interest in women in their fiction, but in the 1890s a distinct topicality emerged in their work. Although they do not articulate a specific feminist agenda, nevertheless, novels such as Hardy's *Tess of the d'Urbervilles* (1891), Gissing's *The Odd Women* (1893) and Moore's *Esther Waters* (1894), with their focus on lower-class women, the sexual double standard and female sexuality, were products not only of the new realism but also of the new feminism in British fiction. Reviewers resisted acknowledging this for some time, frequently downplaying or even ignoring the importance of women in novels by these authors, and focusing instead on some 'larger' theme, or on formal considerations. But as Moore, Gissing and Hardy became more explicitly engaged with issues associated with feminism in their novels, critics were unable to use such a strategy, and their reviews indicate a growing anxiety about what they saw as the 'feminization' of the fiction of England's best male novelists.

Gissing was one of the first English novelists to respond to the call for candor in fiction. In the 1880s, he had battled censors over the frank sexual references in his novels; he shocked Victorian readers by making the heroine of his novel *The Unclassed* (1884) a prostitute, and by depicting her sympathetically. Although Gissing made many statements about women which critics have interpreted as misogynistic, it is evident that his fiction was inspired and energized in important ways by modern women and their changing lives; almost all his novels are concerned with feminism to some degree. He created a wealth of startlingly honest characterizations of women, and instead of focusing solely on educated middle and upper-class women, as the New Woman novelists did, he wrote about women from all classes. The social range of his novels points to the influence of naturalism upon Gissing, as does his remarkable attention to material details and his measured narration; by not taking an obvious stand, he carefully maintains the complex and problematic nature of the issues he addresses. Although his novels contain more social philosophizing than is found in the French naturalists, his fiction is not shaped by polemic in the way that most New Woman novels are.

Gissing's novel *The Odd Women* is his most balanced presentation of feminist ideas. The odd women of the title were also called 'surplus' women in the late nineteenth century, because – owing in part to a high rate of male emigration – there were significantly more women than men in England's population. Thus for a large number of women marriage was a statistical impossibility, but British society refused to accept that they might live on their own and work for a living. These 'redundant' women were as ignored in fiction as they were in life, for they existed outside conventional narratives of romance and marriage, and it was felt that their lack of association with men rendered their lives insignificant. But Gissing boldly chose to center his novel upon these women, and he explores their lives with a devastating and detailed honesty. He grounds his social criticism in economic realities rather than feminist principles, and his portraits of impoverished and unskilled women – suffering from malnutrition, alcoholism and despair, struggling to find decent housing and employment in London – make the rebellion of the typical New Woman seem trivial and naïvely idealistic.

Gissing's version of the New Woman, Rhoda Nunn, has already gone through her initial rejection of social conventions before the novel begins; as an instructor in a secretarial school in London she is successfully living a single and independent life, and helping other women to do so as well. There is a romance plot, but it does not provide the locus of Rhoda's rebellion, or a traditional happy ending; rather, it is a test of her commitment to the way of life she has chosen, and her rejection of romance and marriage is a triumphant – if bitter-sweet – affirmation of her choice. In a secondary plot, Monica Madden is an underpaid and exploited shopgirl who, desirous of financial security and 'freedom', marries an older man who, for his part, is desirous of a submissive and subordinate wife. *The Odd Women* differs significantly from New Woman novels in that Gissing criticizes this kind of misguided and ultimately disastrous marriage by looking at how it affects one of its ordinary victims, rather a self-righteous and articulate New Woman.

One of the most remarkable aspects of *The Odd Women* (and many of Gissing's other novels) is the ordinariness and believability of its female characters. His odd women are not female exemplars, but real people who suffer from doubts and imperfections and jealousies; their world is fully imagined, and the things in it are presented in vivid detail. Rhoda Nunn and her supervisor, Mary Barfoot, seem truly new and modern rather than reworked versions of old Victorian heroines. *The Odd Women* is also exceptional in that it is one of the few feminist novels of the 1890s which succeeds in using traditional narrative forms to present new possibilities, and its conclusion is both realistic and hopeful. Rhoda and Mary are not martyrs for their cause, nor do they feel that the absence of romance and marriage in their lives is a deficiency. The growing strength and success of the two communities of women depicted in *The Odd Women* – the secretarial school and a girls' school – enable Gissing to end his novel with a positive sense of social resurgence without having to rely on the usual device of marriage, or undermining his social criticism.

Like Gissing, George Moore wished to criticize the discrepancies between social ideals and economic realities, and the majority of his novels are also extremely topical in their treatment of changes in women's lives in the late nineteenth century. A disciple of Zola in his early years as a writer, Moore was interested in how social, economic, and even biological forces shape and determine the course of women's and men's lives. In keeping with his theories of realism, Moore resisted idealizing his women characters, or making them outright heroines, to the dismay of many feminists; his women characters, drawn from all classes, are imperfect, at times unpleasant, even amoral; several drink and gamble and are sexually active. But Moore's portraits of women are also honest, balanced and effective; like Gissing, he believed that no matter what the ideological basis, any idealization of women (even that of the New Woman) led to romantic delusions and destructive notions of perfectionism. Most notably in *A Mummer's Wife* (1885) and *A Drama in Muslin* (1886) Moore demonstrated how false romantic ideals can destroy women's lives, and in all his fiction he resists the dominance of the romance narrative. Like the New Woman novelists, Moore struggled with the problem of the ending but, freed from the necessity of expressing a feminist agenda, he was realistic without being completely deterministic; he was able to circumvent any unwelcome interpretations of moral retribution or triumph through his objective narrative stance. For example, though the heroine in *Esther Waters* bears an illegitimate child and faces numerous obstacles in her attempts to support herself, she is eventually able to grow in strength and survive; but Esther is neither an argument for a new ideal of purity (like Hardy's Tess) nor an admonition – she simply *is*. For many, such moral ambivalence on Moore's part was as disturbing as his sexual frankness.

In his fascinating and complex portrait of a New Woman, 'Mildred Lawson', a novella from the collection *Celibates* (1895), Moore was able to resolve the problem of the ending in another way: by taking advantage of the narrative freedom of the shorter form. The narrative begins with the bored and restless Mildred coming to the realization that by 'proclaiming antipathy to marriage she would win admiration, and would in a measure distinguish herself' (228). Adopting a superficial feminism, she is able to avoid the linear path of romance and marriage, but she soon finds she is lost without that familiar narrative. After a series of desultory episodes in which she attempts to find a new ambition in her life, Mildred realizes: 'there was nothing in life except a little fruitless striving, and then marriage. If she did not accept marriage, what should she do?' (233). Mildred's Victorian upbringing makes her incapable of succeeding in any of the alternative narratives she tries, such as being a painter, or a writer for a radical newspaper, for she inevitably warps them into romance narratives which, in her perverse and misguided combination of Victorian prudery and feminist independence, she then rejects. Her growing sense of self yields no accomplishments but, rather, the knowledge that by offering and then withholding sex, she can wield tremendous power over men. The result is an incoherent life of destruction and sexual repression, and appropriately, the story has no climax or resolution; it ends with Mildred writhing on her virginal bed, agonizingly frustrated in her inability to feel any kind of passion.

'Mildred Lawson' has often been read as an attack on the New Woman, but it is actually a condemnation of the Victorian feminine ideal, which teaches women that their true function is their biological one, yet denies them access to their sexuality. Mildred uses feminist principles to justify her chastity, and her chastity to achieve independence and power, all the while unable to perceive herself apart from her sexual appeal to men. In 'Mildred Lawson' Moore dares to confront the contradictions inherent in the conservative sexual ideology of the majority of feminists at the time, and makes the radical suggestion that only when women free themselves from the romantic idealization and sexual values of the past will they be able to envision and enact new and positive endings for their lives.

As Moore discovered, the fragmentary and inconclusive nature of the short story made it the ideal vehicle for some of the most successful fictional explorations of modern women and feminism. It permitted writers to focus on individual episodes, or moments, instead of on causality and resolution, and thus it freed them from some of the narrative constraints of the novel – in particular, that of the ending. Concise and concentrated, the short story was the antithesis of the Victorian novel, so it was appealing to those in search of the new and the modern; a larger social milieu, or the far-reaching implications of a character's actions, were downplayed in favor of a vivid rendering of a moment – of passion, of anger, or of realization. The short story's modernity was reflected in its subject matter as well, for it proved conducive to intimate analyses of individuals, particularly of their psychological and sexual responses.

For example, Victoria Cross, in her short story 'Theodora: A Fragment' (1895), uses evocative details of clothing and physical appearance, and nuances of gestures and words, to convey the intense sexual attraction that arises between a liberated young woman named Theodora and the young man who narrates the story. During the course of two afternoon visits, the young man and Theodora test and tease one another until their mutual sense of tension and excitement culminates in a passionate kiss as Theodora is leaving the man's apartment; at that point, the story ends abruptly in a series of ellipses. Thus Cross was able to portray explicitly a very modern (though momentary) sexual relationship based upon powerful feelings of physical and intellectual curiosity, without having to deal with censorship, moral issues, or the narrative difficulties that an actual liaison would provoke. It was left to the reader to predict what Cross's bold New Woman would do next.

'Theodora' was published by John Lane in his journal *The Yellow Book* (which ran from 1894 to 1897), which, along with the *Savoy* and the many other small literary journals that flourished at the time, was responsible for the popularity of the short-story form in the 1890s. Lane was known for publishing unusual or daring stories, and he created a receptive atmosphere in which writers could combine formal experimentation and sexual frankness to create innovative new fiction about women. He was also associated with the 'feminization' of fiction in that he published a large number of women writers (including Ella D'Arcy, E. Nesbit, Ada Leverson, Evelyn Sharp and Netta Syrett) both in his journal and in his 'Keynotes' series of fiction, and received a great deal of publicity as the publisher of Grant Allen's *The Woman Who Did* (which caused a sensation even though it was actually an anti-feminist novel disguised as a New Woman novel). But conservative critics read the short stories published by Lane as glorifications of egotistical introspection and 'morbid' sexuality, and used Lane's interest in such fiction to confirm their suspicions of an alliance between New Women, decadence and homosexuality.

The Yellow Book, with its yellow wrappers reminiscent of French novels, its shocking Beardsley illustrations, and its Symbolist and Decadent poetry, had consciously cultivated a risqué image for itself, and became synonymous with *fin-de-siècle* decadence. But that decadence had also become synonymous with dandyism, effeminacy and homosexuality; although Oscar Wilde was never published in *The Yellow Book*, he was erroneously associated with it through his work with Beardsley, and the fact that he was arrested with a yellow volume under his arm was proof for many that *The Yellow Book* was a haven for sexual deviants.[30] Many of the men and women published in *The Yellow Book* exemplified, in their writings and in their lives, the kind of blurring of gender distinctions that increasingly came to be seen in the 1890s as a threat to the British nation, if not to the future of the human race itself. *Punch*'s 'Angry Old Buffer' expressed the anxiety of many at the turn of the century: '. . . a new fear my bosom vexes; / Tomorrow there may be *no* sexes! / Unless, as end to all the pother, / Each one in fact becomes the other.'[31] Both the New Women and the Decadents represented disturbing challenges to conventional sexual morality and gender roles; thus, despite their dissimilar artistic aims, they were frequently bracketed together (along with the new realists) as a concerted (and feminized) threat to the stability of society.[32]

The author of the inaugural volume in Lane's 'Keynotes' series epitomized this threat more than any other writer of the 1890s, apart from Wilde. She was Mary Chavelita Dunne, and the short stories she wrote under the pen name George Egerton fascinated the reading public and scandalized the British literary establishment. But her most significant accomplishment was that she realized, in a way that no other woman writer of her time did, that she had to escape the tyranny of novelistic conventions and female stereotypes in order truly to express women's unique sensibility and experiences, and that the way to accomplish that was through new fictional forms. In later years, she reflected back on the genesis of her writing career:

> I realised that in literature, everything had been done better by man than woman could hope to emulate. There was only one small plot left for her to tell: the *terra incognita* of herself, as she knew herself to be, not as a man liked to imagine her – in a word, to give herself away, as man had given himself away in his writings. . . . I would use situations or conflicts as I saw them with a total disregard of man's opinions. I would unlock a door with a key of my own fashioning.[33]

The modesty of this passage is disingenuous and ironic; Egerton knew that what she was positing was not just a 'small plot', but, rather, a whole new literature that would be free from repressive gender definitions and social constraints, taking the lives and concerns of women as its focus. Egerton refused to imitate the writing of men, and her insistence upon making her own 'key' is clearly a challenge to male sexual as well as literary dominance.[34]

Egerton's first collection of short stories, *Keynotes* (1893), was published a few months after Grand's *The Heavenly Twins*, and rivaled Grand's novel in its success and notoriety; Egerton was both heralded and decried as the latest contributor to New Woman fiction. But although she wrote about modern and liberated women, and personally lived the life of a New Woman, Egerton's formal innovations set her apart from other New Woman writers. She consciously crafted her own version of the new realism, deriving the psychological focus and sexual frankness of her stories from modern Scandinavian writers instead of the French naturalists. Her style is controlled and compressed, yet rich in poetic and sensuous details; within the limits of the form, she creates richly imagined worlds with vivid descriptions of rooms, clothing, food, weather, and natural settings. But despite her attention to material reality Egerton was primarily interested in conveying women's experiences through series of 'psychological moments'. In creating these moments, she purposely eliminated the kind of connections and background information readers would normally expect; frequently employing ellipses, she forces the reader to fill in the blanks. Egerton also makes a significant break with conventional modes of characterization in her stories – not just by having her heroine's actions and attitudes challenge gender norms, but also through her narrative emphasis on consciousness and sexual response. In all these innovations, Egerton's fiction anticipates, in important ways, the fiction of modernist writers such as D.H. Lawrence, May Sinclair, Virginia Woolf and Dorothy Richardson.

Instead of focusing exclusively on identifiable New Women, Egerton centers some of her stories around women traditionally deemed not sufficiently significant to be protagonists – divorced women, older women, widows – and depicts friendships between women that are serious and meaningful. Like the New Woman novels, Egerton's stories are sexually frank, but they are also distinctly different from the New Woman novels in that they celebrate female sexuality as a source of identity, strength, and hope for women. Egerton's female characters tend to be physically strong, even athletic, and they are aware of and confident in their sexuality; she even went so far as to give one of her heroines a detailed sexual fantasy (in the story 'A Cross Line'), which was surely unprecedented in British fiction. Maternity is also valorized in Egerton's stories, but not in conventional fashion: she depicts it as an embodiment of women's sexuality and creativity and potency. Finally, in advocating a full life for women, Egerton refused to limit her heroines to the traditional either/or choices between independence and romance, or career and marriage, which dominate New Woman novels; she thought it not only possible but crucial that women should be able to have it all: work, love, and children.

Egerton's philosophy of the complete life is reflected in the formal construction of her stories. She was able to integrate romance narratives into some of her stories by structuring them in a non-traditional fashion, and thus to avoid compromising their feminist content. In several of her stories, a man and a woman meet and fall in love, or at least feel a strong attraction. But rather than let their romantic feelings dictate their course of action (and perhaps the course of their lives), they separate for a length of time, during which they reflect on the situation, evaluate themselves, and generally go on with their lives. Later they meet again – not in the heat of passion, but with a calm self-knowledge that enables them to choose or reject an intimate relationship. Thus the romance, instead of dominating the narrative, serves as a catalyst for character development and other action. But interestingly, Egerton employs this pattern in several different ways. In 'Her Share', the hesitation or postponement stems from sexual repression, and the loss of the moment dooms any potential relationship; it remains ambiguous whether the relationship was better lost anyway. But in 'Now Spring Has Come', Egerton mocks the romantic ideals of beauty and youth which the man values and the woman is unable to sustain over time. When they meet again, the man rejects the woman, who in turn ceases to admire him because of the foolish unreality of his desire. The woman emerges somewhat cynical but wiser, relieved to have been spared a romance which would only have brought pain.

Egerton also used this same pattern to portray strong and lasting relationships, most notably in her long short story 'The Regeneration of Two'. This story is frequently described as a fantasy, and some critics cite it as evidence that Egerton was a utopian writer. But although its ending is the most unambiguously triumphant of all the 1890s fiction dealing with women and feminism, the story succeeds because it is grounded in the psychological and material realism of Egerton's style. The heroine, a bored and pampered widow, meets an angry young poet who denounces modern society, and the artificiality and idleness of women in particular. Although she disagrees with some of what he says, and tells him so, his speech changes her life. She uses her wealth and abilities to found a self-supporting community of women, comprised mainly of unwed mothers and reformed prostitutes, and when the story resumes a few years later she is healthy, active and fulfilled. She encounters the poet again when she rescues him from a blizzard, and after nursing him back to health, she discovers that she has changed his life as well. They decide to live together as 'free man' and 'free woman', with neither abandoning their work. The ending is satisfying and believable in part because Egerton's realistic details of the community make it seem possible, rather than hopelessly utopian. But it is also a powerful ending because although it is clear that the woman's major accomplishment in life is her community, not her relationship with the poet, her independence does not preclude an intimate relationship with the man. Instead, Egerton implies that when women realize their strength they will be able to establish new kinds of relationships with men – mutually beneficial relationships based upon equality and respect.

Egerton's stories provoked a strong public response. *Punch* published a parody called 'She-Notes' by 'Borgia Smudgiton'; Henry James mocked Egerton's interest in a 'larger latitude' in fiction via the character of 'Guy Walsingham', in his story 'The Death of a Lion' (1894). Of all the women writers dealing with the Woman Question in the 1890s, it was Egerton who was both praised most highly for her 'rare artistic power', and denounced most vehemently as the greatest threat to literature and society. Critics were able to dismiss other New Woman writers for the most part by segregating them as an inferior class of popular novelists, trivializing their fiction as 'womanish', badly written and limited in scope, and demeaning them personally as literary amateurs, propagandists, and sexual neurotics. But Egerton was an undeniably talented writer, and her stories did not fit easily into the stereotypes: T.P. Gill, her first editor, was shocked to discover that she was a woman: 'It never once dawned on me that the author of those virile sketches was not one of my own sex...'[35]

Egerton also went far beyond New Woman novelists in her challenges to gender roles and conventional sexual morality: her heroines are strong without being mannish, sexual without being neurotic, womanly but not traditionally feminine or 'pure'. Her new kind of New Woman resists being defined in terms of her relationships with men, and her self-sufficiency and happiness belie the frustrated-spinster image that critics tended to impose upon New Woman heroines. The narrator of James's 'The Death of a Lion' jokes that when one tries to refer to authors who write under pen names of the opposite sex, 'it sounded somehow as if there were three sexes' (29); but part of the critical hysteria surrounding Egerton's stories actually stemmed from a very real fear in the 1890s that New Women were an omen of the emergence of a third sex – that of the 'hateful hybrid'.[36] The outspoken and sensual Egerton personally exemplified such a creature to many of her critics; W.T. Stead wrote that he preferred 'to believe [Egerton to be] hermaphrodite than a typical woman of our time'.[37]

By 1895, the frequency of such outrageous statements in literary reviews was just one sign among many that British fiction had reached a point of crisis. Despite all efforts to the contrary, fiction was dominated by women and feminism, and New Woman novels continued to proliferate and sell; Gosse complained that 'things have come to a pretty pass when the combined prestige of the best poets, historians, critics, and philosophers of the country does not weigh in the balance against a single novel by the New Woman'.[38] Although numerous articles and symposiums on the new realism and on New Woman novels had been appearing throughout the early 1890s, in the course of 1895 they reached a peak of abundance and emotional intensity; 'The Decay of Literary Taste', 'The Tyranny of the Modern Novel', 'Sex in Fiction', 'Sex in Modern Literature', 'The Fiction of Sexuality', 'Literary Degenerates', 'Tommyrotics', 'The Anti-Marriage League', and many other articles with similar subject matter filled the pages of such periodicals as *The Westminster Review*, *The Fortnightly Review*, *The Contemporary Review*, *The Nineteenth Century*, and *Blackwood's*.[39] A few of these articles were written by defenders of realism such as the critic Mrs B.A. Crackanthorpe, who described the public's 'new appetite' for realism and frank discussions of 'the sex problem' as 'healthful and health-giving'. Hannigan argued that 'sex forms one of the greatest facts in human life, and must, therefore, be emphasized by the artist', and warned that critical reaction against realism was 'a recrudescence of Puritanism'.[40] But the majority of these articles were written by conservative critics who opposed the new fiction and protested that its depictions of sex were profoundly detrimental not only to British literature, but to the nation as a whole.

Alerted to the telltale cultural signs of a larger social 'degeneration' by Max Nordau in his popular book by the same name (the translation of which also appeared in 1895), many critics saw modern novels as both products and producers of 'a moral cancer in our midst'. Using Nordau's 'scientific' vocabulary of disease, decay and death, critics issued fevered warnings about the degenerative dangers of the 'morbid' 'fiction of sexual sensualism' being written by 'erotomaniacs'. Mrs Oliphant warned that novels dealing with 'the Sex-question' were a 'national degradation' which threatened 'the foundation of society'. And one critic's xenophobic conclusion that the new fiction of 'the physiologico-pornographic school' was 'the offspring . . . of Continental decadentism' is representative of the sense of moral invasion and national crisis that pervades these articles.[41]

The authors of all these articles, whether opposing or supporting the new realism, tended to focus their fear and anger upon women writers and readers (with the exception of Mrs Crackanthorpe, who complained: 'it is the fashion of the hour to cry that women are here the chief offenders, that the plague of the female scribe infests the land'.)[42] In a rhetorically convenient but paradoxical way, women were brought into these discussions alternately as perpetrators, victims and saviors with regard to the current crisis in fiction. Not only were the '"yellow" lady novelists' to blame for all the 'sex problem' novels, but it was also the readers, the 'neurotic young women of the idle classes', with their 'unwholesome' interest in psychology and physiology, who were accused of popularizing them.[43] And it was also for the *sake* of young women that these novels were condemned, for women were depicted by critics such as Mrs Oliphant as too poorly educated and naive to perceive the false and pernicious aspects of the new fiction. She lamented that 'things are discussed freely and easily which it would a few years ago have been a shame to mention or to think of', and warned repeatedly that the new fiction was 'dangerous' and 'damaging' for the young women who were its chief readers.[44] It was also specifically the depictions of *women's* sexuality which were denounced as unhealthy and hazardous; any threat to the 'purity' of women was interpreted as a threat to the institution of marriage, as well as to British society. The authors of these articles implored women to fear for their own well-being and that of the nation, and placed the responsibility for putting a halt to the 'sex-mania' on women's shoulders: 'In all matters relating to decency and good taste men gladly acknowledge the supremacy of women, and we may surely ask them to give us a lead in discouraging books which are a degradation of English literature.'[45]

The emphasis in these articles on literature was obfuscatory; at the core of the literary crisis of 1895 was a pervasive uneasiness about women in general, and their power to influence and change not only fiction but the social, political and economic structures of England. This uneasiness is evident in the way in which many of these critics express their aesthetic judgements and moral values with gender terms and sexual metaphors. Traditional social norms and literary standards are characterized as 'masculine' and 'natural'; the health and strength of the nation are equated with virility and potency. 'Good sense and manliness' are called for to counteract the current tendency toward the 'effeminate' and 'effeminacy' in literature and criticism, the latter terms being the dominant ones of denigration and devaluation in these essays; the ills of society are described with metaphors of impotence, sterility, weakness and flaccidity. Works as diverse as New Woman novels, the plays of Oscar Wilde and Ibsen, the philosophy of Nietzsche, and the fiction of Zola are all criticized for being 'effeminate', for they exhibit qualities such as introspection, pessimism or eroticism, which are said to have the effect of 'sapping manliness and making people flabby'. The influence of Nordau, who warned that the movement away from distinctive and separate sex roles for men and women was an unmistakable sign of evolutionary reversion, or degeneration, is obvious. One of his devoted acolytes, Hugh Stutfield, called for the resurgence 'of manliness and self-reliance in men, and womanliness in women' in order to rid literature of 'putrid eroticism'; the implication of his criticisms, as well as that of other opponents of the new realism, is that only when men and women have returned to their proper gender roles can literature (and England) once again be 'decent' and 'sound'.[46]

The trouble with fiction was also the trouble with women, and those troubles were seen as emblematic of England's more general malaise at the close of the century. The dominant image of the New Woman in fiction and in the popular press, as well as the actual advances being made by women in education, employment and government, contributed to a general sense that the most basic order of things was being threatened. The subversion of the social and economic structures of England by women seemed imminent, and conservatives felt that it was imperative to stop women before they went too far. It is not surprising that fiction became a primary battleground in the war of the sexes, for while critics complained that the new fiction was responsible for influencing many of the recent changes in women's attitudes and behavior, they also realized that fiction, if properly controlled, had the potential to be a powerful instrument of containment and social regulation. And by 1895, the state of British fiction itself seemed like a portent of what could happen on a larger scale. The conservative critics who encouraged the public perception of a literary and social crisis believed that unless what they saw as the feminization of fiction was stopped, it was only a matter of time before all of England became dominated by women as well.[47]

Many agreed with Mrs Lynn Linton that society had reached a state of 'universal topsyturveydom', and there were several troubling developments which seemed to confirm that impression. In 1894, which the *Lady's Realm* had dubbed 'an *annus mirabilis* in the annals of the enfranchisement of women', the Local Government Act entitled some women to a limited and local vote, giving those who opposed women's suffrage the panicked sense that they were 'nearing the rapids'.[48] Then, in 1895, the publication of Allen's *The Woman Who Did* raised the furor over sex in fiction to a new pitch. Several months afterwards, a highly publicized incident concerning a young woman who was forcibly committed to a mental asylum by her father after declaring her intention to live with her lover without the benefit of marriage was viewed by many as proof that New Woman novels were enticing young women to abandon all moral restraint.[49] Even more disturbing were the trials of Wilde, which not only forced a shocked British public to confront the fact of homosexuality but also validated the predictions of those critics who warned that modern literature was undermining the masculinity of the nation, and would eventually lead to a blurring of gender roles. But there was one event in particular which brought the literary crisis of 1895 to a climax of anxiety and hysteria: the publication in that year of Hardy's *Jude the Obscure*.[50]

Women, sexuality and marriage had always played a significant part in Hardy's novels, and many of his heroines are akin to the New Woman in their intelligence, independence and unconventionality. Hardy was obviously sensitive to the social issues of his time, and as a matter of course he wrote about the social conventions and legal and economic inequities which shaped and restricted women's lives. But for the most part, his social criticism was of a general nature (though he had focused specifically on the issue of divorce in *The Woodlanders* [1887]), and society's effects upon individuals were often subsumed in the larger workings of fate. Like that of the French naturalists, Hardy's emphasis on women and sexual relations had less to do with any particular interest in women's issues than with his artistic desire to portray all of life honestly, unrestricted by conventional moral codes or false notions of literary decorum. In that respect, Hardy's project in *Tess of the d'Urbervilles* resembled Moore's in *Esther Waters* and Gissing's in *The Unclassed*. Like Moore and Gissing, Hardy declined to offer solutions to the problems he raised; even when he advocated divorce, it was only with the sense that it could mollify, not rectify, the problems inherent in intimate and sexual relationships. Nevertheless, *Tess* was also Hardy's response to the contemporary debate about women and sexual knowledge and ideals of purity; its subtitle – 'A Pure Woman' – was a deliberate provocation to readers and critics, and a clear signal that the novel was an expression of Hardy's disdain for conventional sexual morality. As a result, detractors of *Tess* were quick to associate Hardy with the French naturalists, Zola, and Ibsen, and accuse him of writing a *'tendez-roman'*, or a 'novel with a purpose'.[51]

But the passive and unintellectual Tess is by no means a New Woman; although Hardy used her sufferings to illustrate the evils of the sexual double standard and the Victorian feminine ideal, she is an innocent victim, not a purposeful rebel. Hardy had Tess reject Angel Clare's linear narrative of causality and irrevocability, but he did not give her a new narrative in which to live her life; after aimlessly wandering through most of the novel, Tess has no other choice than to rejoin the conventional narrative in the only role available to her – that of the fallen woman. Hardy challenged, through his narration, those social and narrative structures that insist that Tess's sexual relationship with Alec be read as a 'fall', or dictate that Tess must follow an inexorable path to disgrace and death. Yet he also maintained the conventional plot of the fallen woman who, through her extreme suffering, gains the reader's sympathy, but must die in moral retribution for her sexual sin. Hardy, not unlike some New Woman novelists, tried to have it both ways: by manipulating but not discarding traditional narrative structures, he produced a kind of ambiguity in *Tess* that allowed him to make a social critique while appealing to a wide range of readers.

Because of this ambiguity, some critics were able to downplay the sexual frankness and unconventional morality of *Tess* to a certain extent, and it was generally well received. But the bitter denunciations of marriage and the New Woman character in Hardy's next novel, *Jude the*

Obscure, made it almost impossible to dissociate it from recent trends in fiction, and as a result there was a vehement critical outcry. The reviewer for the *Fortnightly Review* spoke for the majority of critics: 'If we consider broadly and without prejudice the tone and scope of the book, we cannot but class it with the fiction of Sex and New Woman, so rife of late.'[52] Although Hardy was probably influenced as much by the social and cultural climate he shared with the new realists as by their fiction, they nevertheless enabled him, as it were, to make an analysis of sexual relations and marriage the primary focus of his novel, and to present it more topically, polemically and frankly than he had been able to do before.[53] New Woman novels in particular provided Hardy with a new type of heroine who could respond both sexually and intellectually to the changing status of women in society.[54] In his 1912 postscript to the preface of *Jude the Obscure*, he confirms this association in part when he agrees obliquely with a German critic that Sue Bridehead is 'the woman of the feminist movement – the slight, pale, "bachelor" girl – the intellectualized, emancipated bundle of nerves that modern conditions were producing, mainly in cities as yet; who does not recognize the necessity for most of her sex to follow marriage as a profession'.

For reviewers, the markings of New Woman fiction were all there: the use of marriage as a tragic beginning to a narrative rather than a happy end; the anti-marriage rhetoric; the blatant sexuality of Jude and Arabella; and most of all, the character of Sue, the modern, neurotic young woman who scorns tradition and talks obsessively about sex. But Hardy's complex and subtle presentation of Sue makes her anything but the typical New Woman heroine; through Sue's insecurities and doubts, Hardy examines the problems inherent in a rebellion which bypasses crucial questions of self-definition and defines itself solely by what it is against. Like Moore, Hardy was fascinated by the contradictions involved in the sexual aspect of women's emancipation, and through Sue's relationships with men, he examines how difficult it is for women to separate sex from subordination or chastity from personal freedom, particularly in the light of the risk of pregnancy that they must face. But such nuances of analysis were lost on the opponents of *Jude the Obscure*, who saw only perverse frigidity and coarse sexuality, as well as the unrelieved bleakness and ugliness of the world Hardy gave them. What was shocking to readers was not only that Hardy had lowered himself to write a sex problem novel, but that he went far beyond the New Woman novelists in his pessimistic anti-marriage stance and his demystification of maternity; to some, *Jude the Obscure* placed Hardy 'as an advocate of celibacy and the extinction of the race'.[55]

For many years Hardy had been considered the undisputed master of the British novel, and his fiction was seen as a good example of exactly the kind of serious, masculine novels that greater candor was supposed to encourage. In 1892 Gosse smugly noted that it was 'men [who] have made Mr Thomas Hardy, who owes nothing to the fair sex; if women read him now, it is because the men have told them that they must'.[56] Hardy's traditional (and manly, considered many) style of realism was not obviously influenced by either French naturalism or feminism; thus even opponents of the new realism found something to admire in his novels. Hardy made the idea of a hierarchy of British fiction feasible for those who were eager to ghettoize women's novels and women's issues as low or popular fiction. So when he chose to ignore the emerging distinctions between serious and popular fiction by focusing upon women and sex in *Tess of the d'Urbervilles* and *Jude the Obscure*, most of the literary establishment was appalled, and his supporters scrambled to distinguish him from writers of New Woman fiction, and place him back up 'at the summit of British novelists'.[57]

The strategy of Richard le Gallienne and others was to bluntly but illogically deny any connections between Hardy and the new fiction: 'Too many reviewers have treated *Jude* as a polemic against marriage. Nothing could be more unjust.'[58] But the extremely negative critical response to *Jude the Obscure* indicated that for many readers and critics, the redemption of Hardy was no longer possible. The reviewer in the *Spectator* insisted that while '*Tess* was unmistakably a novel with a purpose', the 'decadent realism' of *Jude* made it 'too deplorable a falling-off ... to be reckoned with at all'. That Hardy should be 'caught in the fashion of the period'; that 'such august names in literature and art have taken the new ideas under their patronage'; that such 'grossness, indecency, and horror' should come 'from the hands of a Master', was more than conservative critics and readers could bear.[59] As was usual with reviews of the new fiction, reviewers expressed deep disgust at the sexual references in *Jude* (one called it 'steeped in sex'), and shook their heads over the possible corrupting influence the novel might have upon women.[60] In Hardy's case, his literary status made the situation even more serious and dangerous: the reviewer in the *World* complained that Hardy had 'consciously or unconsciously thrown the whole weight of his powerful literary influence into the scale of revolting womanhood ...'.[61]

But *Jude the Obscure* was also a confirmation that 'revolting womanhood' was exerting a strong influence upon Hardy and other established writers. The reviewer in the *Nation* explained that 'toleration [had been] extended to inferior novelists' who wrote about New Women and sexual matters, for they were presumed to have little influence; but *Tess* and *Jude* 'made some people feel and say that our literature was in danger of corruption'.[62] The publication of *Jude the Obscure* made it clear that it was no longer possible to segregate sex and marriage and the concerns of women as inferior or inconsequential subject matter; it was no longer possible to ignore the fact that the feminism that was changing women's lives had the potential to change British literature in a wide-ranging and serious manner. Hardy had disregarded distinctions between serious literature and popular novels, and ignored the rules concerning 'respectable' topics for literature, and the shock of having literary hierarchies challenged by one at the top cannot be overemphasized. But the real crisis of 1895 was that such a literary breakdown seemed emblematic of a larger social breakdown: if literary divisions were destroyed, then gender and class divisions could also be leveled. Hardy's literary crossover was a powerful indication of how far things had gone.

To a certain extent the authors of the crisis articles of 1895 were successful in their efforts. Hardy never wrote another novel after *Jude the Obscure*; New Woman novels declined in production and popularity; there was a resurgence of reticence, romance and idealism in fiction. In his review of *Jude the Obscure* in 1896, H.G. Wells observed: 'It is now the better part of a year ago since the collapse of the "New Woman" fiction began,' for he marked the beginning of the decline with the publication of *The Woman Who Did*.[63] In 1897 the critic Hugh Stutfield noted with relief that 'the literature and the drama of 1896 have shown a distinct improvement upon those of two or three years ago. The protests of the Philistines have not been altogether in vain.'[64] An Edwardian novelist, Maud Churton Braby, looked back on the years following the crisis of 1895 with dismay:

> The cult of literature (!) for the British Home was shortly afterwards in full blast. There followed an avalanche of insufferably dull and puerile magazines, in which the word *Sex* was strictly taboo, and the ideal aimed at was apparently the extreme opposite to real life. It was odd how suddenly the sex note . . . disappeared from the press. Psychology was pronounced 'off', and plots were the order of the day.[65]

Wells later recalled the same period as a time when 'ideas were dead – or domesticated':

> For a little time the world did actually watch a phase of English writing that dared nothing, penetrated nothing, suppressed everything and aspired at most to Charm, creep like a transitory patch of sunlight across a storm-rent universe. And vanish. . . .[66]

Censorship, or merely the fear of censorship, was an important factor in the purgation from literature of references to sexuality and unconventional behavior and relationships. The trials and imprisonment of Wilde had a significant subduing effect upon sexual frankness in literature, as did the suppression of books on sexuality by Havelock Ellis and Edward

Carpenter in the late 1890s.[67] At the same time, there were also renewed attempts to contain the advances being made by feminism. A suffrage bill was defeated, and in highly publicized and vigorously fought battles, women tried and failed to obtain the right to earn degrees at Oxford (1895–6) and Cambridge (1896–7).[68]

But the story does not end there, despite the standard view that the reactionary and conservative tendencies of the late-Victorian age continued into the Edwardian period. The feeling in the final years of the nineteenth century that gender roles had become restabilized and literature remasculinized was short-lived: the fact remained that the lives of women had changed, and the novel had changed with them. The crisis of 1895, instead of marking the end of something, actually marked the beginning of a series of developments in fiction which would culminate in literary modernism. Ironically, the literary (though not the social) predictions of the conservative critics who warned that fiction was being 'feminized' were accurate; the British novel was being transformed by women and feminism in fundamental and perhaps irremediable ways.

It has been generally recognized that the influence of the new realism continued into the twentieth century, but there has been little critical consideration of the continued influence of feminism. Its impact on literature at the turn of the century has come to be so closely identified with the New Woman novels that other, less obvious indications of its literary significance have been overlooked. But the thematic and formal developments in fiction which resulted from the intersection of feminism and realism in the early 1890s did not disappear with the demise of the New Woman novel; they reemerged to unsettle novelistic traditions in the fiction of the Edwardian period and set the stage for the fiction of literary modernism. Ironically, the very aspects of the new fiction of the 1890s that critics condemned as the most decadent and neurotic – such as its subjectivity, its psychological introspection and its sexual frankness – would eventually come to be regarded as essential components of the modernist novel.

By the early years of the Edwardian period, innovations that had been considered controversial a decade earlier were being assimilated into fiction with ease. As one contemporary observer noted: 'It was typical of the Victorian and the post-Victorian ages that up to 1900 everybody pretended that he had not read George Moore, while under King Edward all pretended they had.'[69] The problem novel became the most popular novel genre of the period. Readers of Edwardian novels came to expect a certain level of frankness and sophistication in fiction, particularly with regard to sexual matters. The increasing size and diversity of the reading public made it difficult to maintain the categories that the conservative critics of the 1890s insisted were universal and unalterable; the multifarious fiction of the Edwardian years subverted neat distinctions between popular and serious, art and entertainment, masculine and feminine, and well-respected authors such as Joseph Conrad and H.G. Wells crossed literary boundaries with impunity.

Most significantly, the reemergence of feminism, newly energized and politically focused, during the Edwardian period once again placed modern women and feminist issues at the center of fiction. Feminism, like realism, was no longer considered a corrupting force in British fiction, and rebellious heroines, independent women and unhappy wives became common figures in Edwardian novels. Although some critics complained about 'the flood of feministic fiction' being published, there was no real anxiety that British fiction was being feminized; that particular anxiety was replaced in the public mind by a far more palpable fear of the militancy of the suffragette movement.[70]

But Edwardian writers did not just inherit the thematic innovations of the new fiction of the 1890s – they also inherited its formal problems. No longer having to battle simply to present women with honesty and specificity and sexual frankness, novelists now had to face the inadequacy of the traditional narrative forms of the nineteenth-century novel for narrating the lives of modern women. And it is in this regard, too, that the conservative critics of the 1890s were prescient. Although it was not as direct or simple as they perceived it to be, there was indeed an intimate link between feminist challenges to the social order and artistic challenges to the literary tradition, and that link became an important concern of Edward novelists. The next four chapters take as their subject the variety of representations of modern women and feminist issues in Edwardian fiction, and examine the ways in which these representations forced Edwardian novelists to scrutinize stereotypes of gender, to confront the ideologies of narrative structures and, ultimately, to challenge and break with the formal traditions of the novel.

CHAPTER TWO

Women and the Marriage Problem Novel

Marriage indeed seems to be in the air more than ever in this year of grace;
everywhere it is discussed, and very few people seem to have a good word to
say for it. The most superficial observer must have noticed that there is being
gradually built up . . . a growing dread of the conjugal bond, especially among
men; and a condition of discontent and unrest among married people,
particularly women.

(MAUD CHURTON BRABY, *Modern Marriage
and How to Bear It* [1909])

We of today know that whatever marriage is, it is not an end. We know that it
is rather a beginning, and that the lovers enter upon life's real problems when
those wedding bells are silent. . . . The early Victorian woman was regarded as
a bundle of goods. She passed from the possession of her father to that of her
husband. Marriage was a final event for her: beyond it, she was expected to
find no new development, no new emotion. And so the early Victorian
novelist might reasonably end his book with a marriage. . . . But the woman of
today is quite another person. She is by no means a bundle of goods. . . . She
may marry, but her marriage is most certainly not an *end*, either for herself or
her husband. Their courtship was but a prelude: their wedding is but the
raising of the curtain for the play. The drama of their problems, their
developments, their mutual interaction, is all to come. And how can a novelist
of today, knowing this, end his novel with a marriage?

(E.M. FORSTER, 'Pessimism in Literature' [1906])

An unhappy marriage! No ill-treatment – only that indefinable malaise, that
terrible blight which killed all sweetness under Heaven . . .

(JOHN GALSWORTHY, *The Man of Property* [1906])

What had initially been designated the Marriage Question in the 1890s
came to be perceived during the Edwardian era as the Marriage *Problem*.
The majority of Edwardian women did expect and desire to marry, but
they were doing so later in life and with more personal volition than
women in the nineteenth century.[1] Because of new opportunities for
higher education and employment, more women were leading independent lives before marriage, and were subsequently less tolerant of the
traditional, patriarchal structure of marriage which required subser-
vience, self-abnegation, and a limited sphere of activity and influence.
Maud Churton Braby, a novelist and author of marital advice books,
observed: 'a spirit of strange unrest has come over married women . . .
[who] rebel against conditions which our grandmothers would never
have dreamed of murmuring at'.[2]

Other developments in the early twentieth century also served to
challenge the institution of marriage. As a result of changes in law during
the nineteenth century, married Edwardian women were able to own
property, retain custody of their children, and sue for divorce (given
certain circumstances), and could no longer be imprisoned by their
husbands for refusing conjugal rights. The Royal Commission on Divorce
was formed in 1909 to investigate – among other issues – whether women
should have equal rights with men in divorce cases. There was also a
noticeable trend in the early years of the century toward smaller families
in the middle and upper classes, facilitated by the increasing availability
of information about contraception.[3] There was still a significant 'surplus'
of women in the Edwardian age, but many single women, unlike their
Victorian counterparts, were able to pursue careers and lead independent
lives in the cities; their acceptance of their unmarried status and their high
visibility (particularly in the suffrage movement) were disconcerting to
those who believed that women could be truly fulfilled only through
marriage and motherhood.

These social and legal changes were seen by a great many Edwardians
as specific threats to the stability of the family, and hence of British
society, and more generally as signs of 'the growing dissatisfaction of the
sexes with each other'.[4] But they were also signs of a growing
sophistication among the Edwardians about sex and marriage – a
sophistication that was heralded, in part, by the widely discussed and
controversial new fiction of the late 1880s and early 1890s, which
questioned traditional ideas about gender, sexuality and morality. This
sophistication and dissatisfaction led to the scrutiny of the Victorian ideal
of marriage, and throughout the Edwardian age the institution of

marriage was tirelessly discussed, analyzed and criticized, both publicly and privately; as one literary critic put it: 'The once sacred, the once theoretically indissoluble life-tie between husband and wife has become, in short, an open question.'[5] The result was a heightened self- and social consciousness concerning relations between men and women – a consciousness fraught with tension and doubt.

Thus for many, the marriage problem was that marriage could no longer be viewed as a paradigm of harmony and happiness, or even as a necessary component of a fulfilled life. This shift in attitude is reflected in the large number of Edwardian men who postponed marriage until middle age, or opted to remain bachelors (a situation which prompted some to propose a bachelor tax).[6] It is also indicated by the cynical titles of Edwardian books on marriage, such as Braby's *Modern Marriage and How to Bear It* (1909), or Cicely Hamilton's *Marriage as a Trade* (1909); these books are predicated upon the belief that the desires of men and women in marriage inevitably conflict with one another.

The marital advice of Braby, who also wrote *The Love-Seeker: A Guide to Marriage* (1913) and two novels, exemplifies the contradictory position women found themselves in during the Edwardian years. Starting with the assumption that all 'average, normal' women desire 'to find a mate, build a nest, and rear a brood', Braby set out to teach liberated modern women what she assumed their mothers and grandmothers knew naturally: how to get and keep a man.[7] Although she cautiously praised the recent advances made by women, she warned that the 'tendency of modern ideas and education is to make women less feminine. Those who wish to please men must beware of this and cultivate femininity deliberately, concealing their independence, just as shrewd women often conceal their superior mentality.' Braby advised that women should 'make a cult of self-control and a hobby of self-sacrifice', for 'men should never be reproached or criticized'.[8] Even though she admitted that 'personally, all this "playing up" is repellent to me', she advised women to act in such a fashion because 'men apparently take with an ill-grace women's rebellion against the old man-made conditions', and few men 'are sufficiently educated and evolved to appreciate the advantages of candor between the sexes'.[9] Braby called for women's economic independence and 'a rational code of sex equality', but offered few suggestions for social reform other than better sex education for girls, a 'preliminary canter' for women before marriage, and 'wild oats for wives'. The fact that the 'canter' and the 'oats' are to be strictly chaste however, exemplifies the conventionality beneath Braby's radical veneer; in her books she strove to reinforce traditional gender definitions, and repeatedly stated her belief that marriage and motherhood comprise women's 'highest destiny'.

The conflict between traditional values and modern ideas about women that cuts through Braby's books is characteristically Edwardian, as is her resolution of that conflict: women must find ways to achieve personal gratification without alienating men or sacrificing their social respectability. Recognizing the difficulties of living in a time of transition, Braby advised women to develop a kind of double existence: be modern and liberated in thought, but hide your true nature so that you can enjoy the comfort and stability of conventional social arrangements. Braby's books, with their promises of happiness through compromise and concealment, went through several editions; they obviously appealed to a large number of women who felt torn between the values of their parents, the desire for social acceptance and integration, and a modern awareness of their own needs and abilities.

The increasing tension between tradition and modernity that many Edwardian women felt is also visible in the popular (and, for the most part, conservative) women's magazines of the age. In the midst of romantic fiction, fashion advertisements, and articles on food and housekeeping, many magazines such as *The Lady* or *The Queen* presented a new feature – the 'problem page' or personal advice column – which testified to the pressing need for new rules of behavior for the modern age. Advice to readers in Victorian periodicals had been of a strictly impersonal and factual nature, but Edwardian advice columns were dominated by the personal problems of frustrated daughters, young women in love, and unhappy new wives.[10] These letters chronicle feelings of confusion, disillusionment and loneliness, and suggest that the questioning of gender roles and discontent with traditional relationships were not limited to feminists, suffragettes, or sophisticated New Women. These letters also attest to a rift between generations, for the young women writing them were obviously no longer comfortable appealing to their mothers for advice about courtship and marriage.

Correspondence of a similar nature was also to be found in the pages of the radical feminist newspaper *The Freewoman*, which published lengthy and scholarly articles on such topics as 'The Immorality of the Marriage Contract' and 'The Failure of Marriage'. But the most powerful discussions of marriage in *The Freewoman* were in the letters to the editor, in which women revealed with astonishing honesty and freedom their feelings about sexuality, the indignities of the marriage market, and the frustration of trying to maintain some kind of personal identity while running a household and raising children. Indeed, what unites the letters from the feminists with those from the readers of popular magazines is their repeated emphasis on the conflict between one's individual situation and society's ideals of womanhood and marriage.

Edwardian discussions about the marriage problem also frequently contained references to the problem of 'sex-antagonism' or 'sex-warfare' in modern society – a problem created in large part by the militant suffrage movement. The majority of women who were active in the suffrage campaign were unmarried, and unlike Victorian feminists, many Edwardian feminists were more interested in making a case against marriage and sex than in promoting an ideal of a fair and companionate relationship.[11] They saw the rejection of marriage as both psychologically and strategically necessary, in order to achieve the emancipation of women; in 1912, the feminist writer Lucy Re-Bartlett argued that '[a] period of this kind must be passed through before the old relations between men and women be set aside and the new and nobler ones established'.[12] It was generally accepted among these feminists that change on a personal and private level would occur only after women's votes effected larger and more sweeping social changes. The suffragette Christabel Pankhurst declared (erroneously) in her pamphlet *The Great Scourge and How to End It* (1913) that 75 to 80 per cent of British men had venereal disease, and she implied that it was women's political duty to abstain from marriage and sex in order to liberate women and 'purify' the nation. Radical feminist theorists like Re-Bartlett and Frances Swiney posited a fundamental relationship between sexual intercourse and the oppression of women and, invoking the spiritual superiority of women and the animal nature of men, argued that 'Sex union in the human being should be limited strictly to the actual *needs of creation*'.[13] The sexual disgust evident in the writings of Pankhurst, Swiney, and others came to be unfairly considered as characteristic of Edwardian feminism in general, and contributed to a growing sense that feminists were waging war against marriage and men.

For other feminists, though, the 'problem' with marriage was that it was badly in need of reevaluation and reformation. These feminists recognized the importance of marriage to individuals and to society, but they also criticized its traditional structure, which demanded the subordination of the wife, and the restriction of her activities and interests to domestic duties. Florence Farr, suffragist, actress and playwright, is representative of the more moderate Edwardian feminists who neither hated men nor denigrated sexuality as an 'animal' instinct, but wished to reform relationships between men and women. In her book *Modern Woman: Her Intentions* (1910) she predicted, with optimism and remarkable frankness, that women's economic independence would lead to 'love marriages', more satisfying sexual relations, and healthier children. Farr argued that if women workers were paid better wages, there would be fewer marriages based upon financial necessity, and she suggested that housewives be paid regular wages as well. She warned that the

Victorian ideology of motherhood was dangerously restrictive, and predicted that 'women will specialize in the future', in terms of choosing whether to have children or not (63).

The feminist playwright and novelist Cicely Hamilton also attacked the institution of marriage from economic and sociological perspectives. In her book *Marriage as a Trade* she analyzed marriage as if it were a profession, deploring its unfair working conditions and criticizing society for refusing to train women for any other occupation. Hamilton went so far as to imply that married women sold themselves much as prostitutes did; thus she boldly exposed the sexual economy at the heart of marriage. The criticism of feminists like Farr and Hamilton is indicative of the increasing popularity of the ideal of companionate marriage during the Edwardian years; as marriage became less of an economic or social necessity for women, the desire for a partnership of companionship and mutual respect increased. But this new kind of marriage required men to relinquish their domestic power and authority, and thus constituted yet another disquieting threat to the status quo by women.

It is no surprise that the marriage problem became the dominant subject of Edwardian fiction, given the enormous public interest in the issue as well as the centrality of marriage to the novel genre itself. Sexually frank, critical of social norms, grounded in detailed material and psychological realism, the Edwardian marriage problem novel – or the novel of marital incompatibility, as it was sometimes called – is a direct descendant of the new fiction of the 1890s. But it differs from its predecessors in one significant regard. By the early twentieth century, the controversy over the new realism and New Woman novels had faded, and the thematic innovations of that fiction had become more or less assimilated into Edwardian fiction. Overt expressions of feminist sympathies in fiction were still regarded with some suspicion, and publishers, wary of negative critical and public response, still demanded that their authors delete potentially offensive passages; but in general the atmosphere was far more tolerant than that of the 1890s. It was expected that fiction would be sexually candid, would engage with social problems, and would treat the particular concerns of women with depth and seriousness.

But even though it seemed inevitable that the marriage problem should be explored within a genre predicated upon marriage, there was something contradictory in the project as well. Marriage had been essential to the novel, both as a subject and as a structuring principle, from its inception: marriage served as a paradigm of social integration and stability within the narrative, while the desire for marriage provided narrative impetus and the achievement of marriage offered a means of narrative resolution. To question that paradigm entailed (at least implicitly) a questioning of the narrative conventions and forms that novelists used to depict romance and marriage. Traditionally, marriage had figured in the plots of British novels in one of three basic ways, the most common being the courtship plot, in which the protagonists overcome obstacles and achieve personal maturity in order to enjoy the final unifying triumph. The comic wedlock plot essentially duplicates the courtship narrative within a marital relationship; conflicts and problems are resolved in order to reaffirm the ideal of marriage at the end of the novel. The plot of tragic wedlock depicts an unhappy marriage which is doomed to failure; but its narrative focuses upon the faults and failings of the protagonists, and invariably takes care not to place blame on the institution of marriage itself.[14] The new fiction of the 1880s and 1890s broke with this latter tradition and, using marriage as a bad beginning, attempted to demonstrate the problems of the institution, specifically for women, through a married heroine's experiences. These novels were only partially successful in challenging narrative conventions concerning marriage and narrative closure; in particular, the social critique of the New Woman novels was often contradicted or even canceled by the conservative force of the novelistic traditions their authors employed. Nevertheless, the new fiction of the 1890s marked an important shift in the relationship of the idea and ideal of marriage to the form of the novel.

By the Edwardian age, the public debate on the marriage problem and on divorce reform made it difficult for marriage to function in the novel simply as a happy ending, or as a positive indicator of personal success and social unity; increasingly, marriage in itself was a *subject* for fiction, and all but the most conventional novelists ceased to treat it as an unproblematic ideal. Some critics complained about the new emphasis in fiction and drama on 'the post-nuptial phase of love and marriage', but most agreed with E.M. Forster that marriage should be seen as a beginning, not an end, and that 'the drama of their problems' was the real story that modern readers wanted.[15] Novels that depicted marriage as an uncomplicated and happy romantic relationship, such as E. Nesbit's *The Red House* (1902), were rare; although the author admitted that her tale of newlyweds joyfully sharing housework was 'a fairy tale', she told H.G. Wells that she refused to accept the current notion that marriage was all 'detestable disintegration'.[16] But there was a general feeling that relations between the sexes were breaking down, and it is reflected in the fact that the novels of the period are filled with unhappy marriages; the institution of marriage is relentlessly scrutinized in Edwardian fiction, even in those novels which eventually advocate it.

All marriage problem novelists confronted the limitations of the institution of marriage in their novels; Forster, Ada Leverson, John

Galsworthy, Arnold Bennett, Amber Reeves, Olivia Shakespear and Elizabeth von Arnim went one step further and confronted the limitations (and ideological implications) of the traditional narrative forms at their disposal. Some of the novels that resulted are innovative, even subversive; some are contradictory or regressive. But all their novels exemplify the dynamic struggle with tradition which is characteristic not only of Edwardian fiction, but of the entire Edwardian period.

E.M. Forster complained in *Aspects of the Novel* that novelists are too reliant upon marriage as a plot device; in particular, he objected to 'that idiotic use of marriage as a finale'.[17] Yet Forster's five Edwardian novels demonstrate a fascination with as well as a resistance to marriage; two of them end in marriage (although one is of an unconventional nature) and the others rely heavily upon marriage in theme and plot. This contradiction points to the transitional nature of Forster's work, and of the Edwardian novel in general. Forster wished to be recognized as a 'modern' novelist, and what he deemed modern was a pessimistic attitude and novels which ended with scenes of separation. But he also looked back to the 'healthy simplicity' and optimism of Victorian novels with fondness and longing, despite his recognition of the limitations of Victorian conventions and values.[18]

The predominance of marriage in Forster's novels is contradictory in another way as well. Most of the other Edwardian novelists who wrote about marriage were themselves married, and often had a strong personal stake in the way they depicted marriage in their novels. But Forster was a homosexual who never had any intention of marrying, and he had little personal interest in contemporary debates about the institution of marriage, or the divorce laws: though there are many unhappy marriages in his novels, there is never any mention of divorce. The rights of women, women's suffrage, and indeed, women in general, seem to have been of negligible interest to Forster as well.[19]

Forster himself provided a straightforward explanation for the dominant role love and marriage play in his novels: it is 'the only subject that I both can and may treat – the love of men for women & vice versa. Passion and money are the two main springs of action (not of existence) and I can only write of the first & that imperfectly.'[20] The phrase 'can and may' is telling: the 'can' refers to the limits of Forster's abilities as a novelist and the reading public's demand for novels about love and marriage; but the 'may' has to do with his sense that there is another kind of passion and love that he could write about, but is not permitted to: homosexual love. In one respect, Forster's emphasis on heterosexual relationships can be looked upon as a screen that protected him from any revelation of his own sexuality. The only novel in which he wrote openly about homosexuality is *Maurice* (1913–14), which was not published until after his death. Like the hero of that novel, it seems that Forster, in his fiction, often tried to be conventional and unobjectionable, so as to arouse no suspicion. But heterosexual love and marriage also provided him with a lens through which he could refract his own feelings about love and passion. Though this deception pained him at times, it also – ironically – freed him, and his best Edwardian novels are those that focus on women and love and marriage: *Where Angels Fear to Tread* (1905), *A Room with a View* (1908), and *Howards End* (1910). In these novels, correspondences between the lives of women and those of homosexuals become evident, though seemingly unintentionally: they are linked by their sexual repression, their victimization by social conventions, by simply their otherness. These correspondences result in several sensitive and sympathetic portrayals of women that belie the misogyny which mars Forster's novels about men.

Forster's novels are about a great deal more than marriage, but at the heart of them his interest always returned to the philosophy expressed in his famous dictum 'Only connect'. In that Forster presented conventional marriage as a highly unlikely place for anyone to 'connect', he was commenting upon the marriage problem. But he was not interested in marriage reform; marriage is simply a convenient and familiar context in which to explore a more general conflict between the feelings people have for one another, and all the social conventions and institutions that are designed to contain, categorize, and regulate those feelings. 'Only connect' refers both to social connections and to an individual's personal connections with life, and Forster's characters can be divided into those who embrace life and those who retreat from it. To embrace life for Forster also meant to embrace the physical world – of nature and of one's own body. Underlying Forster's depiction of the stifling social conventions of his class and age is a critique of a society that despises and fears sexuality, a society which tries to prevent people from enjoying what he saw as ideally the ultimate connection – that of sexual relations.

Ironically, the best expression of Forster's philosophy of sexual connection is contained within his most traditional novel – *A Room with a View* – which was the first novel he wrote, but the third published. *A Room with a View* is a courtship novel rather than a marriage problem novel, and Forster presents a classic narrative of two lovers who overcome various obstructions and disapproval to be finally joined in marriage. But the triumphant lovers are not the socially acceptable and conventional couple of Lucy Honeychurch and Cecil Vyse but, rather, the unconventional couple whose 'courtship' has subverted all the social rules: Lucy and George Emerson. Marriage itself, as a desideratum and an ending, is never questioned; indeed, Lucy and George's marriage is celebrated as a natural connection and an inevitable conclusion. But it is the nature of their marriage that is revolutionary in its own way.

In *A Room with a View*, Forster offers a new ideal of wedlock for Edwardian society to consider, for the marriage of Lucy and George is based upon sexual passion and equality. Instead of depicting sexuality as a disruptive, disturbing force that either exists outside of or is tamed by marriage (as so many Edwardian novels did), Forster valorizes sexual passion, and is thus able to subvert the traditional ideology of the courtship novel even while he employs its traditional structure. Tradition also dictated that the novel end when the couple are wed, so the only view of Lucy and George's new marriage that the reader is given is of their honeymoon. But the experimental nature of their marriage ultimately makes the ending an open one rather than a traditional one, for how Lucy and George's ideal of equality will fare in practice, especially after they return to England and Lucy's disapproving family, one can only guess. Yet for Forster, who believed that 'the *end* is of supreme importance in a book', the structure of *Room*, and particularly its ending, ultimately diluted the social criticism contained within it to the extent that he eventually dismissed it as merely 'a nice story': *A Room with a View*, he said, 'will gratify the home circle, but not those whose opinion I value most'.[21]

Two years before the publication of *Room*, in a speech to the Working Men's College Old Students' Club on pessimism in literature (quoted in the epigraph to this chapter), Forster had insisted that to end a novel with a marriage was old-fashioned and unsatisfactory. He explained that although in life people seek 'what is cheerful, and noble, and gracious, even if it is transitory', an author 'looks for what is permanent, even if it is sad' (138); to be modern, a novelist must be a pessimist of sorts, and end his or her novel with a 'scene of separation'. Forster never demonstrated satisfactorily why a scene of separation imparts a greater sense of permanence than a marriage; also, he did not take into account either the formal difficulties of accomplishing such ends, or his own personal impulse toward connection. It is significant that Forster's aesthetics were rarely actualized in his own novels; he clearly struggled with the endings of all of his other Edwardian novels, and was forced to resort to sudden (and often unbelievable) deaths to bring his narratives to a climax. The strong pull of narrative closure, particularly that achieved through social integration and regeneration, is evident in the dénouements of all Forster's Edwardian novels. It is also possible that Forster's theories were predicated in part upon his own personal antipathy toward marriage and its dominance in the novel, for it was a happy ending he could never partake of. It is telling that when he came to write *Maurice*, it was extremely important to him that it have a happy ending – that of the 'marriage' of the homosexual lovers.

Only *Where Angels Fear to Tread*, Forster's first published novel, follows his formal prescription exactly. It begins with a marriage, from which all subsequent events can be traced, and ends with a separation. The marriage of the young British widow Lilia Herriton to Gino Carella, the son of an Italian dentist, is ill-considered, brief and tragic, but it does provide Forster with an opportunity to depict 'the drama of their problems' in a modern and pessimistic fashion. Forster uses Lilia's disastrous marriage to reveal how little difference there is between the seemingly barbaric customs and beliefs of rural Italy and those of suburban Sawston. Although for Philip, Lilia's British brother-in-law, Italy is a romantic land of glorious freedom and brotherhood, Lilia soon discovers that by moving to Italy and marrying an Italian she has 'only changed one groove for another – a worse groove' (77). She is repressed, controlled, and given no personal independence or credence; there is no romance in Italy for her, and she dies in childbirth. The chapter in which Forster traces the breakdown of Lilia's marriage is perhaps his most intimate investigation of marital relations, but it is predominantly a psychological portrait of Lilia: the relationship between Lilia and Gino remains puzzling and almost unimaginable. The novelist Elizabeth von Arnim, an acquaintance and former employer of Forster, once commented in her diary that Forster's 'non-comprehension of the love of men and women' lies 'like a smear across his work'.[22] Indeed, what is described in *Howards End* as 'the astonishing glass shade ... that interposes between married couples and the world' (174) proved a major obstacle for Forster in the novels in which he chose to use marriage as the beginning of a story rather than the end.

Of all Forster's novels, *Howards End* is the one most obviously involved with the subject of marriage and family relationships: there are five engagements and three weddings, and four children are born. It is also the novel in which Forster most explicitly addresses the Woman Question. It was written in 1910, the year in which the militant suffrage movement began its disruptive campaign of property destruction, and Forster presented a paper to Vanessa Bell's Friday Club on 'The Feminine Note in Literature'. In *Howards End* there are numerous topical references to the women's suffrage movement, careers for women, and women's rights. The two heroines, the sisters Margaret and Helen Schlegel, are Edwardian New Women – intelligent and independent: Helen has a brief affair and bears a child out of wedlock; Margaret rebels against her husband and 'the lopsidedness of the world', and effectively becomes the head of her family (331).

But although *Howards End* appears to be a novel with feminist sympathies, the large amount of discussion in it, by both narrator and characters, about what constitutes feminine and masculine characteristics points to Forster's ambivalent attitude toward women. In this novel Forster valorizes the feminine, but his concepts of femininity and masculinity are very traditional and restrictive: it is the men who are identified with work and public life, who are active and powerful, whose 'hands [are] on all the ropes' (103); the women are intuitive and impractical, and associated with personal relations and nature. There is also a rigidity to these definitions, which is unexpected given Forster's own sexual orientation: the masculine is never tempered with feminine characteristics, and the women characters, though quite varied, are all alike in their lack of masculine qualities. Only Evie and Tibby subvert these categories, and their abnormality is commented upon and implicitly criticized: it is repeatedly emphasized that Tibby is not 'a real boy' (43), and 'handsome' Evie cuts herself off from the female tradition of Howards End when she heartlessly throws Miss Avery's pendant into the pond.

Though Margaret and Helen possess the requisite sensitivity to see that similarities do exist between the sexes (such as when Margaret insists to Mr Wilcox that women experience sexual desire too), the men in *Howards End* are depicted as too imperceptive to realize such correspondences. This inflexible opposition that Forster creates through his gender definitions ensures that no man in the novel is even remotely appropriate for someone with the sensibilities of Helen and Margaret. Helen asserts, only half-jokingly: 'If I marry, it will either be a man who's strong enough to boss me or a man whom I'm strong enough to boss. So I shan't ever marry, for there aren't such men' (194). Forster suggests that the extreme differences between the interests and sympathies of men and women lead not to complementary relationships but, rather, to misunderstanding and alienation.

The epigraph to *Howards End* is 'Only connect', but Forster's main focus in the novel is on the *attempts* people make at connection rather than on any actual successes. Marriage or sexual relationships are shown to be misguided, doomed attempts at connection, for they come up against 'the barrier of sex' (65). It is the spiritual connection, such as exists between Margaret and Mrs Wilcox and Miss Avery, that is important, not the social or physical connections that exist between husband and wife, or between lovers such as Helen and Leonard. The marriages of Charles and Dolly, and Leonard and Jackie, are notable for their meanness and triviality; Charles's policy is to give Dolly 'all his affection and half his attention' (95). Mrs Wilcox is never fully appreciated or understood by her husband, who is unfaithful to her, and never realizes that she is terminally ill. Mr Wilcox marries Margaret mainly as a replacement for Evie, and he rewards her devotion with lies and bullying. When Helen and Margaret become involved with men, they act as if they have been reading Braby's advice books: they quickly drop their independent ways, say things they don't mean, let their opinions be 'knocked into pieces' (6), and generally become submissive and self-effacing. After her marriage, Margaret, reminding herself that 'comment is unfeminine', quietly accepts Mr Wilcox's patronizing and censorship, and resorts to 'the methods of the harem' (230) to get her way with him.

Unlike his contemporaries, Forster did not criticize marriage because he had an ideal in mind or any particular dislike for the institution or its laws. He did not object to marriage as a useful legal arrangement that protects property rights and heirs, or provides social legitimacy, as in the case of Jackie. Marriage can even usefully serve as a career for someone like Margaret, who marries Mr Wilcox in order 'to make him a better man' (243). But marriage as a significant connection, given the utterly dissimilar qualities of those involved, is inevitably a failure. Perhaps this is why Forster showed no interest in the psychological dynamics of courtship and marriage, and why intimate marital interaction is so rarely depicted in the novel. But ultimately, the unrealized nature of the relationships between Mr Wilcox and Margaret, and Leonard and Helen, makes them unsatisfactory.[23] It is no wonder that Helen declares at the end that she is no longer interested in attaining the love of a man. *Howards End* is not so much a marriage problem novel as a novel that condemns all heterosexual relationships.

Thus it is inevitable that Margaret's marriage with Mr Wilcox eventually deteriorates into a battle of 'women against men' (290), with the rights of the pregnant Helen as the rallying point. Margaret and Helen triumph, and they become the inheritors of the female world of Howards End, as it was before the Wilcoxes invaded. All is brought together in the final chapter: the past is summed up, future plans are made, inheritances are settled, and the two women, like the nature around them, are praised as forces of renewal and rebirth. As the mower cuts the meadow in circular swathes, the novel also circles to a close, with Margaret and Helen reunited, and Helen's child replacing Tibby as the third in their reassertion of their matriarchal family structure. But the triumph of the women is troubling, for it has been achieved only at the great expense of the men; no compromise is ever reached, and categories of gender are never questioned or blurred. The masculine has been ousted: Leonard is dead, Charles is in prison, Evie and Paul are alienated from the family, and Mr Wilcox, 'broken' and beaten, is now dependent upon Margaret, lacking connection with both his former life and the natural world of Howards End. But he remains conveniently in the background to handle the business matters, while a male neighbor is retained to do the physical labor.

The victory of the women is also disturbing in that Margaret and Helen admit to no error, experience no change, and apparently learn no lesson from all the 'tangle' they have been through. Their smug, privileged self-confidence has been constant from beginning to end, while they have played carelessly with the lives of other people. They treat Leonard and

Mr Wilcox as human experiments, but as in the case of the Basts' being financially ruined through Helen's thoughtlessness, they never have to face up to the damage they have done. In retrospect, they, and most of the other characters in the novel, are distinctly unlikable, which raises the question whether Forster ever fully put his heart into this story of female triumph. Despite his obvious preference for the values characterized as feminine in the novel, there is a subtle thread of disapproval of the women themselves (especially the overly intellectual and 'bloodless' Schlegels) throughout. Forster's comments on *Howards End*, written forty years after its publication, offer a revealing summary: 'Have only just discovered why I don't care for it: not a single character in it for whom I care ... their barrenness has become evident. I feel pride in the achievement, but cannot love it, and occasionally the swish of skirts and the non-sexual embraces irritate...'[24]

The antagonism toward marriage and women that lies beneath the feminist surface of *Howards End* is also evident in Forster's two Edwardian novels which deal with homosexuality: *The Longest Journey* (1907), written for public consumption, treats the sexual preferences of its hero covertly; while *Maurice*, which Forster knew would not be published until after his death, is explicit. In these novels it becomes very clear that Forster's critique of marriage is unique among Edwardian novelists in that he sees marriage as a symbol of the dominant heterosexual values which make him an outcast. In *The Longest Journey* the effeminate Rickie, whose clubfoot substitutes for the sexual 'deformity' Forster can only hint at, becomes engaged to Agnes in a moment of confusion about his sexuality and his future. Their marriage is a disaster of incompatibility and misunderstanding, but Forster places all the blame for the failure of their marriage and of Rickie's life on Agnes. She is presented as a heartless embodiment of all the social conventions and expectations that force Rickie into conformity and prevent him from ever expressing himself artistically or sexually. Rickie's best friend Ansell is fond of proclaiming that 'Man wants to love mankind; woman wants to love one man' (89), and both young men quote (and interpret misogynistically) a poem by Shelley which criticizes monogamy (and from which the title of the novel comes). But these assertions of masculine spiritual superiority cannot completely distract from the fact that Ansell and Rickie love one another, and that what they are criticizing is not really monogamy but the fact that *they*, who should be married, cannot be.

In his 'Terminal Note' to *Maurice*, Forster wrote: 'A happy ending was imperative. I shouldn't have bothered to write otherwise. I was determined that in fiction men should fall in love and remain in it for the ever and ever that fiction allows' (250). The novel is the story of Maurice, a young homosexual suffering from repression and guilt, who finds sexual satisfaction and love with Alec Scudder, the gamekeeper on the estate of

Maurice's Cambridge classmate (and first love), Clive Durham. The novel ends with Maurice giving up everything to be with Alec. Originally, the last chapter depicted Maurice and Alec several years later, living happily together as woodmen in a forest hut; but most of those who read the manuscript agreed with Lytton Strachey's assessment that the relationship 'would only last six weeks' (252), and the chapter was deleted. But the end of the novel is still full of the prospect of love and happiness, like the ending of *A Room with a View*, and for the same reason – we never see the daily 'married' lives of the lovers, 'the drama of their problems'.

Forster does, however, offer a brief glimpse of Clive's conventional heterosexual marriage, so as to compare it unfavorably (and unfairly) with the relationship between Maurice and Alec. The physical relationship between Clive and his wife Anne is revealed to be a failure; but instead of noting the similarity between their sexual shame and ignorance and that which once crippled Maurice, Forster instead cruelly condemns their marriage as emblematic of the shallow and dishonest nature of heterosexual relations. As in *The Longest Journey*, there is a great deal of misogyny in *Maurice*; women are presented as the instigators and upholders of social convention. Maurice hates to return home to his mother and sisters because they pull him down to their level, and 'sap his strength' (82): 'Home emasculated everything' (52). Whereas in his other Edwardian novels, Forster seemed (perhaps unconsciously) aware of the correspondences between the marginality of women and that of homosexuals, in *The Longest Journey* and *Maurice*, novels written with great speed and personal emotional involvement, his sympathy deteriorates into hostility.

Forster occupies an anomalous place among the Edwardian novelists who wrote about marriage and its problems. Although he includes marriage among the social conventions he satirizes and criticizes, he does not show with any particularity or intimacy the ways in which heterosexual marriages are unsatisfactory. He demonstrates no impulse toward social reform, nor does he hold to any ideal of heterosexual marriage. What Forster's novels do reveal is an aversion to marriage motivated predominantly by his own sexual orientation and a formal disapproval of marriage as a novelistic convention; yet when he was free to imagine a homosexual marriage, he celebrated the relationship and featured it as a traditional ending. Forster's sympathy for the predicament of women in Edwardian society was inconsistent; but when – as in the case of Lucy in *A Room with a View* – he is able to recognize their feelings of frustration and self-doubt and sexual confusion as being like his own, then his characterizations of them are impressively sensitive and insightful. In all his novels Forster makes a plea for greater tolerance and flexibility in sexual and social relations, but he is able to offer little hope. The happy endings of *A Room with a View*, *Howards End* and *Maurice* are possible only because the characters have fled from society to 'an exile they gladly embrace'; it is painfully clear that the havens they create for themselves cannot last.[25]

In contrast, the novels of Ada Leverson are firmly located within society and intricately involved with society's numerous and rigidly codified rules of decorum. There is no question of escape; life would be meaningless to her characters without dinner parties and concerts and theatre and shopping and gossip. Leverson – most notably in her trilogy, *The Little Ottleys* – depicts brilliantly the pretension, vanity, pettiness and hypocrisy of the upper classes, all the while delighting in their idiosyncratic absurdities and sense of style. The subject of all her six novels (written between 1907 and 1916) is marriage – or rather, 'married unhappiness'.[26] For marriage in her novels has little to do with happiness or love; it is a social arrangement, a circumstance of one's life that one must bear with as much style and grace as possible, differing from a pairing at a dinner party only in its duration. In Leverson's novels, people marry because they are bored or jealous or in need of money, or – as in the case of Sir Charles in *Love's Shadow* (1908) – they become engaged 'through a slight misunderstanding in a country home', and do not have 'the courage to explain away the mistake' (48). Rarely does someone use feelings as a guide to behavior – it is far too risky. Social conventions and rules of etiquette are the safe and acceptable ways of determining how to act and whom to marry.

The conflict in Leverson's novels is not whether to marry (or stay married) or not but, rather, how to reconcile one's desires as an individual with the requirements of marriage. Edith Ottley, the heroine of the trilogy, is married to Bruce, a monster of immaturity, selfishness, vanity and hypochondria, whose awfulness is always dangerously on the verge of overwhelming the comic nature of his role. But since he is her husband and the father of her children, Edith feels absolutely bound to stay with him, despite his numerous faults; it is a matter of duty, honor, character – even style – for her to make the most of her marriage. Edith is invariably charming, imperturbable, patient; she survives through humor and discreet manipulation and, at times, deception. To those who do not know her well (including her husband) Edith is the epitome of the gentle, somewhat helpless feminine woman; yet she is actually strong and intelligent and utterly in control – she is the head of her family.

Almost all the women in Leverson's novels adhere to the social and cultural dictates of gender, yet quite a few of them realize the artificial nature of those dictates, and are clever enough to use stereotypes of conventional femininity for their own ends; one of Leverson's favorite themes is the double life that these women must lead as a result. She rarely categorizes or generalizes by sex, and there is an obvious equality among the intelligent and witty men and women in her novels, as there is among those who are stupid and silly. But for the women, every day is like a fancy-dress ball, with dressing up and role playing; they must pretend to be other than they are, even though some of them, like Edith, are self-conscious and sophisticated about the game they are playing. The advice Bruce's mother gives Edith in the first novel is typical (and reminiscent of Braby's advice): 'Never contradict. Never oppose him. Agree with him, then he'll change his mind; or if he doesn't, say you'll do as he wishes, and act afterwards in the matter as your own judgement dictates. He'll never find out' (81).

Edith has often been described as Leverson's self-portrait, and there are important similarities between Edith's social methods and Leverson's own technique as a novelist. The cardinal rule in Edith's world is to maintain one's style, and never show any effort or strain; as a woman, she is required to exercise power unobtrusively so as to not to disturb the masculine ego or the relations between the sexes. Similarly, Leverson's style is so light and graceful and charming that it seems effortless and easy; and thus some critics have misread it as empty. She has also been trivialized because her social critique is never harsh or blatant – it is as if she gives the reader the option of noticing it or not. However, Leverson is completely committed to and in control of the highly mannered and artificial surface of her fiction; she manipulates masterfully the tension that results when her humor unexpectedly reveals rather than obscures disturbing and unpleasant realities. But the tension that occasionally emerges in the character of Edith is less controlled and less satisfactory, for Edith's investment in the artificial constraints of her society is a matter of survival, not stylistic choice. A kind of sad reality keeps pushing up against the brilliant surface of her personality, and of the novels themselves – the reality of loneliness, of unloving sexual relations, of natural, honest responses that are being stifled beneath a veneer of sophistication and control.

In the first novel of the trilogy, *Love's Shadow* (1908), Edith and Bruce are secondary characters, but their marriage serves as one of several 'shadows' thrown across the romance of the main couple; the narrative of their married life works to undermine the main narrative of courtship. The heroine, Hyacinth, goes through a process of initiation into the realities of marital relations, and learns to manage and manipulate her husband just as Edith manages and manipulates Bruce – learning what Margaret in *Howards End* called 'the ways of the harem'. As with all of Leverson's novels, there is very little plot or character development in *Love's Shadow*, but there is a great deal of witty repartee; various combinations of characters and usually obvious complications of plot provide the fuel for the narrative, along with much of its humor and charm. The short chapters of Leverson's novels are like scenes in a play: these episodes usually occur in interior domestic settings; they are dominated by dialogue, and populated with just a few characters at a time. Thus, Leverson's novels purposely work against any mimesis of domestic continuity or stability; even though several years pass during the course of the trilogy, Edith's relationship with Bruce always feels disjointed and unsettled.

The second novel, *Tenterhooks* (1912), places Edith and Bruce at the center, and 'the drama of their problems' now moves from the friction of their daily interactions to the possibility of both of them entering into adulterous relationships. Bruce is motivated by a non-specific desire for an affair, and he latches on to the nearest adoring young woman – first the governess, then a young art student of questionable morals. Edith falls in love with Aylmer Ross, a handsome, intelligent, sensitive widower, but refuses to consummate their relationship or leave Bruce. The birth of Edith and Bruce's second child, with which the novel opens (during which Bruce has retreated to a spa with 'an indisposition of his own'), startles the reader into realizing that their marriage is not merely a social arrangement, but a sexual relationship as well. In the first novel, Edith's humor and intelligence had seemed so to distance her from the boorish and unappreciative Bruce that their son Archie was a kind of pleasant anomaly. But the birth of another child underscores the illusive quality of that distance: Edith cannot make herself completely inviolate, and she is subject not only to Bruce's querulous interruptions but also to his sexual advances. It is only after a 'very strong mutual physical attraction' develops between Aylmer and Edith that she is able to reject Bruce sexually (263): she begins to be conveniently plagued in the evenings by headaches which necessitate 'solitude and darkness' (239).

But despite Leverson's sophistication, even cynicism, about marriage, she nevertheless felt that it should be a lifelong commitment; although her husband left her to live in America with his illegitimate daughter, Leverson could never bring herself to suffer through divorce proceedings. Similarly, Edith refuses to give Bruce a divorce, both for the sake of the children and because of her horror of the public scandal which divorce entailed. But Edith's love for Aylmer forces her to face up to the inadequacies of her particular situation, and she declares her dissatisfaction to Bruce for the first time:

> 'I'm twenty-eight years old, we've been married eight years; you leave the
> housekeeping, the whole ordering of the children's education, and heaps of
> other quite important things, entirely to me; in fact, you lead almost the life of
> a schoolboy, without any of the tiresome part, and with freedom, going to
> school in the day and amusing yourself in the evening, while everything
> disagreeable and important is thought of and seen to for you. You only have
> the children with you when they amuse you. I have all the responsibility . . .'
> (284)

She also realizes that Bruce and her children 'did not nearly fill her life': 'Bending down to a lower stature of intelligence all day long would make one's head ache; standing up on tiptoe and stretching would do the same; one needs a contemporary and a comrade' (303). But although Aylmer is obviously this ideal comrade, there is no way for Edith to enjoy his companionship; she will not leave Bruce, and Aylmer is unwilling to be a 'house cat' and live on the fringes of her life. Even though Edith's marriage has been severely challenged and criticized, the novel ends at an impasse, circling back to where it began, with Edith resigned to a life of married unhappiness. Acknowledging that neither social nor novelistic conventions allowed women much chance to escape from their marital commitment, this circular narrative structure recurs frequently in Edwardian marriage problem novels.

But everything changes in the final volume, *Love at Second Sight* (1916), which was written and takes place during World War I. The narrative structure is a variation of the courtship plot, with Bruce serving as the 'wrong suitor' and Aylmer as the 'right suitor'.[27] But unlike Victorian courtship novels, it is not male guidance which steers Edith to a happy ending but, rather, her own maturity, which allows her to take a second look at her situation, and act as she truly desires. In the first two novels Edith is depicted as an exceptional and admirable woman, and as such, her motives are rarely analyzed by Leverson. But in *Love at Second Sight* Leverson gives her heroine a new degree of psychological interiority, and with it, self-doubt: Edith's manipulations begin to seem more dishonest than disarming, and her enslavement to convention and self-sacrifice is criticized. The war has turned everything upside down, and Edith's previous values and concerns, including her fear of the scandal of divorce, suddenly seem unimportant. The ending of *Love at Second Sight* is unabashedly happy, and the messy complications of marital break-up, custody and divorce, as well as the war, are completely elided in favor of fantasy: Edith and Aylmer are engaged to be married, the children gleefully accept Aylmer as their new father, and Bruce runs off with a woman who promises to give him all the misery he deserves.

In the light of the fact that *Love at Second Sight* is the final novel of a trilogy, as well as Leverson's last novel, and a novel written in wartime, it is not surprising that Leverson opts for the comforting reassurance of traditional narrative closure. While she demystified romance and criticized marriage as an institution, she never abandoned the ideal of a true companionate relationship, and it is a fitting reward for her heroine who, after all, has no desire other than to find happiness as a wife and mother. In this respect, Leverson recalls Sarah Grand, who made an equitable marriage the ultimate goal of her feminist heroines. But neither the happy ending of the final novel of the trilogy nor her pervasive sense of humor detracts from the power of Leverson's feminist social critique. Her novels expose the ways in which upper-class wives were twice suppressed – limited not only by British society's general ideals of femininity and marriage but also by the sensibility of their social class, which encouraged and valued artifice, idleness and duplicity.

Like Leverson, John Galsworthy wrote about romance, marriage, adultery and divorce among the wealthy; but whereas Leverson was influenced by Oscar Wilde and the *Yellow Book* writers, Galsworthy followed in the realist tradition of George Moore and George Gissing. Many Edwardian writers, most notably George Bernard Shaw and H.G. Wells, were reformers whose writings were not only social critiques but programs for social change. But although Galsworthy was similarly attuned to the problems of his age, his social criticism was usually not prescriptive.[28] Like Moore and Gissing, he was an admirer of European and Russian literature, and he valued narratorial objectivity and precision of observation; in his novels he holds his emotions aloof, advocating sympathy and sensitivity but offering no solutions. The narrative voice of *The Man of Property* (1906) and *The Country House* (1907) is quite often that of an anthropologist viewing a completely alien culture, the tone a striking combination of cynical aloofness and wide-eyed wonder. By coolly dissecting its subjects, this scientific method of narration reveals the constructed nature of all orders – legal, social, familial, sexual. Galsworthy differed from Moore and Gissing in his almost exclusive focus on the upper middle classes; but his social scrutiny, like theirs, inevitably involved the role of women in society and the institution of marriage.

Galsworthy's interest in the marriage problem stemmed in part from the circumstances of his life. He fell in love with his cousin's wife, Ada Galsworthy, when he was twenty-six. It was generally known in the Galsworthy family that Ada was miserable in her marriage, and she and John Galsworthy soon began a secret affair that lasted ten years. For fear of scandal, Ada obtained a divorce only after Galsworthy's father died; she and Galsworthy were married shortly thereafter. But Galsworthy's exposure to the intimate details of Ada's marital sufferings led to an obsession with the 'physical and spiritual agony of the unhappy marriage'.[29] While he did not deny 'the value and beauty of a perfect union', Galsworthy refused to keep from his readers 'the shrivelling hell of the opposite': 'my gorge rises within me when I encounter that false glib view that the vow is everything, that people do better to go on living together ... when one of them, or both, sicken at the other'.[30] In all his Edwardian novels marriage is revealed to be a trap, particularly for women; with a passion that brings to mind the New Woman novelists, Galsworthy repeatedly condemned the institution which requires from women a 'nightly denial of their own birthright to give themselves only where they love'.[31] Galsworthy, like Forster, recognized the intimate connections between marriage and money, property, convention and social status, but he was deeply skeptical about the relation of marriage to love or happiness.

The Forsytes, the large, prosperous and self-satisfied upper-middle-class family that is the central focus of *The Man of Property*, base their morality upon the worship of property and their actions upon the requirements of convention. The 'sanctity of the marriage tie' is proclaimed by several Forsytes, but the phrase is an indication not of religious beliefs but of the conviction that marriage is first and foremost a matter of property – not just in their eyes, but legally and socially as well. Divorce is out of the question, for it is not only a social scandal but the 'jettisoning of . . . property' (264). It is in the context of these materialistic values that the unhappy marriage of Soames and Irene Forsyte is presented. Soames, a collector of art, first sees Irene as a beautiful object made for his acquisition, and after a courtship which is likened to 'hammering the iron till it is malleable' (55), she becomes 'his property'. At the time of their engagement, she asks for a promise 'that if their marriage were not a success, she should be as free as if she had never married him' (105); but when the failure of their marriage becomes apparent, Soames refuses to give up his prized possession, even though 'he could do no more than own her body' (65). Infuriated by Irene's growing love for Bosinney, the architect of their country house, Soames feels that he must assert his right of ownership; thus he rapes his wife – 'the supreme act of property'. Through this brutal act, Galsworthy demonstrates how thin the veneer of civilization is: the social, legal and religious sanctioning of marriage cannot disguise the fact that it is, at its core, a primitive relationship based upon power and subordination, and governed by animal instincts.

Virginia Woolf famously faulted Galsworthy (along with Arnold Bennett and Wells) for his materialism, but the predominance of buildings and objects in *The Man of Property* is essential; they are the currency of power as well as the source of suffering and defeat. Alarmed by the growing independence and mobility of women (the novel is set in the late 1880s), Soames plans to build a country house so as 'to get Irene out of London, away from opportunities of going about and seeing people, away from her friends and those who put ideas into her head! That was the thing!' (56). When Irene finally leaves Soames, what shocks and hurts him most is not the fact of her leaving but the fact that she does not take any of the jewelry and clothes he has given her. Irene's rejection of Soames's possessions and gifts does not free her, however; she is forced to return 'to the cage she had pined to be free of' (289), for when Bosinney dies, she has absolutely nowhere else to go.

The final scene of the novel powerfully demonstrates that Soames has become Irene's jailer, and his elegant house her prison. When Soames's cousin Jolyon comes to offer his sympathies to Irene, Soames turns him away by saying, 'This is my house . . . I manage my own affairs . . . we are not at home' (291). Soames's house is the material façade he wishes to be judged by, and within its walls he *is* the master. The final slam of the door cuts off any chance of escape for Irene, and brings to mind her previous, futile attempts to retain her autonomy by locking her bedroom door. The end of the novel is an ironic allusion to the final slamming of the door in *A Doll's House*: in the world of the Forsytes, women have no hope of flight or freedom. But the language of Soames's final speech inadvertently reveals that his triumph is actually a failure: Soames and his wife are not 'at home' because his house will never be a home, and because Irene will never accept him as a lover, there remains one 'affair' that Soames cannot manage.

In *The Man of Property*, Galsworthy demonstrates a keen sensitivity to the ways in which women are objectified, repressed and frustrated within British society, but his characterizations of women, especially Irene and June, Bosinney's fiancée, are barely developed. This is due in part to Galsworthy's stated intention to show how personal and social circumstances had rendered Irene completely passive. Irene's only opportunities for escape or change come through the agency of men; her desire for freedom can be realized only in terms of romantic desire. But Galsworthy's primary interest in *The Man of Property* was not the psychology of women but the man-made laws and traditions which he believed were responsible for the marriage problem. He sought to criticize those laws and traditions by studying those with the most interest in maintaining them; thus the perspectives of men dominate the novel. This focus, and his examination of marriage as an institution which replicated the domination and inhumanity of other social institutions based upon male power, set him apart from the majority of marriage problem novelists. As a result, Galsworthy's treatment of 'larger' issues such as poverty and the class structure earned him a reputation for high purpose and seriousness which would not have been possible had he dealt solely with the issue of women and marriage.

Edward Garnett, Galsworthy's editor and friend, was appalled by the ending of *The Man of Property*: he believed that the Forsytes should be defeated by the happiness of Irene and Bosinney, who, he suggested, might run off to Paris with Irene's jewels. Galsworthy rejected this advice with a defense of his 'negative' method: 'the only way [to defeat Forsytism] is to leave the Forsytes the masters of the field. The only way to enlist the sympathies of the readers . . . to leave property as an *empty shell* – is to leave the victory to Soames . . .'[32] Galsworthy saw that in order to make his social criticism effective, he had to jolt his readers into awareness by purposely disappointing their expectations. In *The Man of Property* he creates a circular narrative which, after dispelling disruptive forces, returns to where it began, with the stasis of the established order reasserted. But the circularity is deceptive, for only the surface of things remains the same; by the end the reader sees the structures of order differently, for they have been undermined and exposed by the events of the novel, and especially by the critical narrative voice. The illicit relationship between Irene and Bosinney provokes the Forsytes into revealing just how petty and dangerous they are, and through their responses Galsworthy demonstrates both the strengths and the weaknesses of a social order based upon property and male dominance. The issue at the heart of the novel – the marriage problem – is left unresolved, and that thematic openness subverts formal closure. Marriage, like property, is left an 'empty shell', and can therefore no longer function as a 'happy ending'.

But although the narrative obviously places moral integrity above the legal, social and religious claims for the institution of marriage, there are no clear-cut, unambiguous villains or heroes in the novel. Unlike the plays about 'the modern Society conjugal problem' which Soames frequently takes Irene to see, Galsworthy's narrative offers neither the triumph of the strong husband nor the tragedy of the wayward wife. For Galsworthy, such an outcome, like the proposed romantic escape of Irene and Bosinney, would have been an unrealistic palliative, a dilution of his social criticism. Ultimately, he felt that any *conclusive* ending would have been complicitous in the continuation of the status quo, for the resultant narrative satisfaction would subdue – if not cancel – the troubling questions raised within the novel. Instead, Galsworthy created an open, disquieting ending which induces discomfort, indignation, perhaps self-recognition, but offers no solace and no answers.

The Country House, written the year after *The Man of Property*, began as a novel entitled *Danaë*, in which Galsworthy intended to focus upon an unhappily married young woman, 'unburdened with a moral sense', who engages in an extramarital affair. But that narrative of the dramatic and public failure of a marriage fell into the background; the story of Helen Bellew and her lover George Pendyce provides an essential point of conflict in the plot of *The Country House*, but their characters and their relationship are never fully realized. Instead, Galsworthy turned his attention to an examination of the quiet, intimate unhappiness of daily married life, as exemplified by George's mother, Margery Pendyce. As in *The Man of Property*, he adopts a narrative stance of disingenuous scientific objectivity, looking beneath the surface of the lives of the rural gentry, leaving few values or conventions unquestioned. The outward world of the country house – hunting, shooting, fishing, presiding over farm and village – is overwhelmingly male; thus one of the ways in which

Galsworthy exposes the hypocrisies and limitations of this world is by contrasting it with its private, domestic side – that of the women.

Almost all the women in the novel, with the exception of Mrs Bellew, have repressed their own feelings and desires in order to fit into the social roles required of them; when they married, they 'had parted with their imaginations and all the changes and chances of this mortal life' (59). Although the ostensible project of the work is a satirical examination of the rural aristocracy's attitudes to class, property and morality, the stories of the women keep disrupting that narrative. But since the women have been taught not to speak for themselves, it is predominantly the narrative voice which testifies to the burdens of married life, the pain of childbirth and motherhood, and the suffocating limitations of the domestic sphere.

Mrs Pendyce is a most unexpected heroine: the middle-aged wife of a country squire, 'for thirty odd years she had waited at once for everything and nothing; she had, so to say, everything she could wish for, and – nothing, so that even waiting had been robbed of poignancy' (158). She is the perfect wife, quiet and unassuming, following the daily routine of her country house as if 'a heavy horseman [was] guiding her with iron hands along a narrow lane' (111). Every night Mr Pendyce wakes his wife when he comes to bed, and every night Mrs Pendyce is unable to get back to sleep for several hours; the entire nature of their relationship is summed up by the fact that Mr Pendyce never realizes this, and Mrs Pendyce never tells him. But Mrs Pendyce retains bits and pieces of her individuality, and never completely gives herself up to her marriage. The fact that she has three hundred pounds a year of her own secretly sustains her, and every spring she dreams of making a trip to London alone, even though she knows it will never come about. But when her husband threatens to disown their son because of his involvement with Mrs Bellew, all Mrs Pendyce's suppressed anger and frustration explode, and she rejects her husband and his obsession with property and punishment; realizing that the matter had moved 'beyond mother love' to 'self love', she leaves her husband and 'all that had been to her like prison' (237–9).

When Mrs Pendyce first arrives in London, she is happy and excited; Galsworthy movingly conveys her astonished delight at being completely independent for the first time in her life. But as the novelty of the situation fades, she begins to feel 'utterly adrift, cut off from all the world': she comes to the realization 'that she had lived too long in the soil that she hated; and was too old to be transplanted' (247). After helping her son, Mrs Pendyce returns to her husband, who, though dismayed by her absence, begins to take her for granted again almost immediately. Mrs Pendyce's 'odyssey' of self-discovery is placed in pointed contrast to Mr Pendyce's obstinate obtuseness, which makes it all the more troubling that she must return to his world. She resumes 'her habit of subordinating her feelings to the feelings of others' (256), and resigns herself to the fact that no one will ever know who she is or what she feels. Ironically, Mrs Pendyce is finally the one who acts decisively to restore order in her rural society, even though it is an order which denies her power and autonomy. Throughout the novel the men have dominated the discussions about divorce, forbidding women even to voice an opinion, but they never do anything but talk: only Mrs Pendyce has the courage to persuade Mr Bellew to stop his divorce proceedings, and thus save her son from involvement in a scandal.

As with *The Man of Property*, Galsworthy prevents the circular structure of rebellion and return in *The Country House* from being construed as an approbation of the status quo; his criticism of the small-minded hypocrisy of the rural gentry is unmistakable, at times even 'cruel' (as Bennett characterized it). But although Mrs Pendyce's return underscores the ways in which ideologies of gender and class limit one's outlook and choices in life, it also points to the powerful pull of the past, of tradition, of habit, even when those traditions and habits are hateful; in that respect the ambiguity and divided perspective of the novel are quintessentially Edwardian. Although Galsworthy focuses on her for only a third of the novel, his characterization of Mrs Pendyce is unique in his portrayals of women characters for its imaginative depth and sensitivity; she emerges as a figure for Galsworthy's own sensibilities, in that she is gifted with clear vision but frustrated by her inability to act upon it.[33] Her love of the pleasures in her life conflicts with her recognition of the compromises she has had to make in order to enjoy them. The ending, like Mrs Pendyce's life, is quietly sad; she is bound by 'the custom of the country', and must leave it to subsequent generations to find new ways to live (247).

The ambiguous nature of the endings of these novels did not lessen the impact of their social criticism for Galsworthy's Edwardian readers and critics; he was considered a preeminent social critic, and regarded by some as a 'revolutionary' and a 'dangerous man', although he strenuously denied the characterization.[34] His analysis of the institution of marriage as yet another social and legal system of property and male power was radically demythologizing, as was his presentation of women (of all classes) as an oppressed underclass. Although sexual frankness was becoming increasingly common during the Edwardian years, Galsworthy's references to adultery, marital rape and childbirth were bold for the age, as were his casually intimate scenes of married couples dressing or in bed together. Because of his deep skepticism about 'the sanctity of the marriage tie', Galsworthy broke with novelistic tradition and welcomed adultery's disruptive challenge to authority: Giles Legard in his first novel, *Jocelyn* (1898), contributes to his invalid wife's death, yet is allowed to find happiness with his lover Jocelyn; in *The Country House* Mrs Bellew is clearly a survivor, not a victim, and her adultery is never punished; and in *The Man of Property* young Jolyon, who left his wife and daughter for a 'foreign governess', eventually enjoys social acceptance and financial success.

But these illicit relationships are isolated, self-contained; they have no significant effect on the social order. Galsworthy's pessimism about marriage ultimately left him at a creative impasse, as his novel *Fraternity* (1909) demonstrates: devoid of any possibility of escape or change, it is a depressing account of married celibacy and sex-warfare, in which three unhappy couples battle psychologically and physically. In the case of *Fraternity*, the open ending is neither provocative nor aesthetically satisfying but, rather, seems to indicate Galsworthy's own irresolution and discouragement in the face of the marriage problem.

In Galsworthy's fiction, and in many other Edwardian novels, divorce hovers in the background as a potentiality – a threatened social scandal or a longed-for release – but it is rarely realized in the plot. Talk of divorce reform was in the air during the Edwardian age: in both fiction and actuality, there was a growing acknowledgement of the fact of marital incompatibility, and a growing debate about the inequity of divorce laws. But the issue of divorce remained at a stalemate, and the age saw neither legal reform nor any increase in divorce.[35]

The last time Parliament had significantly altered marriage laws was with the Matrimonial Causes Act of 1857. The Act was important in that it granted the possibility of divorce (although realistically divorce was very difficult and expensive to obtain), but it also served to reinforce the moral double standard in its different requirements for men and women: a wife's adultery was sufficient grounds for divorce for a man, but a man had to be guilty of extreme cruelty, incest, bigamy, rape, or desertion lasting two years or more, in addition to adultery, in order for his wife to sue for divorce. By the turn of the century there began to be vocal and organized opposition to this legal double standard, as well as to the restrictive conditions of the divorce laws and the expensive and criminal nature of divorce proceedings. Lord Russell submitted divorce reform bills to Parliament in 1902 and 1903; on both occasions, the bills were defeated with indignation and outrage.[36] In 1909, a Royal Commission on Divorce was appointed to investigate marriage and divorce laws; but when it issued its report in 1912, the Commission was split: the Majority Report advocated reform, while the Minority Report, using rhetoric similar to that employed against women's rights in the 1890s, warned that such reforms would lead to the proliferation of divorce and immorality, and the subsequent deterioration of the nation. As in the 1890s, the unknown outcome of such fundamental changes in social organization was sufficient argument in the mind of the anxious public for maintaining the status quo.

Edwardian feminists were conspicuously ambivalent on the issue of divorce reform. Although most feminists (including women as diverse as

Florence Farr and Maud Churton Braby) believed that women and men should have equal rights in divorce cases, they preferred to focus upon marriage reform instead of divorce reform as a solution to the marriage problem; many worried that more liberal divorce laws would exacerbate the problem of male sexual irresponsibility. In general, the public was apprehensive and unsure about the controversial topic of divorce, and most novelists treated it cautiously. There were anti-divorce novels such as Mrs Humphry Ward's *Daphne* (1909) and John Oliver Hobbes's *The Dream and the Business* (1906), but there were very few novels that were clearly and pointedly pro-divorce. Those novelists who wished to demonstrate their sympathies with divorce reform might have their characters discuss or suffer from the inequities of the laws (as Galsworthy does), but they were clearly not comfortable promoting divorce as a source of happiness or a positive step toward social transformation.

Arnold Bennett's *Whom God Hath Joined* (1906) is one of the first British novels to focus exclusively on the issue of divorce. It is a sober, realistic account of the personal turmoil and public humiliation that divorce entails, and while it suggests no legal reform, it criticizes the public and sordid nature of divorce proceedings. While newspaper accounts of sensational divorce trials of public figures were not uncommon, no one before Bennett had chronicled the ways in which divorce affects ordinary people. *Whom God Hath Joined* is the story of two divorce actions – one brought by Lawrence Ridware, a solicitor's clerk, against his wife; the other brought by the solicitor's wife, Mrs Frears, against her husband, Charles; both cases are prompted by the discovery of an adulterous relationship, and both ultimately fail in court. Although Bennett makes it clear that the legal world is a man's world, and that women have little hope of triumphing there, he carefully structures the novel to present several different perspectives on the divorce issue. His moral position is similarly balanced and relative: Phyllis Ridware's adultery is based upon genuine love for another man, so it is not condemned in the way that Mr Frears's careless philandering is. Bennett shows that legal concepts of right and wrong, the moral absolutes of the Frears's daughter, Annunciata (who discovers her father's adultery), and the romantic ideals that Ridware has acquired from novels are all inadequate for dealing with the real and complicated lives of men and women.

As with Galsworthy, Bennett's interest in women as fictional subjects, along with the objective realism of his style and his social criticism, point to the influence of the fiction of the 1890s upon his work, so it is not surprising that a reviewer labeled *Whom God Hath Joined* a 'sex novel'.[37] But despite its subject matter, sexual frankness and moral relativity, the novel was not considered particularly shocking or scandalous, partly because its detached narrative voice and its ending allowed Bennett to remain safely ambiguous about his actual opinions on women, marriage and divorce.[38] The novel is repeatedly punctuated with generalizations about 'women as a sex' – condescending or derogatory generalizations that begin 'she was one of those women who...', or 'like all women, she...'. Yet these statements are frequently expressed in such a way as to make it unclear whether they are the narrator's opinions or the narrator is ironically 'speaking' for one of the characters, or for a general social attitude. Thus it is impossible to pin Bennett down: he may have wished to indicate that the ignorant stereotypes which treat women as a separate species are a significant source of the 'sex-discord' in British society; yet it seems equally possible that he is offering these generalizations as proof that the marriage problem is rooted in the very nature of women and men, rather than in social or legal structures. In all his novels which focus upon women, Bennett seems torn between a modern desire to particularize and psychologize his women characters, and a Victorian impulse to understand 'Woman' by characterizing and categorizing women as a group.

In a 1910 essay in which he admired the 'adult' and 'subtle' sexuality of d'Annunzio, Bennett observed: 'English novelists cannot deal with an Englishwoman – or could not up till a few years ago. They never get into the same room with her. They peep like schoolboys through the crack in the door.'[39] Clearly, Bennett felt that he himself was one of the few English novelists who was able to 'deal' directly and honestly with Englishwomen; yet despite his good intentions, his characterizations of women, as in *Whom God Hath Joined*, are often disappointing in their ambiguity and superficiality. Bennett obviously does not think that Phyllis Ridware is a villainess, as her husband does; she is not punished by the court for her adultery, nor is she explicitly condemned by the narrator for seeking to escape from a disastrous marriage. But she is not given any interiority or voice, either; the reader sees her only as Ridware sees her – aloof and inscrutable. Nor does Bennett imagine a life for Phyllis after her marriage ends: her lover and her mother die, and after Ridware finally obtains a divorce in Scotland, she is never heard from again. Autonomous and mobile as few Edwardian female characters are, Phyllis moves out of the domestic sphere (which she had always despised) but also out of the narrative; her independence cannot exist within social or novelistic norms. Like Renée, the French governess who has an affair with Mr Frears, Phyllis's illicit sexuality and lack of domestic affiliation render her subsequent life unnarratable: she 'disappear[s] as completely as Renée Souchon had disappeared' (391).

Bennett's sympathy for Mrs Frears is more clearly indicated, but she too is denied any interiority. In the scenes in which she stands up to her husband and his domestic demands, the emphasis is on Mr Frears's thoughts and emotions, not those of Mrs Frears. Frears is the quintessential Edwardian patriarch, a domestic tyrant around whom the household revolves. He is astonished that family life can go on without him, and inordinately hurt when his estranged wife shows no interest in whether he has had his dinner or not. Confronted with his wife's new-found anger and strength, he can only think selfishly: 'She was destroying his ideal of her' (356). But the reader never learns how Mrs Frears feels about that ideal – either when she rejects it and leaves her husband, or when she restores it by returning to her husband when the divorce action fails (due to Annunciata's inability to testify in public against her father). Like Mrs Pendyce, Mrs Frears bends to the demands of social stability, and sacrifices herself in order to protect her children, but her rationalizations are never specified in the text. The women's side of married unhappiness remains theoretical and generalized. Although Bennett clearly delights in depicting in detail the thoughts of Annunciata, who is a kind of monstrous ideal of the Victorian virgin daughter, his imagination fails when he is faced with the feelings and motivations of an adulteress or a rebelling wife; he never gets 'into the same room' with them.

Like *The Man of Property* and *The Country House*, *Whom God Hath Joined* circles back to where it began, and ends with a troubling feeling of retreat and irresolution. Ridware and Annunciata, both deeply disillusioned about marriage and disgusted by the 'terrific and ravaging' power of sexual passion, choose lives of celibacy. Mrs Frears, her dignity and independence compromised, resumes her 'comfortable' relationship with her husband – one which ensures social respectability while accommodating his discreet adultery. In a way that recalls the later novels of Hardy, sexual passion moves through the novel as a dark, disturbing, subversive force: it is 'odious and revolting', a 'damnable' thing which 'destroys calm'; yet it is also 'the sole genuine interest in life'. The institution of marriage is revealed to be little more than a practical social and economic arrangement, which is unable to regulate or contain sexuality. Although Bennett clearly advocates a more humane and private divorce process, he never implies that divorce will mitigate what he depicts as a fundamental discord between the sexes. The final scene of *Whom God Hath Joined* shows Ridware and Annunciata conversing politely, resigned to their celibacy, carefully avoiding any emotional involvement with one another. They are caught in a characteristically Edwardian limbo – having rejected the institution of marriage, they are unable to create anything new with which to replace it.

In many of his other Edwardian novels, Bennett set out to 'deal' with Englishwomen with frankness and originality, but his own contradictory feelings about women and sexuality hampered him – as did, apparently, his consciousness of the demands of the marketplace, most notoriously in the sensationalistic 'shocker' *Sacred and Profane Love* (1905). Bennett read and wrote about the New Woman fiction of the 1890s, and his novels *Leonora* (1903) and *Hilda Lessways* (1911) may be seen as Edwardian adaptations of that genre.[40] In his preface to *The Old Wives' Tale* (1908), he explained: 'I had always revolted against the absurd youthfulness, the unfading youthfulness of the average heroine'; so, as 'a protest against this fashion', he wrote *Leonora*, the story of a forty-year-old woman with grown-up daughters who falls in love. He further detailed the origins of the novel in a letter to an acquaintance: 'That women of forty . . . long to be young again is an undoubted fact. That they are particularly, peculiarly, & specially passionate & prone to sexual excitement is an undoubted fact. It was the discovery of these piquant truths which led me to write "Leonora".'[41]

In *Leonora*, Bennett goes behind the social and novelistic conventions which insist that the drama of a woman's life ends with her wedding, and reveals Leonora, a vital, attractive and passionate woman who does not wish to resign herself to 'the grayness of an impeccable and frigid domesticity' (291). Leonora's husband is consumed by his business affairs, and scarcely pays any attention to her; their marriage, like that of the Frearses, is merely a comfortable arrangement, having nothing to do with passion or even mutual interests. Bennett describes in effective detail the daily domestic routines of Leonora and her family, and sympathetically conveys how stifling and limited the life of a middle-aged, middle-class wife can be. As her husband and her daughters rush off to their various appointments and activities, Leonora, with no outside interests of her own, is left alone amidst the emptiness of her perfectly appointed house.

But unlike Ibsen's Nora (whom Bennett obviously wanted to recall with his heroine's name) Leonora has no desire for freedom, no interest in escaping her domestic sphere. Her rebellion is that she wishes to be loved again, and she finds that love in Arthur Twemlow, her husband's business associate. All the potential problems that this love raises – her husband's financial ruin, the scandal of running away with Arthur, her children's alienation – are swept away by the convenient suicide of Leonora's husband, which allows her to marry Arthur and live happily ever after as a 'slave' to her husband, 'supine' and content. There is no irony when the narrator describes the day of Leonora's engagement to Arthur as 'the last day of the dramatic portion of Leonora's life'; no acknowledgement that she ends up essentially back where she began; no recognition that this passion, too, will inevitably cool into marital familiarity. The tensions created by Leonora's critical examination of her married life are obliterated by her achievement of a new ideal of marriage.

Although in *Whom God Hath Joined* Bennett used the circular pattern of rebellion and return to criticize women's limited choices in life, in *Leonora* he uses the same basic pattern to reinforce the status quo. He withdraws from a criticism of the institution of marriage to a criticism of one particular marriage; thus – conveniently – he is still able to use marriage to end his narrative. As a result, *Leonora* is not unlike some of the romantic fiction that Bennett published in *Woman*, the popular women's magazine he edited from 1894 to 1900. Leonora is the ideal magazine heroine, totally obsessed by her appearance, her possessions, her clothes, and her feminine powers of attraction; she feels of value only when she herself is an object of desire. Despite his intentions, what Bennett depicts in *Leonora* is not really the sexual passion of a mature woman, but a rather immature woman finding a way to feel twenty again; ultimately, gender roles and stereotypes are reaffirmed, not challenged.

However, Bennett's choice of an older woman for a heroine did mark an important break with novel tradition (which he continued in *The Old Wives' Tale*). To make a romantic heroine out of a middle-aged, married woman was unprecedented and controversial, as is evident from one reviewer's response: 'There is something so offensive about the clandestine love affairs of a woman of forty with grown-up daughters that it is difficult to read certain parts . . . without a feeling of absolute nausea.'[42] Writing about *Whom God Hath Joined* and *Leonora* in 1931, Rebecca West recalled: 'In their day both were not only good but daring. One did not write about divorce, for it was too full of sensuous possibilities; and for the opposite reason one did not write about a woman of forty.'[43] These novels *were* daring, but in a characteristically Edwardian way, for they raised controversial issues only to retreat from them, seeking refuge in either a traditional ending or a mood of defeated ambiguity.

In general, the male writers who wrote about the marriage problem – such as Galsworthy, Bennett, Ford Madox Ford and D.H. Lawrence – were more comfortable being 'daring', and writing about women's adultery and divorce, than female novelists. Women writers who wrote about sexuality were often still hampered by a sexual double standard which placed great value on feminine propriety and reticence, and a critical double standard which gave men far more leeway in their choice of fictional subjects and the frankness of their treatment of them. But the sexual explicitness of these male writers did not necessarily translate into psychologically intimate depictions of marriage, for they all had difficulty creating realistic and persuasive female characters. Gender stereotypes about female nature and behavior continually impede the characterizations of women in the novels of these men – whether blatantly, as with Bennett's truisms about 'Woman' in *Whom God Hath Joined*, or more subtly, as in the novels of Ford, in which women rarely fall between the poles of sexual voraciousness and sexual purity. Their explorations of the dynamics of sexual relations within marriage gave these novels a complexity and modernity that were often missing from the more reticent and traditionally romantic marriage problem novels written by women; yet they rarely allowed their female characters to voice their own particular perspectives on love, sex and marriage.

Instead, it was the popular marriage problem novels written by women writers such as Mrs Henry Dudeney and M. P. Willcocks which specifically articulated women's grievances against marriage: disillusioned and unhappy, the wives in these novels criticize the restrictions of domesticity, the trials of maternity, and the tyranny of marriage laws, and express their need for independence and personal growth. But their protest is usually carefully constrained by both the demands of the conventions of the novel and those of the reading public. The majority of marriage problem novels are structured along the lines of *Leonora*: within a context of realistic social criticism, they combine the comic wedlock plot with the novelistic convention of the two suitors.[44] The husband functions as the 'wrong suitor', whose actions and values point to more general problems inherent in the institution of marriage. But in the comic wedlock tradition these problems are overcome and the romantic ideal is preserved, through the heroine's acceptance of the 'right suitor'; with him she establishes a new relationship, a new and better kind of marriage. Although adultery and divorce are discussed and contemplated as possible solutions in these novels, they are rarely realized; instead, most marriage problem novelists relied upon plot twists, such as the death of Leonora's husband, to free their heroines from unhappy marriages. This traditional narrative structure offered several advantages: it permitted novelists to write about contemporary social problems while satisfying their readers' expectations of a happy ending; it also enabled them to criticize marriage without offending social and sexual mores.

The concept of the indissolubility of marriage was a powerful and deeply rooted one in British society, especially for women; conservative sexual morality and traditional romantic ideals taught women that they should have but one true love, to whom they should remain committed for life.[45] The idea of a woman having adulterous sexual relations, or even multiple sexual relations through multiple marriages, was extremely disturbing to the average Edwardian. As a result, most marriage problem novels go to great lengths to avoid associating their heroines with divorce, or with any kind of illicit sexuality. An extreme example of this kind of reticence is *Studies in Wives* (1909), Marie Belloc Lowndes's collection of short stories about marital incompatibility and breakdown: despite the title, all the stories focus on the husband's perspective, as if Lowndes found the point of view of women involved in adultery or divorce either so unimaginable or so distasteful that she had to leave their stories untold.

Rhoda Broughton's *Between Two Stools* (1912) typifies the sexual caution of Edwardian marriage problem novels written by women. The heroine is in love, not with her husband, but with one of her husband's friends; the marriage problem is characterized as the conflict between social and religious insistence on the permanence of the marriage tie, and the reality and validity of the heroine's feelings. The issue of divorce is safely avoided, for the husband is an invalid, and the wife must stay with him to care for him. But the husband's handicap also enables the author to ensure that he is incapable of a sexual relationship with the heroine; thus she is able to remain 'pure' for the man who is to be her second husband. In *Between Two Stools*, as in *Leonora*, marriage is transformed from a problem into a happy ending when the heroine's husband dies, and she is able to marry her 'right suitor'.

The narrative of separation and return is also frequently used in marriage problem novels. As in *Whom God Hath Joined*, this narrative often takes the form of actual judicial separation which, being easier and less expensive to obtain, was far more common at the time than divorce. By using separation as a means of transforming the husband from the wrong suitor to the right one, marriage problem novelists were able to evade the moral complications of multiple sexual relationships. In Mrs Dudeney's *A Runaway Ring* (1913) and Margaret Legge's *A Semi-Detached Marriage* (1912), the wives separate from their husbands until the husbands sufficiently improve and broaden their attitudes about women and marriage; the heroines happily reunite with their 'new' husbands, enjoying what amounts to a second marriage, without having to form a sexual relationship with a different man. Willcocks varied this structure in *The Wingless Victory* (1907) by having the wife be the one who must readjust her expectations of marriage; but the happy ending of this novel, like that of the others, is dependent upon the wife's realization that her husband is indeed the right man for her. Florence Farr's *The Solemnization of Jacklin: Some Adventures on the Search for Reality* (1912) is daring in that the heroine actually divorces her first husband and marries another man; but it ultimately aligns itself with the dominant narrative pattern in that the second husband proves to be the wrong suitor, and Jacklin decides to return to her first, 'true' husband.

There is one particular Edwardian genre, however, in which the sexuality of married women is treated quite boldly by women writers: Elinor Glyn, Victoria Cross and Dolph Wyllarde wrote extremely popular sensation novels in which the heroine's sexual feelings are paramount, and adultery is commonplace. Although the New Woman novels of the 1890s prepared the way for the sexual sophistication of the sensation novels, there was little similarity between the two genres; sensation novels had far more to do with the Edwardian vogue for 'smartness' and 'naughtiness' than with the Woman Question. The public was greatly interested in the activities of King Edward VII and his set, who were known for their style, their wealth, and their discreet but adulterous sexual affairs, and sensation novels capitalized on that interest; with their detailed descriptions of exotic locales, luxurious clothes and expensive food, these novels were pure escapism.

Glyn's phenomenal bestseller *Three Weeks* (1907) is a classic example of the genre: it tells the story of a young Englishman on holiday in Switzerland who meets a mysterious and beautiful queen from a Balkan country; she proceeds to spend three weeks teaching him all about lovemaking and sexual pleasure. Her sexual power is never threatening, for she is purely an object, with no interiority or psychological reality; enigmatic, changeable and desirous of domination, she is a fantasy creature who combines stereotypical femininity with unrestrained sexuality. After the young man has learned 'how to LIVE', he returns to England with renewed interest in working for the good of his nation. But the adulterous woman must 'pay the price', and she is killed by her jealous husband. Thus the reader is able vicariously to enjoy forbidden pleasures, complete with tiger skin and champagne, yet is ultimately left with the familiar comfort of a conventional and morally correct ending. Glyn's novels, along with those of the other sensation novelists, were innovative in their frank acceptance – and even glorification – of female sexuality, yet they always retreated into resolutions in which that sexuality is somehow punished or domesticated. They also usually took care to distance their readers from the menace of their heroines' unconventional morality by locating their novels outside England and, indeed, outside recognizable reality. But the most regressive aspect of these novels was that their authors believed that 'life means love-making', as one critic complained about Victoria Cross; the narrative desire of the women characters is reduced from traditional romantic desire to purely sexual desire. Rather than reflecting the ways in which women's lives and interests were expanding, the sensation novelists instead diminished women's sphere of influence to the dimensions of a bedroom.

Many popular marriage problem novels resemble New Woman novels in that they function primarily as a polemical platform: the characters and plot exist as illustrations of the marriage problem, and there is little psychological realism or thematic complexity. But the endings of most marriage problem novels are more like those of sensation novels, for the heroine's desire to fight the inequities in marriage is transmuted into a romantic desire which, when realized, has the effect of canceling out all her previous complaints; the troubling ambiguities raised by the novel's critique of marriage are lost amidst the sense of stability and coherence that the resolution imparts. Novelists like Dudeney or Willcocks tried to criticize marriage while uncritically utilizing a narrative form predicated upon the ideal of marriage, and the results are inevitably contradictory and strained.

Willcocks's *Wings of Desire* (1912) exemplifies the contradictions that resulted when novelists relied upon conventional narrative structures to write about the marriage problem. Sara Bellew, Willcocks's protagonist, faces numerous difficulties related to the marriage problem: she is trapped in an unhappy marriage, in love with another man, frightened by the social scandal of divorce, unable to pursue her career as a concert pianist, and doubtful whether a woman can have both a career and children. But by the end of the novel all her difficulties have vanished, all tensions are reconciled, and narrative satisfaction is granted: Sarah has triumphantly returned to her career, is determined to face her divorce bravely, and plans to marry and have children with her 'right suitor'. Willcocks accomplishes this by transforming what are initially presented as social problems – restrictive gender roles, the sexual double standard, the inequities of the institution of marriage – into personal problems, which Sara is then able to solve through sheer will and the power of love. Willcocks evidently meant to inspire women to create their own, similarly modern marriages, but by glossing over the very real obstacles which prevented women from achieving such a relationship, she reduces her novel to little more than a fairy tale.

There were, however, a few women writers in the Edwardian age who dared to confront the complex dynamics of marital relations and refused to mitigate their criticisms of marriage with the narrative of romantic desire. Amber Reeves, Olivia Shakespear and Elizabeth von Arnim were three exceptional Edwardian novelists who rejected the social and novelistic traditions which placed romantic desire as the dominant desire in a woman's life. The marriage problem about which these three women wrote was the conflict between married women's need for independent purpose and achievement in their lives and the social ideal of wifely submission and self-sacrifice. The heroines they created who experience that conflict are not idealized New Women or romantic heroines but are ordinary, fallible and recognizable. In their marriage problem novels, Reeves, Shakespear and von Arnim reverse the nineteenth-century narrative pattern which subsumes the adolescent female's *Bildungsroman* into a marriage plot. They begin with a traditional marriage plot, but then transform it into a kind of delayed *Bildungsroman*; thus their novels are not only marriage problem novels but also novels of awakening, in which their mature heroines grow and come to understand themselves only after they have confronted the limitations of marriage and maternity.[46]

Amber Reeves was the daughter of two prominent members of the Fabian Society; she graduated from Cambridge University with a degree in moral sciences. She was extraordinarily open-minded and independent, and had an infamous affair with H.G. Wells (who used it as the basis for his novel *Ann Veronica*) while she was still a student; she married a college friend, Rivers Blanco-White, when she became pregnant with Wells's child. Her first novel, *The Reward of Virtue*, was published in 1911; in it, she vehemently criticizes the limited opportunities for modern young women. For her second novel, *A Lady and Her Husband* (1914), she took as her premise a situation much like the one in *Leonora*: Mary Heyham is forty-five, and feels confused and useless now that all her children have grown up and moved away. Yet unlike Leonora, she does not search for romance to renew her interest in life; instead, at the urging of her socialist daughter, Mary begins investigating the working conditions in her husband's chain of tea shops, and soon becomes an advocate for the rights of working women.

As Mary begins to understand the economic basis of her comfortable married life, and realize the moral compromises her husband must make to earn a profit, she decides to leave him and live on her own. Reeves is careful to make Mary neither unusually intelligent nor particularly modern; her awkwardness and confusion make her transformation from complacent wife to social activist both delightful and believable:

> She was not a fine lady, she did not care for a fine lady's life. She was an ordinary middle-class woman, who preferred doing practical work to being kept in the house to be beautiful and mysterious and tender and all the rest of it to any man with half an hour to spare . . . She was surprised at the resentment that she discovered in herself when she thought of this aspect of the life she had led. . . . She knew that she had not seen the matter like this before, and yet this was not, she felt convinced, a new resentment. She must have disliked her position all along, if only she had known it. (357)

Mary, like Leonora, has been taught to believe that the narrative of romance and marriage is the supreme one in a woman's life; but unlike Leonora, she realizes that that narrative is a cheat, and that women's lives do not end with marriage or children. Leonora puts off dealing with the problem of what to do when her children are grown up and romantic passion fades; Mary finds a new narrative of work and social commitment that will fill the rest of her years, and satisfy her as her marriage and children no longer can.

Like Amber Reeves, Olivia Shakespear has become known for her romantic association with a prominent male writer (in her case, W.B. Yeats) rather than for her own works, but she was the author of six novels, and collaborated on two plays with Florence Farr.[47] Her last novel, *Uncle Hilary* (1910), is generally considered her best; despite its title, its focus is not on the wise and tolerant Uncle Hilary but on his ward and wife, Rosamund Colston. The novel deals with such issues as marriage laws, divorce and bigamy, but it is not a conventional marriage problem novel. The problem at the center of the novel is the ideal of romantic love which shapes women's ideas about marriage and life, and through Rosamund, Shakespear demonstrates the ways in which that ideal leads to disillusionment and resentment.

Rosamund is an intelligent and quietly unconventional young woman who has grown up believing that 'love [is] the one essential thing in the world' (76). Although she is confused and distressed when she witnesses the calculated and prosaic reality of her cousin's engagement, she shrugs off her doubts about the viability of romantic passion when she meets Colonel Henry, and is soon off to India to marry him. But the Colonel quickly becomes involved in his military work, and Rosamund realizes that men and women view marriage in very different ways: 'a man seeks love as a rest from his activity, a quiet harbor; to a woman love is the activity, into which she comes from a state of quiescence, of expectation' (81).

Before Rosamund has a chance to become too dissatisfied with her life, however, it is revealed that her marriage to Colonel Henry is invalid, because he was once married to her mother. Rosamund, now pregnant, returns to London, and Uncle Hilary, though significantly older than she is, offers to marry her to protect her reputation and give her child a name. He explains that their marriage will be just a 'form', and that she will be utterly free; he emphasizes that Colonel Henry is her true husband, regardless of what the law says. The baby eventually dies, but surprisingly, that does not render Rosamund's marriage to Uncle Hilary pointless; instead, their relationship takes on a life and significance of its own. Rosamund and Hilary are shown to be intellectually and spiritually compatible and, freed from any romantic or sexual expectations, they find great joy in one another's company. Others are puzzled by their relationship, but Rosamund now realizes that marriage is best seen as an 'arrangement' rather than the product of an overwhelming passion.

Rosamund is seduced by the ideal of romance one more time, however, and after her mother's death she decides to live in a remote seaside cottage with Colonel Henry, 'free from conventions'. Hilary supports her decision, although he will not divorce her, for he sees – as she cannot – that her relationship with Colonel Henry will not last: 'Love is the worst slavery that exists – not only sexual love, but any love: it is the most persistent of the illusions. Some day it will fall away from you . . . then you will find yourself isolated, in spirit, but possibly, still bound by chains of circumstances . . .' (240). Without his work Colonel Henry is soon restless, and Rosamund realizes that love is not only insufficient to fill a man's life to the exclusion of all else, but insufficient for women as well:

> . . . she had given herself to him, wholly; to find that the gift was one no man really desires. She had recovered possession of herself, as it were, and could look on him now with tranquil eyes, unmoved by passion. Perhaps love, stripped of its glamour, was nothing but a matter of the senses . . . (295–6)

She arranges for Colonel Henry to return to India without her, and goes back to Uncle Hilary with a new sense of peace and happiness, freed from the 'burden' of love.

While many marriage problem novels deal with the romantic disillusionment that comes with marriage, they do so in order to criticize the institution of marriage, not the ultimate value of romance; *Uncle Hilary* is unique in its powerful rejection of the ideal of romance itself. Love is depicted as merely a temporary emotion, something to be experienced and then 'outgrown'; Shakespear emphasizes that for both men and women, love is no substitute for 'the realities of life'. She also makes it clear that the different expectations men and women have of marriage are the result of cultural conditioning, not nature; and she suggests that when women are allowed to have other significant interests in their lives, as men do, they will no longer be so dependent upon love and marriage. But as in the novels of Bennett and Galsworthy, there is ultimately a kind of resignation to the fact that the relations between men and women present insoluble problems. Rosamund is able to find in her relationship with Uncle Hilary satisfaction, her spiritual growth and her intellectual development, and it is never intimated that she is in any way incomplete without children or a traditional husband. But her relationship with Hilary is admittedly exceptional, and is made possible only through a series of unusual circumstances. Instead of offering solutions to the marriage problem, Shakespear complicates the issue further: if romantic passion should not be the basis of marriage, what should be? Should women experience and outgrow their passion through premarital or extramarital affairs? Why should people marry at all? Even though Uncle Hilary can be viewed as the 'right suitor' for Rosamund, the happy ending achieved through their reunion challenges rather than comforts the reader, for all the troubling questions raised by the novel are left unresolved.

Surprisingly, the most remarkable of the Edwardian marriage problem novels was written by an Australian woman living in Europe. Elizabeth von Arnim (born Mary Annette Beauchamp) was best known for her first book, *Elizabeth and Her German Garden* (1898), a chatty and charming autobiographical account of life on her husband's country estate. The book, published anonymously, became a bestseller, and thereafter all von Arnim's books were credited on the title page to either 'Elizabeth' or 'the author of *Elizabeth and Her German Garden*'. But von Arnim's novel *The Pastor's Wife* (1914) is a marked departure from that first minor work. Though it is charming in its own way, and very funny, *The Pastor's Wife* is a powerfully frank and detailed marriage problem novel.

Despite the fact that the novel is geographically distanced from modern-day England, and its heroine has little knowledge of the Woman Question, or of issues such as divorce reform or contraception, *The*

Pastor's Wife is far more relevant to the specific concerns of Edwardian women than most other marriage problem novels. Von Arnim does not focus on the 'larger' issues of social or legal reform; rather, she looks at what the marriage problem means for women on a private, personal level; she writes of the same problems that appear in the problem pages and letters to the editor of women's magazines and journals. Her heroine, Ingeborg, is confused about sex, feels lonely as a new wife, experiences the discomfort of pregnancy and the pain of childbirth, suffers from the exhaustion of motherhood, and worries about her husband's indifference. *The Pastor's Wife* is unique in its privileging of these topics as suitable for serious fiction. The domestic life of women was denigrated as trivial and inferior subject matter by the male literary establishment, and women writers who wished to be taken seriously tended to avoid dwelling on strictly domestic issues; even New Woman novelists had refrained from specific discussions of domestic complaints in favor of 'larger' issues. But von Arnim rejected such value judgements, and mocked them within her novel. Ingeborg's husband, Herr Dremmel, emphasizes to Ingeborg that his work involves 'great things, great interests, great values', while her problems in comparison, are 'minor concerns' (280). Yet this male/female, work/personal life hierarchy is nicely undercut by the fact that Herr Dremmel's 'great' work is the study of manure. Von Arnim dared to make Ingeborg's 'minor concerns' the central focus of her novel, and by so doing she provided one of the few detailed narratives of the realities of a married woman's life in Edwardian fiction. Completely avoiding polemics, *The Pastor's Wife* succeeds where other marriage problem novels fall short, for it gives a recognizably human face to the feminist issues of the day.

The novel is divided into three books, each of which corresponds to a different narrative pattern: the first is a courtship narrative; the second is a marriage problem narrative which mingles elements of comic and tragic wedlock plots; and the third is a narrative of romantic rebellion and return. Von Arnim employs the conventions of all three narratives ironically, and continually points to the discrepancies between traditional narratives and the real lives of women.

Ingeborg is introduced as a 'pliable', self-effacing young woman, 'trained in acquiescence' by her father, the Bishop, who expects her to devote her life to being his secretary. But when she finds herself alone for the first time in her life on a trip to London, she is soon, like Galsworthy's Mrs Pendyce, both intoxicated and disoriented by her complete independence and freedom. Forgetting 'that her movements had all first to be sanctioned', she impulsively signs up for a tour to Lucerne, where she meets Herr Dremmel, a German pastor, who soon determines to marry her (9). Although she does not love him, and at times feels 'engulfed' by him, Ingeborg nevertheless finds Herr Dremmel like 'a brisk invigorating wind' compared to her domineering and repressive father, and she simply lets her engagement happen to her (45). It never occurs to Ingeborg that she could rebel against the life planned for her by her father on her own; having been taught that she has no intrinsic value, she accepts the marriage offered to her as an opportunity for freedom and personal fulfillment. She has few romantic illusions about marriage (having been forbidden to read novels), but she never even considers that she is trading one tyranny for another. She finds the prospect of living in East Prussia with a man who keeps himself locked up in a laboratory all day appealing; she imagines that she will have 'space, freedom, quiet', and lots of time to read.

The second part of the novel is 'the drama of their problems', in which Ingeborg discovers what marriage is really all about. True to his word, her husband Robert works on his experiments most of the day and night, requiring little from Ingeborg, and for a while she enjoys a delicious freedom, unlike anything she has ever known. But Robert does expect to have children, and it is with her first pregnancy that Ingeborg's life changes: 'She who had never thought of her body, who had found it the perfect instrument for carrying out her will, was forced to think of it almost continuously. It mastered her' (210). While von Arnim does not dwell much on the sexual relations between Ingeborg and her husband (Ingeborg thinks of her sex life as 'a series of clutchings'), she does pay a great deal of attention to Ingeborg's experience of pregnancy and childbirth, and to Robert's varying states of interest and detachment during the process. Von Arnim pointedly contrasts the reality of Ingeborg's physical discomfort with Robert's ideal of a big family and his clichés about the 'holy' experience of childbirth. It is not until late in her pregnancy that the naïve Ingeborg realizes with horror that 'some very appalling convulsion' is going to be necessary to get the baby out of her body, and with a frankness unprecedented in British fiction von Arnim describes that 'convulsion' and its attendant pain and fear:

> . . . courage and unselfishness and stoicism and a desire to please Robert – who was Robert? – were like toys for drawing room games, shoved aside in these grips with death . . . she was battered into being nothing but a writhing animal, nothing but a squirming thing without a soul, without a reason, without anything but a terrible, awful body . . . (236).

The experience of motherhood is never sentimentalized either; Ingeborg is profoundly ambivalent on the subject of children, and devastated when she discovers that she is pregnant for the second time. The next seven years of her life are quickly passed over as she bears one child after another, losing several at birth or shortly after. Von Arnim refuses to valorize this passive, numb existence of continual childbearing, or even to narrate it, and with her refusal she indicates that such an existence is not really a life at all. The constant demands of pregnancy and motherhood cancel out Ingeborg's sense of self even more completely than her father's domination ever did, and for a time, she seems in danger of disappearing.

The third section begins with Ingeborg's insistence, at the age of thirty, that she stop 'this wild career of ... unbridled motherhood'; consequently, she refuses to sleep with her husband any more (290). Robert discovers, just like Ingeborg's father before him, that the 'servile' are capable of 'sudden rare tremendous insurrections ... more devastating than the steady fighting of systematic rebels' (294). After the initial shock, he trains himself to think of Ingeborg as a sister, and as a result he pleasantly but completely ignores her. Ingeborg is crushed by the discovery that her husband, like her father, does not love or value her for herself, only for what she can provide for him. With her children at school, Ingeborg faces the same confusion and aimlessness that Leonora and Mary Heyham face, but before long she resolves to fashion a new narrative for her life:

> It was useless to depend on others; it was useless to depend, as she had done in her ridiculous vanity, on others depending on her. . . . If she let herself be beaten back this time into neglect of herself and indifference she would be done for. There was no one to save her. (332–3)

She begins to order books and journals from England, and her days are soon filled with reading and thinking and long pleasant walks. But this new narrative is interrupted by the appearance of the famous painter Ingram, who subsequently falls in love with Ingeborg. He tries to force her to follow his own narrative of romantic escape and adultery, and lures her on a trip to Venice with him. Ingeborg agrees to go, but without any 'sex-consciousness', and when she eventually realizes Ingram's true intentions, she quickly returns to her husband – who, of course, has not even noticed that she was gone. But Ingeborg's return is not tragic: like that of Mrs Pendyce, it is just quietly sad. Although she welcomed Ingram's love and admiration, she also discovered that it was a kind of tyranny in itself; if she had stayed with him, he would have forced her to sacrifice her nascent sense of self and conform to his romantic feminine ideal. But ultimately, she never even considers breaking her commitment to Robert; he gave her her freedom, and she will remain faithful to him, even if he no longer wants her.

Because Ingeborg has been shown to be wonderfully resilient and resourceful, her return at the end of the novel does not have the effect of closure; there is no sense of defeat, or that her life is over. But there is a sense that she now knows that the happy endings her father and her husband and Ingram offered her were all fictions, and that she is going to have to write her own ending if she is to be truly happy. The novel lies open at the end, waiting for Ingeborg to complete her story herself.

The Pastor's Wife is exceptional not only in the psychological reality of its heroine but also in the degree of interiority given to the three men in the narrative. Although the narrative focus is predominantly on Ingeborg, the men's points of view are also presented in key scenes of conflict; von Arnim attempts to understand their motivations and desires, and though she might mock them, she never reduces them to male stereotypes or patriarchal monsters. Thus she is able to depict the dynamics of the relations between men and women with a sympathy and complexity that are missing from most marriage problem novels. But what is most exceptional about *The Pastor's Wife* is that it deals with the two 'problems' in marriage which feminists felt were essential to resolve, but which were absent from almost all marriage problem novels – work and children. The Bishop, Robert and Ingram all state outright that their work is the most important thing in their lives, and they value Ingeborg only in relation to how she can help them to achieve that work. But Ingeborg is not allowed to have any independent purpose or work in her own life; she does not choose to be a secretary, or a mother, or a muse, and none of those roles fulfills her, least of all that of mother. The humor of the novel cannot quite distract us from the fact of Ingeborg's painful loneliness, and neither her husband nor her children are enough to assuage it; her marriage completely isolates her from people and ideas and activities that are meaningful to her. Like Reeves and Shakespear, von Arnim rejects the ideology of noble and all-consuming motherhood, and demonstrates how the narrative of love, marriage and maternity is insufficient to fill the days of a woman's life. For a great many Edwardian women, the insufficiency of that narrative *was* the marriage problem, both in fiction and in life.

The New Woman novelists praised the novel's ability 'to carry the pressure of the moral question into the sacred enclosure of marriage itself'; they believed that 'much of the solution of our problems lies within those sacred precincts'.[48] Edwardian novelists continued this feminist and literary project by making the marriage problem the central subject of their fiction. The marriage problem was no longer considered a specialized concern of a small group of women; it became accepted as a product of modern life which affected men and women of all classes. Edwardian marriage problem novels did not center on New Women and their principled rejection of the institution of marriage, but depicted recognizable men and women, in realistic situations, struggling to reconcile their individual needs to the requirements of marriage.

The Edwardian marriage problem novelists were confronted, however, with the formidable obstacle of novelistic conventions of character and narrative structure. Male novelists such as Forster, Galsworthy and Bennett found it difficult to imagine women outside traditional gender roles, or to depict women's negative responses to the limitations of marriage and motherhood with psychological complexity. Male novelists also often chose to approach marriage as a social problem rather than analyze its private dynamics: instead of focusing on intimate, psychologically nuanced scenes between husband and wife, they opted for discussions of marriage and divorce laws which emphasized their serious social purpose. Women novelists such as Ada Leverson, Mrs Dudeney, and M.P. Willcocks were also hampered by their acceptance of gender stereotypes, as well as their reluctance to let go of the ideal of romance. They attempted to criticize marriage, while preserving it as the ultimate reward for their heroines; the results were often contradictory and confusing. All marriage problem novelists found it difficult to reconcile their desire to present sexual relations candidly with the basically conservative nature of the reading public. Even though many actual married couples – such as H.G. and Catherine Wells, or E. Nesbit and Hubert Bland – developed unconventional living arrangements that allowed for extramarital affairs, no comparable relationships are explored in Edwardian fiction.[49]

The marriage problem novelists also had to contend with literary standards which insisted that the daily, domestic concerns of women were not interesting or significant enough to be the subject of fiction. Even though the issues of household management and childcare were crucial for feminists and socialists, they were rarely explored in fiction. Similarly, even though many Edwardian women were pioneers in their attempts to combine careers and marriage, their stories were not translated into fiction. The relation of children to marriage and divorce reform was a particularly emotional and troubling issue, as was the falling birth rate, but these issues are also avoided in most Edwardian novels about marriage, and children are strangely absent. Only a few novelists, such as Amber Reeves and Elizabeth von Arnim, treated the demands of household and children seriously; they were also among the few who chose to write about women's desire for economic independence and work outside the home.

In most Edwardian novels about marriage there are self-conscious references to traditional novel plots of love and marriage, and the expectations they engender in their readers; these references point to the authors' awareness of the inadequacy of novelistic conventions for conveying the reality of complex sexual and marital relations. In their recognition of that complexity, their sexual frankness and their moral relativity, the marriage problem novelists were innovative and modern. But they found it difficult to match their modern content with formal innovations; the conventions of the novel proved as formidable and tenacious as the conventions of society, and while they could be criticized or challenged, they persisted as the dominant structures within which one operated. Most Edwardian novelists who wrote about marriage adopted a strategy similar to the one Braby recommended to young wives: their modern ideas about marriage are couched in traditional forms which conceal the radical nature of their critique and appease the demands of the reading public. But what resulted in fiction (and presumably something similar occurred in Edwardian marriages) were tensions, ideological contradictions, and narrative instabilities.

An enormous number of novels were published each year to compete for the attention of an increasingly large and diverse readership; even the most serious Edwardian novelists were unwilling to disregard completely the demands of critics and the expectations of readers, which were, with regard to conventions and plot, conservative. The primary narrative desire for women remained romance and marriage; the dominant narrative structure relied upon linearity and closure. As a result, in traditionally structured marriage problem novels such as those by Bennett, Dudeney and Willcocks, any challenges to the status quo are ultimately circumscribed by the social values inherent in the novel's form; social criticism is voiced only to be canceled by the stasis and stability of the ending.

This fluctuation is most evident in the women characters; they realize their discontent within marriage, perhaps they even act upon it, but owing to the constraints of British society and the novel form they cannot truly escape their situation, for there is nowhere for them to go. This circular pattern of rebellion and return dominates Edwardian novels about marriage: Margaret in *Howards End*, Lilia in *Where Angels Fear to Tread*, Irene in *The Man of Property*, Mrs Pendyce in *The Country House*, Mrs Frears in *Whom God Hath Joined*, and Ingeborg in *The Pastor's Wife* all leave their marriages, only to return. The one exception is Phyllis in *Whom God Hath Joined*, who chooses divorce and independence, and refuses to return; but by so doing she places herself outside social and novelistic conventions and disappears from the novel, her future being unimaginable and unnarratable.

In some cases, novelists used this pattern of rebellion and return self-consciously, as an analogy for and a criticism of the limitations in women's lives, and their novels mark an important stage of literary development. Galsworthy, von Arnim, and occasionally Bennett were sensitive to the pressures that the form of the novel exerted on their social critique, as well as the ways in which their subject matter might reshape the novel's structure; as a result, they refused to use marriage to achieve closure and restore equilibrium. The open endings of *The Man of Property*, *Whom God Hath Joined* and *The Pastor's Wife* underscore the unresolved nature of the marriage problem itself, and anticipate the openness and irresolution that are characteristic of modernist fiction. The questioning of the institution of marriage was inevitably related to the questioning of the very nature of British social organization, and in that respect the marriage problem novel, with its distinctive moods of dissatisfaction and alienation, is indicative of a new, modern sensibility which was radically suspicious of tradition and received ideas.

Generally, by the end of the era, novels about 'the drama of their problems' had become the norm, for the social ideal of marital union could no longer effectively function as an unproblematic or unquestioned basis for fictional or social order. This trend is obvious in D.H. Lawrence's *Sons and Lovers* (1913) and *The Rainbow* (1915), in which marriage does not signal maturity or social integration or personal contentment but, rather, is a locus of frustration, confusion, unhappiness and violence: marriage is an unsettling rather than a stabilizing force in these novels. The marital relations of the Morels and the Brangwens shape their children's ideas about gender and sexuality, and are presented as an essential key to understanding Paul's and Ursula's motivations. But through their intimate knowledge of the realities of their parents' marriages, both Paul and Ursula come to realize the insufficiency of romantic desire, and find it impossible to view marriage as an ending, let alone a happy one.[50]

Ford Madox Ford's *The Good Soldier* (1915), more than any other novel of the time, marks the juncture between the Edwardian marriage problem novel and modernist fiction. There are many similarities between Ford's novel and Edwardian marriage problem novels: *The Good Soldier* is about the failure of marriage, about adultery and celibacy, about the impossibility of love in the modern world (and it has a character named Leonora). But Ford pursues, where Edwardian novelists did not, the full implications of the connections between marital, cultural and social breakdown. His story of the adulterous and deceitful relations of two married couples is told by an unreliable narrator, within a narrative which is non-linear, unchronological and unresolved. The narrator repeatedly emphasizes how the traditional narrative structure of stories is a cheat, for it attempts to give the impression of causality, coherence and resolution where none exists. But his statements about narrative are also implicitly statements about marriage, and they indirectly express the narrator's painful realization that the ideal of marriage is a cheat as well.

It is not just the novel, though, which becomes destabilized when marriage no longer exists as a focal point of order and stability; the social order, culture – even basic notions of truth and reality – are all revealed to be shams, façades constructed to cover up the alienation, confusion and meaninglessness at the core of human existence. Those who write about the emergence of a distinctively modern sensibility in British culture rarely discuss the importance of the marriage problem, but the collapse of the marital ideal precipitated an important crisis of belief, the evidence for which is abundant in the fiction of the late nineteenth and early twentieth centuries. In Hardy's *Tess of the d'Urbervilles*, Angel Clare's fundamental sense of reality is altered when he realizes that his marriage to Tess is not what he thought it was:

> ... the complexion even of external things seemed to suffer transmutation as her announcement progressed. The fire in the grate looked impish ... the fender grinned idly ... all material objects around announced their irresponsibility with terrible iteration. And yet nothing had changed since the moments when he had been kissing her; or rather, nothing in the substance of things. But the essence of things had changed. (297)

In two remarkably similar scenes, both Ford and Bennett represent the connection between marital breakdown and this larger shift in perception through the disillusionment of an innocent young girl. In *Whom God Hath Joined*, the discovery of her father's adultery irrevocably changes the way Annunciata sees the world: 'the very aspect of the senseless chairs straddling on the drawing-room carpet seemed to cry aloud that all was changed; and that they were no longer the same chairs' (149). In *The Good Soldier*, Nancy becomes completely disorientated when she realizes the existence of adultery and divorce for the first time: 'In her eyes the whole of that familiar, great hall had a changed aspect ... the burning logs were just logs that were burning and not the comfortable symbols of an indestructible mode of life' (220). By the end of the Edwardian period, marriage itself could no longer function, as it once had, as a 'comfortable symbol of an indestructible mode of life'; the essence of things had changed, and marriage, like the novel which was so dependent upon it, would never again be the same.

CHAPTER THREE

New Maids for Old

It is highly ironical, this spectacle of the serious masculine alarm lest the 'sex novel' (as the journalists twenty years ago dubbed it) 'should undermine Marriage' – the fact being plain that underneath the alarums and excursions of outward unconventionality, practically every one of these novels was a secret hymn, an inner pleading for married happiness! . . . And yet the masculine reviewers could never see it! So perturbed and scared were they by the cry of the revolted daughter that they never noticed that her predestined path led, circling and winding . . . to the Matrimonial Altar!

(EDWARD GARNETT [1910])

I am sick of every one thinking that I would marry any man for his possessions. I would not stoop to marry a king if I did not love him. As for trying to win a man, I would scorn any action that way; I never intend to marry. Instead of wasting so much money on me in presents and other ways, I wish you would get me something to do, a profession that will last me all my life, so that I may be independent.

(MILES FRANKLIN, *My Brilliant Career* [1901])

No single figure comparable to that of the New Woman of the 1890s served to symbolize the modern Edwardian woman. As more women actually began to lead new and modern lives – pursuing higher education and careers, marrying later in life and having fewer children, or not marrying at all – the New Woman of fiction and the popular press lost her mystique and power. Independent, 'new' women were becoming a reality, and feminism was influencing an increasing number and variety of women's lives. As the suffrage campaign developed, it became obvious that there was not just one coherent feminist movement, nor was there only one way of being emancipated; feminism had a variety of expressions and participants and beneficiaries, and no single image could embody them. Several new images or types emerged which reflected this diversity of Edwardian female independence; these included the suffragette, the Freewoman, the college girl, the typewriter girl, and the spinster.[1] These figures were employed by both 'sides'; those opposed to feminism or women's suffrage used them negatively in satirical cartoons and anti-feminist novels, while supporters of suffrage and feminism depicted some of these types as avatars of feminist progress, and used others, such as the spinster, to illustrate the current inequities of the British social and political system.

Edwardian fiction also began to reflect this variety in its representations of modern women. Owing in part to the Edwardian novelists' strong interest in the new realism and in social criticism, both the conventional romantic heroine of nineteenth-century novels and the idealized New Woman of the 1890s began to be replaced with a multitude of female characters who represented a range of classes, ages, and feminist philosophies; at the same time, increasing numbers of novels depicted women outside the traditional narratives of courtship and marriage. There are numerous Edwardian novels about adolescent girls, young career women, spinsters, widows, and other women whose lives did not fit neatly into the social patterns privileged by the nineteenth-century novel. Some of these novels dealt with the suffrage movement, and made a radical break with tradition by placing their narratives of women's lives in the public sphere: they will be examined in Chapter 4. But there were also many novels which sought to break free from romance-centered narratives and the conventional closure of marriage or death, while remaining more or less in the traditional female realm of the personal and the domestic. Most of these novels enact women's struggle to create a life apart from marriage; they also depict particular experiences and times in women's lives that were usually considered not significant or 'universal' enough to merit serious fictional treatment. Writers such as Mary Findlater purposely worked in opposition to such standards, and set out to write about what she ironically called 'the particularly trivial details of a narrow life';[2] this revelation in fiction of the previously hidden and silent lives of women was important to the development of both British feminism and British literature.

Courtship, marriage and childrearing were generally regarded by British society as the key experiences in a woman's life; in terms of fictional narratives, only the first of these was considered of interest during the nineteenth century, for women characters were deemed viable only as long as they were involved in dynamic relationships with men. Once marriage was achieved, women retreated into a world of female domesticity which was usually regarded as too limited and mundane to serve as a fictional topic (although, of course, women were expected to find it personally fulfilling). The marriage problem novel, which first became popular in the early 1890s and dominated Edwardian fiction, increased the range of a woman's narrative activity, and Edwardian novelists such as Arnold Bennett, Ellen Thorneycroft Fowler, Lucas Malet and Amber Reeves made a significant departure from tradition by writing novels about older married women or widows. But with the exception of Reeves's *A Lady and Her Husband*, most of these novels still relied upon romantic desire as the central motivation, and used romance and marriage as indicators of their heroines' worth.

The centrality of romance and marriage in narratives about women was challenged, however, by the large number of novels which emerged in the Edwardian age about another type of older woman: the spinster. Although the spinster had been a familiar figure in nineteenth-century fiction, she was usually little more than a stereotype, functioning in a secondary, and frequently admonitory, role. The spinster most often represented unnaturalness and uselessness, and lived a kind of death-in-life; she served as the specter of what the heroine might become if she did not marry. Her querulousness and pettiness reinforced the idea that a woman's natural role was to marry, and bear and nurture children; without such duties, women were doomed to unhappiness. But in the late 1880s and early 1890s, increasing interest in realism and the Woman Question prompted writers such as George Gissing in *The Odd Women*, and George Moore in *A Drama in Muslin*, to place spinsters at the center of their novels, and to portray them with sympathy and psychological complexity, particularly with regard to their position as social misfits. Many Edwardian novelists followed suit, and made spinsters the central focus of their novels.

This shift in fictional representations of unmarried women is symbolized by the two very different spinsters in Forster's novel *Where Angels Fear to Tread*. Harriet Herriton is the stereotypical nineteenth-century spinster: her single status has left her unusually attached to her mother and her home, and her lack of contact with the world, or any feelings of passion, has narrowed her perspective, and made her peevish and cruel. She represents unnatural, atrophied womanhood, and significantly, Lilia and Gino's baby dies after being held in her arms. But Forster contrasts Harriet with another spinster, Miss Caroline Abbott, and, by so doing, reveals the deficiencies of the stereotype. Miss Abbott is not a liberated woman in any obvious way, but she strives to retain an open mind, and remain receptive to new sensations and experiences. Thus, she does not automatically condemn Lilia's engagement to the young Italian Gino, and later, she dares to make an unchaperoned visit to him; her delight in helping Gino to bathe his baby demonstrates that even an unmarried woman can enjoy maternal feelings. Miss Abbott eventually admits to Harriet's brother Philip that she feels a sexual attraction to Gino, but she is realistic about how far she will allow herself to step outside the social restrictions placed upon her, and ultimately she does nothing about it. Miss Abbott is a not a New Woman, but she is not a typical old maid either; it is clear that her willingness simply to experience her feelings for Gino has made her life immeasurably richer than Harriet's will ever be. Forster's sympathy for Miss Abbott, his depiction of her sexuality, and his desire to place her inhibitions and limitations within a social context are all representative of the trend in Edwardian fiction toward more complex, realistic and compassionate portrayals of unmarried women. By contrasting the two spinsters in *Where Angels Fear to Tread*, Forster shows that even though the stereotype of the spinster is often actualized, it is neither natural nor inevitable; he suggests that one of the best ways to escape the constraints and conventions of society is first to reject the stereotypes by which society defines and regulates its members.

An important project of Edwardian feminists was to change both the public perception and the self-image of the unmarried woman and, by so doing, allow her a fuller life and a more significant role in society. Unmarried women had been considered 'superfluous' or 'redundant' at least since the mid-nineteenth century, when census figures revealed what was referred to at the time as a significant 'surplus' of women. This imbalance was viewed as a major social problem by the vast majority who were unable to conceive of any other role for a woman than that of wife and mother.[3] But feminists cited the census figures in support of their argument that women should stop being considered only as potential wives and mothers, and be educated and trained for useful careers. Opportunities for such training and education did gradually increase by the Edwardian age, but social attitudes toward women and marriage were slow to change. The majority of women in the Edwardian era still longed for marriage and motherhood – not only because society idealized them as the only natural careers for women, but also because marriage remained the most accessible and economically practical option. As she had been in the Victorian age, the unmarried woman or spinster continued to be a figure of pity and even ridicule in Edwardian society; Maud Churton Braby, author of advice books on love and marriage, was typical in her characterization of single women as 'the undesired', and in her assumption that their lives were tragedies.

Increasingly, there were women who actively chose not to marry – usually in order to have a career, or because of their political beliefs; but for every successful and self-supporting single woman, there were many other women who lived solitary, impoverished and unhappy lives, believing themselves to be useless and unwanted. Most feminists were united in their desire to obtain respect, legal rights, employment opportunities and, in general, a useful place in society for unmarried women; but there was much debate over the best way to attain those ends, as is demonstrated by the lengthy and passionate exchanges on the subject in the feminist journal, *The Freewoman*. Those involved in the suffrage campaign believed that unmarried women could best achieve the social equality they desired through the vote; others emphasized how education and work could give meaning to women's lives as well as marriage and motherhood did; still others insisted that the ways in which men and women were socialized must be altered, in order for single women to stop perceiving themselves in terms of limitation and failure. In the first issue of the journal there was a bitter essay entitled 'The Spinster. By One': the author condemned society for fostering the desire for romance and 'the right man' in women, and then telling 'one perhaps in every four ... "Thou shalt not"'. The author insisted that even a life of meaningful work could not make up for the feelings of inadequacy and sexual frustration that resulted.[4] This essay prompted numerous letters in which women insisted that such a view was self-pitying, and only helped to encourage the outdated and dangerous stereotype of the repressed and unwanted spinster. Others wrote in with accounts of spinsters enjoying richly fulfilling lives, or with personal testimony that an absence of romance and sex in one's life was not physically or psychologically harmful.

The issue of the relationship between sex and the single woman was a particularly emotional and troubling one. Most Edwardian women tended to view their options in absolute, either/or terms. It was generally believed that women had to choose between marriage and a career; similarly, most accepted that for a woman, being unmarried also meant being celibate. But some feminists began to question this assumption, and there was much debate in the correspondence pages of *The Freewoman* about the sexual needs of single women. To admit to the existence of such needs was a radical break with the stereotype of the spinster, and the very term 'spinster' soon began to seem inadequate and outdated. Rebecca West used the term pejoratively in a review, and when a reader wrote in to protest, West explained that to her way of thinking, 'spinsterhood is not necessarily a feminine quality. It is simply the limitation of experience to one's own sex'; she went on to cite the novelist May Sinclair as an example of an unmarried woman who was not a spinster, and Walter Pater and A.C. Benson as examples of men who were.[5]

For West and others, the term spinster was indicative of a frame of mind, an acceptance of limitation; as such, it was no longer useful as a general description of all unmarried women.[6] But it was not such an easy thing (in either practical or moral terms) to gain experience (carnal or otherwise) of the opposite sex outside courtship and marriage. Unmarried women found it extremely difficult to escape the restrictions imposed upon them by society, or to redefine themselves apart from traditional social values. But as the exchanges in *The Freewoman* indicate (and the issues raised there were echoed in other journals, and in novels), the problem of the spinster forced Edwardians to confront crucial questions about gender, morality and power. By insisting that women could lead happy and fulfilling lives apart from marriage, women subverted the patriarchal social order; by suggesting that sexuality is an important part of a woman's life, whether she is married or not, they presented a significant challenge to traditional morality and its power to determine women's behavior; and in formulating how best to live a life apart from marriage, they were forced to question social and cultural definitions of femaleness, and explore as never before what it is essentially to be a woman.

This ongoing debate about the spinster and her role in British society transformed the issue into yet another popular social 'problem' suitable for fictional analysis; as a result, a wide variety of novels, all seeking to reveal the hitherto unexplored life of the unmarried woman, were published. The most notorious were two by Hubert Wales – *The Yoke* (1907) and *The Spinster* (1912) – which were shockingly liberal for the time in their positive depiction of sexual desire as a strong but natural physical need of both men and women. In *The Yoke*, Angelica Jenour, a forty-year-old 'maid', has an affair with her ward, Maurice Heelas, the son of her dead fiancé. Their relationship serves the dual purpose of preventing Maurice from turning to prostitutes and contracting venereal disease, and giving Angelica a chance to experience physical passion for the first (and presumably last) time in her life. Like Bennett's *Leonora*, *The Yoke* was radical in its depiction of a middle-aged woman as a sexual being; the fact that Maurice is only twenty-two was also a challenge to conventional ideas about age and attractiveness. Angelica does not suffer, nor is she punished: she and Maurice are very happy together, and she gladly gives him to a young woman he loves when he is finally in a position to marry.

But despite the insertion of several polemical sections which treat the unavailability of a sexual outlet for unmarried women as a social problem, *The Yoke* has more in common with *Three Weeks* and other sensation novels than with serious problem novels. There is an aura of unreality about it, and clearly, its main function is to titillate. There is no consideration of the social complications that would normally have been involved in such an affair, nor of the emotional cost to Angelica. And while such an explicit declaration of female sexual desire can be seen as liberating in one sense, it is also restrictive. Sex becomes the absolute determinant of value, of fulfillment – even of womanhood: without it, Angelica would have been just another useless, shrivelled old maid; with it, she can hold her head high. It is only after her affair with Maurice that Angelica thinks: 'her life was no longer meaningless, the reproach of enduring maidenhood was removed, she had fulfilled her destiny, she was a woman' (143).

The National Vigilance Association, an organization dedicated to protecting the public's morals, took John Long, publisher of *The Yoke*, to court, citing its 'obscene' nature, and Long subsequently removed it from circulation.[7] But Wales later returned to the theme of an unmarried woman's sexuality in *The Spinster*. This time, his justification of his novel as a work of social concern and journalistic observation was more credible, for he does provide a rare picture of the life of a thirty-seven-year-old working woman. Mabel Christopherson has worked for fifteen years as a nurse in a London hospital, and is on the verge of a promotion to a supervisory position when her brother insists that she return to their rural home to care for their recently widowed mother. As was typical at the time, Mabel's career and personal desires are not given any weight at all by her brother; as a single woman, she is completely subject to the needs of her family. But the novel soon moves from social realism to sensationalistic melodrama: Mabel has a brief affair, becomes pregnant, is ostracized by her family, causes her mother's death and her brother's failure, miscarries, and is reduced to singing in the street for pennies. The man who seduces her, Horace Register, tells her explicitly at the start of their friendship that he is a 'confirmed widower'; he offers her a new kind of relationship outside marriage, but Mabel refuses, feeling that 'marriage was the end to which nature had designed her' (9). The object of Wales's critique is confusingly vague; while he condemns conventional sexual morality, he never questions Mabel's belief that hers is a failed 'makeshift life' without marriage. His 'feminist' sympathies and social criticism ultimately seem little more than the means by which he sought to disguise his sexually sensational material, and Wales himself emerges as an Edwardian Grant Allen. As with *The Yoke*, what appears on the surface to be a radical treatment of women and sexuality is finally quite conservative in import; Wales makes it clear that both Mabel and Angelica are unable to find true fulfillment except in a relationship with a man.

Although Wales's novels are not particularly well written, they serve as useful examples of both the common strategies and the failings of most Edwardian novels about unmarried women. In writing about spinsters, novelists were, by definition, unable to end their novels with marriage; thus they were forced to work in opposition to the dominant narratives of romance and marriage which had traditionally been used to tell stories about women. But with few exceptions, authors of spinster novels still managed to include some kind of romance plot, even though it usually compromised the realism of their characterizations. The romance plot was appealing to the novelist in that it helped to sustain narrative interest, and satisfied the expectations of the reading public; but it was also important in that it was one of the most traditional and easily comprehended methods of validating the worth of the heroine. Many women, in reality, were spinsters for such mundane reasons as demographics or physical unattractiveness or lack of money or just bad luck, but none of those was likely to engage the sympathies of the reader. Instead, by creating a romance for the spinster that either occurred in the past, or fails in the course of the narrative, the novelist signals to the reader that the spinster is worthy of interest, for she has been loved by a man, but has been separated from married happiness through some dramatic and heart-rending tragedy.

As with the New Woman novels, this compromise results in a tension within novels about spinsters between the author's desire to portray an unmarried woman realistically and the novelistic ideal of the physically attractive, romantically appealing heroine. Anthony Hope's popular novel *The Great Miss Driver* (1908) features a strong young woman who determines never to marry, but the appeal of her character is based almost entirely upon the fact that she once had a lover who died fighting a duel for her honor. She also considers her greatest business asset to be the fact that she is perceived by men as 'marriageable'; this secures her respect and cooperation that an unmarriageable (that is, physically unattractive) woman could not expect, and paradoxically contributes to her success as an independent woman.

The abrupt, contrived endings of Wales's novels are indicative of how difficult it was for novelists to find alternative endings to replace the traditional ones of marriage or death. Of course, the death of the heroine was used as an ending by some authors, such as Violet Hunt in her novel *White Rose of Weary Leaf* (1908), in much the same way it was used by the New Woman novelists – as a pessimistic conclusion intended to reinforce the novel's social criticism. Positive or constructive endings presented more of a challenge; the self-realization or social integration with which heroines had traditionally been rewarded in fiction were almost entirely predicated upon romantic love and marital union. Those unmarried women in the Edwardian age who were old enough to be termed 'spinsters' were of a transitional generation which did not, for the most part, have the education, training or motivation to pursue careers; thus, in fiction as in real life, Edwardian spinsters had shockingly limited opportunities for any kind of personal or social fulfillment. One of the most common ways in which novelists solved this narrative dilemma was through the literary device of the inheritance, for it not only satisfied readers' demands for a happy ending, but did so without challenging traditional gender roles. The heroine of *The Great Miss Driver*, for example, inherits a fortune, and through it attains independence and power; but because she never does anything actually to earn her wealth, and because she delegates the entire management of her fortune to her male employees, Miss Driver is able to remain conventionally (and non-threateningly) passive and feminine.

To some novelists, however, the marginality of the spinster gave a fresh perspective from which to view gender roles, traditional narrative structures, and the values and institutions of British society. When novelists such as Mary and Jane Findlater and F.M. Mayor chose to focus on the lives of spinsters, they not only opened up a whole new realm for fictional exploration but also began to push against the constraints of narrative conventions concerning women. The fact that their spinster heroines live outside the normative narratives of courtship and marriage enabled them to create new narratives which were not only formally innovative but functioned as critiques of the ideologies upon those normative narratives are constructed.

The sisters Mary and Jane Findlater made their careers writing, together and individually, about spinsters. They were popular and respected novelists in their time, making a successful American publicity tour in 1905. The sisters knew of the life of the spinster at first hand, for neither of them ever married; yet they were more fortunate than most in that they enjoyed an extremely close relationship. Mary broke off her engagement when she realized that she would have to be parted from Jane; afterwards, both women would joke: '*we* could only marry a Mormon'.[8] Similarly, the spinsters the Findlaters wrote about were also single by choice, yet as the novels movingly convey, that choice did not preclude their suffering from feelings of marginality, loneliness and sexual frustration.

The first novel the Findlaters wrote jointly, *Crossriggs* (1908), is also their richest exploration of a spinster's life. It is the story of Alex, a thirty-year-old woman who is forced to repress her own desires in order to support her widowed sister and her five children, as well as her aging and eccentric father. Only when her sister eventually remarries does Alex fully realize that her life of self-sacrifice has left her with nothing to call her own, and no hopes for the future. She is devastated by the sudden departure of her surrogate children and the abrupt cessation of her responsibilities. Alex is saved from a complete breakdown by the timely arrival of an inheritance, but the Findlaters use this conventional device to empower their heroine to lead an unconventional life. Alex comes to realize that independence affords her a kind of strength and happiness that she had never achieved through relationships, and the novel ends with her making plans to travel round the world. The ending is thus open, both in terms of narrative structure and with regard to Alex's ultimate destination. The reader is left with the sense that Alex is moving out into a realm of possibilities, far away from the society which has sought to impose its limits upon her.

Alex, as well as the heroines of Mary Findlater's novels *The Rose of Joy* (1903) and *Tents of a Night* (1914), serves as a deliberate challenge to traditional expectations of how a female protagonist should look and behave. There are none of the usual concessions to make her appealing or attractive: she is angry and resentful at the demands of her family, she refuses to groom and dress herself in ways that brand her as 'marriage-able', she is outspoken in her contempt for the compromises women make in order to attain financial and social security through marriage, and she refuses to make similar compromises herself. There are repeated references to how Alex looks her age, or to how tired she looks, and these remarks are clearly intended to valorize her, to make her more real and substantial than the women in the novel who do nothing but worry about their hair and their clothes. The Findlaters' novels follow in the tradition established by Charlotte Brontë, in *Jane Eyre* and *Villette*, in which the heroines' inability or unwillingness to conform to conventional ideals of feminine beauty is presented as an indication of their superiority and value, thus subverting the ideology which insists that the worth of a woman is determined by her appearance. So although Alex's dresses are unfashionable and her face is lined, the two men in the novel prefer her over other more outwardly attractive women, whose consciousness of the physical impression they make is associated unfavorably with deception and destructive sexuality. This is not to say, however, that the Findlaters' heroines do not agonize over their looks: every time they look in the mirror, there is a struggle between their own sense of self-worth and their consciousness of their shortcomings in the eyes of society. But more often than not these heroines seem quite willing, even relieved, to have their unconventional looks determine their destiny, for they exempt them from the competition of the marriage market, and free them to live an independent life.

For all their appealing rebelliousness and autonomy, however, the heroines of *Crossriggs*, *The Rose of Joy*, and *Tents of a Night* are given little psychological depth. In all three novels, it is revealed in a curiously indirect and annoyingly belated fashion that the heroine is in love with a particular man; once revealed, this love is never discussed or analyzed either by the narrator or by the heroine herself. Although both narrator and heroine tend to be outspoken in their social criticism, they become coy, even dishonest, when it comes to the heroine's personal desires and emotional crises. One reason for this, perhaps, is the discrepancy between the authors' conventional reliance upon a romantic attraction to validate their heroines, and the heroines' eventual rejection, within the narrative itself, of romance and marriage. It is as if the authors are embarrassed by the narratorial necessity of romance, and thus treat it in an oblique and perfunctory fashion. But the omission of the heroines' personal responses also seems to be a way for the Findlaters to avoid any exploration of the enormity of the choice to remain single, and the emotional toll of such a choice. That the authors know the painful and difficult nature of the decision is evident in their depiction of their heroines' constant irritability, repeated periods of illness, and hysterical reactions to sexual advances or to displays of sexual feeling in others. But though the Findlaters dared to allow their heroines 'unfeminine' outbursts of anger and dissatisfaction, they were unable to confront openly the most intimate ramifications of this kind of social rebellion for women. Anxieties about what is naturally or essentially female, sexual fear and frustration, regrets about never having children – all these hover around the edges of the novels, but are never dealt with directly.

The narratives of *Crossriggs* and *Tents of a Night* are implicitly shaped by the limited number of vocations available for unmarried middle-class Edwardian women, but this problem also is never confronted candidly by the authors or their characters. Both Alex, and Anne in *Tents of a Night*, are full of inchoate longing for some kind of new life, but unable to say what they will do with their lives in lieu of marriage. Anne wonders: 'Was there something better, happier even, than any mere fulfilment of passion – than the attainment of any earth-born desire?' (262). During a holiday in France she decides that the answer is yes, and rejects both the possibility of romance with the exotic Dragotin Voinovich, and the offer of marriage from the stolid Jimmy Fordyce, but the terms of her rebellion are ill-defined. Like Alex, Anne is frequently critical, bad-tempered and depressed; she is unable to confront her ambivalent feelings about what she is giving up, or the vagueness of what she is searching for. Her travelling companion, Barbara, a much younger woman, is full of plans for the future: she wants to learn to fly, run a dairy-farm, maybe even be a 'spin' and have her own business; to Anne, Barbara is the 'perfect embodiment of a new spirit' of confidence and freedom which feminism has imparted to young women. But Anne is stuck in her own transitional generation, and feels unable to partake of that confidence; while she can make the decision that she is not going to seek her 'home in another heart', she is unable to imagine herself doing anything else. In a characteristically Edwardian fashion, the novel ends at an impasse: Anne knows she wants a 'richer experience' than marriage, but she has no idea where or how she will find it.

Only in *The Rose of Joy* was Mary Findlater able to ground her heroine's desire for an independent life in the realities of work. The narrative of *The Rose of Joy* is initially that of a marriage problem novel: Susan Crawford, feeling trapped by the drudgery and poverty of her home, forms a miserable marriage with Darnley Stair, bears a child who dies shortly after birth, discovers that Darnley is already married, and has her marriage invalidated. But what seems to be a tragedy turns out to be the occasion for Susan's rebirth, for she is an artist, and her marriage had all but ended her career. Findlater reverses the stereotypes, making the married woman the admonitory figure in the book, and the spinster the figure of admiration and emulation. Susan's mother provides a horrifying picture of how marriage and childrearing deplete a woman, both physically and intellectually, while the 'old maid', Miss Mitford, exemplifies longed-for freedom and independence: 'She had lived to be sixty and was still free; her life had never been broken into.... A shaft of envy shot through [Susan]' (132–3). Marriage and motherhood are represented as ruptures, as violations of personal integrity and private destiny; in her art and her life, Susan can achieve the control, order and clarity she desires only after her marriage ends (and her baby dies). Through her insistence that marriage and motherhood inevitably entail self-denial and intellectual dulling, Findlater reinforces the conventional either/or opposition between marriage and vocation. But as a result, Susan is more secure in her choice of a single life than the Findlaters' other heroines – not only because she has experienced marriage and motherhood and found them wanting, but also because she has a vocation, a purpose in her life that Alex and Anne do not. By its end, *The Rose of Joy* has transformed itself into a *Künstlerroman*: Susan is living in Miss Mitford's former house with Darnley's unmarried sister, supporting herself through the sale of her drawings. The final image of two unmarried women enjoying a life of companionship, comfort and dignity together, apart from their families, recalls Gissing's *The Odd Women*, but is nevertheless rare in British fiction.

The Findlater sisters deliberately chose to write in a realistic mode about unmarried women who were ordinary and imperfect, rejecting both the conventional nineteenth-century romantic heroine and the idealized New Woman of the 1890s. Yet it was clearly important to them that their heroines not simply be resigned to their unmarried state but triumphantly choose to remain single; thus at the end of their novels realism is abandoned in favor of a mild form of fantasy: their heroines shift from being familiar in their insecurities and dissatisfaction to being exceptional in their resolute and confident independence. In contrast, F.M. Mayor, in her novel *The Third Miss Symons* (1913), is unequivocal in her refusal to make similar kinds of concessions either to her readers' expectations or to feminism. Her depiction of a spinster's life is unflinchingly honest and, as such, offers a more powerful social critique than the Findlaters' conventionally satisfying narratives.

Mayor, like the Findlaters, never married, and in both her major novels (the other was *The Rector's Daughter*, published in 1924) she endeavored to break with novelistic conventions, and treat the lives of unmarried women with seriousness and specificity. The spinster at the center of *The Third Miss Symons*, Miss Henrietta Symons, is not redeemed by a past romance, neither does she find any happiness, let alone triumph, in her life. The message that Henrietta gleans from *Jane Eyre* and *Villette*, 'that the plain may be adored too', proves to be a lie, and she waits pathetically for a Prince Charming who never comes. Mayor's realism is uncompromising; Henrietta is thoroughly unexceptional and banal, like the women one sees in the Tube:

> . . . women with dark-brown hair, brown eyes, and too-strongly-marked eyebrows; their features are neither good nor bad; their whole aspect is uninteresting. They have no winning dimples, no speaking lines about the mouth. All that one can notice is a disappointed, somewhat peevish look in the eyes. Such was Henrietta. (20)

In his preface to the novel, the poet and playwright John Masefield praised Mayor for lighting up 'so many little unsuspected corners in a world that is too plentifully curtained'. More than any other novel of the age, *The Third Miss Symons* presents with painstaking (and painful) detail the texture of the daily life of a spinster as she moves through her existence completely bereft of purpose, interests or usefulness. On the first page, the reader is told that Henrietta's life 'attained its zenith' when she was five; after that, her prettiness fades and her value in the world declines. The attributes which are considered 'naturally' feminine are not natural to Henrietta, and her quick temper and loud voice soon make her a 'pariah'. She is courted briefly by a suitor who forsakes her for her more attractive and vivacious sister; although she initially expects that other suitors will follow, none ever does:

> Henrietta realized forcibly, though perhaps not forcibly enough for the truth, that the years between eighteen and thirty were her marrying years, which, slowly as they passed from the point of view of her happiness, went only too fast, when she considered that once gone they could never come back, and that as they fled they took her chances with them. (38)

After her one opportunity is lost, Henrietta simply tries to get through the next forty-three years, fighting off loneliness and boredom by managing her father's household, doing church work, traveling, playing cards, and reading novels; none of these things does she do with any interest or skill. She has mobility and financial independence, but they do not make her happy, or give her any sense of freedom. She has been trained to live out only one narrative – that of marriage and motherhood; when that narrative fails to materialize, she is left without a substitute. Henrietta's life has no conflict, no complications, no climax, no resolution – it is completely, horrifyingly empty. Thus, by daring to write the actual narrative that British society offered to spinsters – one almost entirely lacking in dramatic incident – Mayor powerfully conveys the true superfluousness of a spinster's life.

But Mayor is careful not to blame Henrietta's situation entirely on the social system which has limited her expectations and opportunities; 'inscrutable fate' plays as big a part in Henrietta's dismal life as social circumstances do. Henrietta's sense that it is 'the all-sufficing condition of existence to love and be loved' (22) is presented as a human intuition, not an exclusively female one; her tragedy is that she has no chance to experience such a relationship. What Mayor does criticize implicitly is society's failure to encourage girls and women, through socialization and education, to develop interests, skills and ambitions unconnected with marriage and motherhood. Throughout the novel, the narrator hints that if only Henrietta had to support herself, if only she knew shorthand or typing, if only she felt a desire to do something, then she could actually have lived a real life. It is taken for granted that her brothers will work, that they will have purpose in their lives; but since Henrietta has no need to work, it never occurs to her or anyone else that she might do so. As a result, the protected, comfortable, shallow existence that young women were expected to live between school and marriage stretches out instead for Henrietta's entire lifetime.

The Third Miss Symons provides an excellent illustration of the ways in which the new kinds of characters and the new themes in Edwardian fiction – its modern content – worked to reshape the form of the novel. Though Henrietta is not a rebellious woman, her very existence reveals the inadequacies of the traditional social order. Concomitantly, Mayor's narrative of Henrietta's life self-consciously reveals the inadequacies of traditional modes of characterization and narrative which are founded upon the traditional social order. Mayor, unable to use the usual narrative punctuation of romance or marriage or motherhood, chose instead to fit the novel within the span of Henrietta's life, and end it with her death from old age. Scrupulously avoiding sentiment, Mayor refuses to make the ending of her novel tragic or triumphant, or even particularly meaningful: 'death had not changed Henrietta; there had been no transfiguration to beauty and nobility, she looked what she had been in life – insignificant, feeble, and unhappy' (141). But Henrietta's death does not impart a feeling of closure, for the problem of her existence remains unresolved. The fact of her abiding insignificance endows her with a paradoxical kind of power: by refusing to make meaning where there is none, Mayor ensures that Henrietta's senseless life will unsettle the reader even after the narrative ends.

The disturbing and indeterminate ending of *The Third Miss Symons* is indicative of a distinctively modern sensibility, and points to the connections between this work and modernist fiction. In her deliberate choice to portray the unexceptional and the unloved, Mayor's project is similar to Joyce's in his *Dubliners* stories, and the styles of the two authors are similar as well. Like Joyce, Mayor's diction is precise, her tone is coolly objective, her prose is deceptively simple, her characterizations are brutally honest and psychologically complex, yet also deeply sympathetic. But by writing a very brief work about the most insignificant of women, Mayor, unlike Joyce, risked encountering the criticism commonly applied to women novelists: that they work on too small and personal a scale, and are unable to treat topics of universal significance. Mayor however disproved such stereotypes, for in *The Third Miss Symons* she movingly and disturbingly comments upon and illuminates not only the life of a spinster, but the human condition as well.

With lives such as Miss Symons's visible in fiction and reality, it is no wonder that young Edwardian women looked upon the prospect of life without marriage with dread. Marriage and motherhood continued to be equated with womanly fulfillment, and were idealized as the only natural course of life for women. The concept of women having careers was still a new one; education and career training were viewed by most as temporary measures, or as something to fall back on in case no marriage proposals materialized. Despite the increasing number of working, unmarried women, positive role models for young women were rare; with limited financial and social resources, the life of a working woman was not glamorous or appealing in obvious ways.[9] Young women who attended girls' schools and women's colleges during the Edwardian years were often disappointed by the fact that their teachers or school administrators paid so little attention to their appearance, and their work-centered life seemed to be dreary and lonely.[10]

The scarcity of single women who escaped the stereotypes and created new kinds of lives for themselves reinforced a young woman's sense that she had an either/or choice – to get married or be a spinster, albeit one with a job. But the rise of feminism, and in particular its critique of marriage, further complicated this choice for young women. The situation of Rosemary, a modern, well-educated young woman in Reeves's *A Lady and Her Husband*, serves as an illustration of this dilemma. She is terrified at the prospect of marriage, even though her fiancé has promised to make her his 'equal, his mate and his comrade':

> When you married . . . you lost your sense of the freedom, the spaciousness of life. . . . It wasn't that she didn't love Tony, she loved him so much that she was happy to be giving up everything for him, but she regretted herself, the

self that was soon to be changed into a wife and mother. She liked the world,
she liked adventures; a wife is shut away from adventure, a mother shuts the
world away from her children. She consoled herself by thinking that every
woman who marries young has had these thoughts. (155)

By the Edwardian age, few educated young women could be entirely free
from such doubts about marriage; not only had they experienced
independence such as their mothers had never known, but they were also
far more conscious than previous generations had been of the inequities
in relations between the sexes, and the limitations of a life of childbearing
and housekeeping.

This distinctively Edwardian dilemma, characteristic of a transitional
age – being aware of the faults of the old forms but as yet not having any
new forms to replace them with – led to a group of Edwardian novels best
described as anti-courtship novels. Like traditional courtship novels, they
focus on the time between childhood and marriage; like Jane Austen's
novels, or *Jane Eyre*, they also employ elements of the *Bildungsroman*, for
they are concerned with the ways in which the heroine develops and
matures. But as the heroine of an anti-courtship novel attains maturity,
her first inclination is to move away from marriage rather than toward it;
in the anti-courtship novel the heroine consciously resists the dominant
narrative of romance, and refuses to accept marriage as the inevitable
ending to her story. The Findlaters' novels fit this pattern in some
respects, yet they differ from the majority of anti-courtship novels in that
their heroines are able to move beyond the romance plot to a quest plot,
although the latter is not actually depicted; their novels end as their
heroines begin their search for a new and independent way of life. But the
usual pattern of the anti-courtship novel is that the heroine comes to
realize the limitations of traditional gender roles and social conventions,
and thus rejects them, but is then unable to proceed beyond that
rejection. Her actions are predicated on opposition, not exploration or
innovation: she knows what she doesn't want, but she doesn't know
what it is she wants. Like so many of the Edwardian marriage problem
novels, most anti-courtship novels circle back to where they began, with
the heroine ultimately unable to formulate any narrative desire other than
that of romance. But whereas some marriage problem novels – most
notably those by Galsworthy, Bennett and von Arnim – use a circular
narrative pattern to criticize the lack of options for women, most anti-
courtship novels represent the heroine's return to the status quo as a
happy ending.

E.F. Benson's *Dodo the Second* (1914) is a typical anti-courtship novel,
and its heroine, Nadine, is the epitome of the thoroughly modern
Edwardian young woman: she smokes, discusses social reform novels,
reads Swinburne and Plato, and entertains young men in her sitting-

room unchaperoned late at night.[11] Like the Findlaters' heroines –
indeed, like most modern young women in Edwardian novels – she is
achingly full of unspecified desires to do something with her life, to be
significant somehow:

> I am something beyond and back of the things I like, and the people I like.
> Something inside me says 'I want; I want.' I daresay it wants the moon, and
> has as much chance of getting it as I have of reaching up into the sky and
> pulling it down. (197)

But Nadine's desires remain vague throughout the novel. She never
considers that she might have a career, and although she protests that she
doesn't want to be a spinster, living in a flat and reading at the British
Museum, she doesn't want to marry her boyfriend, Hugh, and settle
down to a conventional (and, by implication, boring) life either; thus, she
spends most of the novel running away from him. Nadine briefly
entertains the idea of marrying the effete and affected Seymour, whose
homosexuality seems to guarantee that she can avoid traditional social
and sexual arrangements; Seymour predicts that when they are married,
'I shall do embroidery in the evening, after dinner, while Nadine smokes'
(285). But after a crisis in which Hugh rescues a drowning boy and almost
dies, Nadine has an 'awakening to womanhood', and realizes that her
true destiny is to marry the man she loves, and have his children. Benson
creates a lively and humorous modern heroine, but does not furnish her
with a new narrative; consequently, Nadine, unable to understand
herself and her desires independently, must return to the conventional
narrative of romance and marriage to give her life definition and
meaning.

Independent women who insisted that they wished to remain
unmarried – women like Nadine (before her change of heart), or the
Findlaters' heroines – constituted, for a great many Englishmen and
women, a significant social threat. That women would choose to live
outside the prevailing patriarchal system was alarming in itself to those
who believed that system to be integral to the order and stability of the
nation; but the problem was exacerbated by the fact that most of the
women who eschewed marriage were well educated and from the middle
and upper classes. At a time when social theorists of all political
persuasions were warning about the decline of the British race (and the
British Empire), it was considered something of a national crisis that
precisely those who should be marrying and propagating the race, those
who were presumed to be the best and the brightest of British
womanhood, were the ones who were remaining single. Theorists as
various as Emma Goldman, Ellen Key and Havelock Ellis insisted that the
health of the nation depended on women accepting their natural duties as

wives and mothers; the novelist Lucas Malet spoke for many Edwardians when she worried anxiously about how society could 'charm the New Woman – sexless, homeless, unmaternal as she increasingly is – back to the store-closet and the nursery'.[12] In this context, the anti-courtship novel can be seen as a kind of lure for young women. Like most marriage problem novels, anti-courtship novels were appealingly modern and liberal in their sympathetic depiction of women's need for autonomy, and in their social criticism, particularly their criticism of the inequities of marriage and traditional gender roles. But also like many popular marriage problem novels, anti-courtship novels allowed their modern young heroines to have it both ways: they are able to enjoy both the adventure of their rebellion and the romance of a happily-ever-after ending. This inevitably entailed some awkward narrative twists, but eventually contradictions are brushed aside, the status quo is reaffirmed, and as in Nesbit's *The Red House*, the once fiercely independent Girton girl is darning her husband's socks before she knows it (and loving it, too).

In *Max* (1910) the popular novelist Katherine Cecil Thurston created an interesting variation on the anti-courtship theme. Her heroine, a Russian princess who has run away to Paris, dresses as a young man so that she can pursue her career as a painter without prejudice or restrictions; her disguise makes her feel 'infinitely free, infinitely unhampered'. After meeting Ned Blake, she has a new reason to maintain the deception, for – like Angelica in Grand's *The Heavenly Twins* – she wants to experience friendship with a man without the intrusion of romantic love. But after Ned falls in love with Max's self-portrait of herself as a woman, Max begins to lead a double existence, as Max and Max's 'sister'. A crucial source of conflict in this novel, as in *Dodo the Second*, is the heroine's fear of sexual love; both heroines desire to keep their relationships with men on a Platonic level, and both novels imply that this fear of sexuality is characteristic of modern women, as are their independence and egotism. Like Sue Bridehead, these women do seem excessively fastidious about sex, yet it is important to place their emotions in a social context. For Edwardian women, sex was inextricably connected with marriage and pregnancy; it did not mean pleasurable liberation but, rather, the cessation of independence, the limitation of opportunity, and the loss of privacy and mobility. What is stressed in both *Dodo the Second* and *Max*, however, is that a desire to avoid sex (and, by association, marriage and motherhood) is unnatural and unwomanly. In the case of Max, that unnaturalness is underscored by her male clothing and short haircut; her disguise gives her freedom, but the implication is that such freedom will not satisfy her forever. Even though Max is depicted as undeniably talented, her powerful desire for artistic achievement is eventually supplanted by the stronger and supposedly more natural one for romantic love; significantly, the possibility that the two desires could coexist is never considered. As in *Dodo the Second*, the initial movement of this narrative is away from romantic love, but Max, like Nadine, after discovering her 'true' feminine nature, willingly gives up her dream of accomplishment and activity, and circles back to accept marriage and motherhood as her destiny.

Forster's *A Room with a View* (1908) is also an anti-courtship novel, and its heroine's acceptance of her sexuality also coincides with her acceptance of marriage; but by challenging traditional relations between the sexes, and by positing a new kind of marriage, Forster attempts to link Lucy Honeychurch's decision to marry with sexual liberation and personal freedom, rather than with an acceptance of a traditional social order. At the beginning of the novel, Lucy is a conventional young woman without 'any system of revolt', living a quiet suburban life. When the very unconventional George Emerson comes along, and stimulates her both intellectually and sexually, she retreats into a Victorian world of female passivity and asexuality by becoming engaged to Cecil Vyse. Lucy's choice of Cecil is like Nadine's of Seymour; although there is no explicit recognition of his homosexuality, Lucy has an intuitive sense that he is 'safe', and will not impinge upon her sexually.

But Forster demonstrates that Lucy's retreat from sexuality is a retreat from life itself, which she herself soon realizes. Significantly, it is Cecil's physical failure which precipitates the failure of the romance; his stilted kisses, his priggishness, even his supercilious refusal to play tennis, all repel Lucy, and she breaks off their engagement. Like Nadine and Max, Lucy runs away from courtship and romance, but doesn't know exactly what she wants; she isn't, as her mother suspects, interested in a life of typewriters and latchkeys, nor do the unmarried women she knows (her spinster cousin Charlotte and the novelist Miss Lavish) offer appealing models of the single life. But Lucy differs from Nadine and Max in that she is ultimately able to articulate what she does want, and act upon it; Lucy becomes 'a rebel who desired . . . equality with the man she loved' (108). When she finally agrees to marry George, it is not due to any acceptance of her natural destiny as a woman, nor does it signal a triumph of traditional gender roles and social arrangements; she sees marriage as the only place where she can experience sexual passion and equality.

Lucy's transformation begins when she discovers that George's awkwardness moves her more than Cecil's confident superiority: 'men were not gods after all, but as human and clumsy as girls; even men might suffer from unexplained desires, and need help' (148). When George courts Lucy by telling her ' "I want you to have your own thoughts even when I hold you in my arms" ' (162), she realizes that he is offering her 'the comradeship after which [her] soul yearned' (149). But Forster does not use marriage to domesticate Lucy's passion into a more socially acceptable desire for wife and motherhood. Unlike the authors of *Dodo the Second* and *Max*, Forster presents Lucy's modernity as her salvation, not her problem; it is her desire for autonomy and equality that allows her to form a revolutionary new kind of relationship with George, and find happiness. But the only view of the marriage the reader is given is of the honeymoon; in this, his first novel (although it was published third), Forster declined to depict 'the drama of their problems', and highlighted instead the triumph of his modern couple's rebellion.

Although such a positive portrait of sexual fulfillment was rare in the Edwardian age, the questions about personal and sexual liberation that Forster raised were very much a part of the feminist debate at the time. There was what was known as the Sex Question as well as a Marriage Question, and it encompassed a large range of issues around gender, sexuality and morality; but one of the most volatile debates among feminists was concerned with the relationship between sex and women's liberation. Diaries and letters from the time, as well as autobiographies and biographies of young women who came of age in the Edwardian years, indicate that young single women of the middle and upper classes were beginning to consider seriously (although not necessarily acting upon) the possibility of having a sexual relationship outside marriage.[13] Braby's emphasis on the need for sex education for girls in her advice manual *Modern Marriage and How to Bear It*, and her suggestion that a 'new style' woman who has sown some 'wild oats' before marriage will make a much better wife than an inexperienced woman, are signs of how much thoughts about female sexuality had shifted since the Victorian age. Several factors led to this situation: more women were living independent lives away from the supervision of their families, owing to new opportunities for higher education and employment; there was still a large discrepancy between the number of men and women in England, and single women increasingly acknowledged the possibility that they might never marry; and there was both a growing sophistication about sexual matters and a decline in the moral influence of traditional religion.

But there was little consensus among feminists as to whether women would benefit from greater sexual freedom. Some feminists who opposed the institution of marriage supported the idea of free unions and the endowment of motherhood by the government, and called for a radical restructuring of social organization. Others felt that sexual freedom was not only morally but also strategically wrong, for it made women dependent upon men for their liberation. The topic was complicated and controversial, and although it was much discussed among feminists, it rarely appeared in novels of the period – except in sensation novels, which had escapist, not feminist, agendas. Although sexual frankness in fiction was tolerated and even expected to a certain degree during the Edwardian age, there was still a stigma attached to fiction which used explorations of female sexuality to challenge conventional social and moral values.

D.H. Lawrence was one of the few Edwardian writers who risked censorship and negative critical response by choosing to write frankly about unmarried women and sexuality. Following in the path of Hardy and other authors of the new fiction of the 1890s, Lawrence was interested in writing about the changing role of women in modern society, and how it influenced relations, particularly sexual ones, between men and women; his letters indicate his enthusiasm for Olive Schreiner's *The Story of an African Farm* and *Women and Labour*, George Gissing's *The Odd Women*, and George Moore's *Evelyn Innes*, among other late-nineteenth-century works, and his early novels are clearly influenced by them. Although Lawrence's first two novels, *The White Peacock* (1911) and *The Trespasser* (1912), had generally positive critical receptions, most of the negative reviews focused upon the author's alliances to naturalism and 'the exotic writers of the nineties'. In particular, many critics were disturbed by Lawrence's 'needlessly frank' depictions of sexual relations, and one complained that Lawrence did not know 'the value of a decent fig-leaf'. Reviewers also noted that Lawrence paid particular attention to the psychology of his female characters in *The White Peacock*, which led at least two of them to guess that he was a woman.[14]

Lawrence's interest in writing about women was also due in part to another important influence upon him at this time – his circle of female friends; most of them were independent, well-educated feminists, and a few of them were active in the suffrage movement. Some of these relationships were Platonic, some developed into romances and even engagements; all of them were exceptionally frank relationships, even when it came to discussions of sexual feelings. This intimate exposure to the desires and fears of modern young women proved be extremely useful to Lawrence in his early novels. But there was a tension between Lawrence's indebtedness to his female friends and his need to assert his independence from them, and this tension is evident in the one particular relationship which was central to the writing of his second novel, *The Trespasser*.

Lawrence had become close to Helen Corke, a fellow schoolteacher, in the fall of 1909, after her lover, Herbert Macartney, a music teacher and a married man, killed himself. Lawrence was intrigued by Helen's story, and persuaded her to let him use her experience and her diaries as a basis for his next novel. During the period of composition, Lawrence apparently became quite interested in the theme of women's sexual emancipation; his letters indicate that he read Moore's *Evelyn Innes* and *Sister Theresa*, and H.G. Wells's *Ann Veronica*, at this time.[15] But also during the writing of the novel, he became sexually attracted to Helen, who rebuffed his advances; partly as a result of this personal conflict,

Lawrence increasingly came to identify and sympathize with the character of Siegmund (who represents Macartney in the novel). Although he had access to Helen's intimate accounts of her side of the story, the resulting novel is critical of rather than sympathetic to Helena, Helen's fictional incarnation; the focus falls instead upon Siegmund, and how he is destroyed by his love for a modern woman.

Most of the action of the novel takes place during a five-day holiday that Helena and Siegmund take on the Isle of Wight. Afterwards, Helena goes on a trip to Cornwall with some friends, while Siegmund returns to the squalor and misery of his suburban home, where he hangs himself. Lawrence makes it clear that Siegmund chooses suicide as a way out of the trap he feels himself to be in: he is unable to leave his wife and children for Helena, but he is also unable to tolerate life with them. But implicit in the novel is the idea that Siegmund does not so much destroy himself as be destroyed by the women in his life. His wife Beatrice hates him for his infidelity, and teaches their children to hate him as well; it is their rejection which makes life finally intolerable to Siegmund. But Beatrice not only survives, she profits from Siegmund's death, and is able to make a fresh start in life as the popular and successful mistress of a boarding house. Although Helena is indicted in less obvious ways than Beatrice, ultimately she too is shown to be culpable for Siegmund's death.

Siegmund assumes that he and Helena will consummate their love physically during their holiday, but Helena reveals that she has no desire to do so; she is characterized as belonging to 'that class of "dreaming women" with whom passion exhausts itself at the mouth' (30). When she finally does submit to Siegmund, it makes him feel 'the full "will to live",' while 'it destroyed her. Her soul seemed blasted' (56). It becomes clear that this conflict of desires between Helena and Siegmund is insurmountable, and that their relationship is doomed. One morning, Siegmund meets a strange man, his 'Doppelgänger', who stuns him with his analysis of the situation, and his prediction of Siegmund's fate:

> 'The best sort of women – the most interesting – are the worst for us. . . . By instinct they aim at suppressing the gross and animal in us. . . . We, as natural men, are more or less degrading to them and to their love of us; therefore they destroy the natural man in us – that is, us altogether.' (84)

Like Hardy's Sue Bridehead, like Moore's Mildred Lawson, Helena represents the cold, intellectual and unnatural modern woman who can literally kill a man through her sexual unresponsiveness. The end of the novel reveals her a year after the fateful holiday, and it is evident that she too has profited from Siegmund's death, for she actually seems to relish her romantic role as tragic heroine. Siegmund is now the wholly spiritual lover she had always wished him to be, and she can use her memories of him both to hold the interest of an adoring young man, Cecil Byrne (a figure for Lawrence), and to stave off Byrne's physical advances.

Rebecca West, in her enthusiastic review of *The Trespasser*, called Helena 'the spinster through and through', and blamed her 'extreme fastidiousness' and 'icy distaste for life' for Siegmund's death.[16] West accepted Lawrence's categorization of Helena as a 'type' of woman, frigid and life-denying, who prefers sentiment over passion, and she used her review of the novel as an occasion to expound on the failings of spinsters. West followed Lawrence in failing to consider Helena as an individual, and in never addressing the real dangers a sexual affair with a married man holds for her. Lawrence's characterization of Helena is additionally complicated by the fact that Helen Corke was a lesbian who was uninterested in turning her close friendships with men into sexual relationships. Although for some single women at the time having sexual relations with another woman was one possible answer to the Sex Question, it was not a solution that was discussed openly in fiction, nor was it one that Lawrence could ever view with any sympathy.[17] So instead, he uses Helena's lack of sexual response to execrate independent and intellectual modern women; he also interprets it as proof of some kind of essential – even eternal – conflict between the sexes. Lawrence's profound skepticism about relations between men and women in *The Trespasser* resembles that of Bennett in *Whom God Hath Joined*; he indicates that the only time men and women can truly come together is in sexual union, but even that is somehow doomed, for their desires are founded in difference, not affinity.

The psychological complexity of Lawrence's portrait of Helena, and the fact that Helena's love for Siegmund is neither punished in the traditional fashion nor safely domesticated, does indicate his general sympathy for women, and his interest in their struggle for personal freedom. But ultimately, Lawrence's view of modern women as cold and unnatural is just as conservative as that of Benson in *Dodo the Second* and Thurston in *Max*, and his criticism, like theirs, conceals a fear of women's independence – a fear that modern women do not need men as much as men need them. All three of these writers failed to consider in their fiction either the powerful social influences which shape women's behavior and values, or the very real consequences, such as pregnancy or venereal disease, which made women wary of sexual relationships. But these consequences were not absent from Edwardian fiction; in fact, a number of Edwardian novelists (the majority of whom were women) chose to center novels upon the subject of extramarital pregnancy and single motherhood.

For most women at the time, the only female sexual desire they were comfortable acknowledging (at least publicly) was the reproductive and maternal instinct. The ideology of maternity was a very powerful one, and feminists and conservatives alike used it to justify their positions on women's rights – the former emphasizing the need for society to value and respect its mothers; the latter arguing that women must focus their energies solely on their most sacred duty. Although some unmarried feminists bridled at the assumption that they were somehow less fulfilled or natural than their sisters with children, most feminists firmly believed that motherhood was a woman's ultimate experience.[18] A recurring theme in spinster novels is that of the regret unmarried women experience at never having children; these novels emphasize that the loss of potential children is felt far more acutely than the loss of a lover or a potential husband. Ellen Key, a prominent Swedish feminist, went so far as to suggest that bachelor motherhood should be encouraged, in order to allow unmarried women to enjoy the fulfillment that is their birthright. Although Key's suggestion was most probably never seriously considered, it is symptomatic of the heightened interest in the Edwardian age in women's reproductive behavior, and in particular, how that behavior might be controlled, through such schemes as eugenics or endowed motherhood.[19]

It was inevitable that the controversial topic of single motherhood would be translated into fiction. A correspondent to *The Freewoman* declared that 'the two great tragedies of womanhood' were 'the misery of the unmarried mother and the bitter cry of the unmated woman', and many writers, even if they disagreed with the negative cast of these descriptions, were eager to create narratives based upon these two 'tragedies', which had, in the past, been ignored or suppressed.[20] Marginalized by society for the lack of a conventional relationship with a man, victimized by the sexual double standard, the unwed mother, like the spinster, served as a useful symbol of the ways in which all women suffered from a male-dominated society. Most of the novels about unwed mothers depict the heroine nobly enduring social ostracism, and emerging triumphant by virtue of the strength and sacredness of her maternal instinct. As Hardy did in *Tess*, these authors emphasize that their heroine's sexual experience and pregnancy in no way detract from her essential purity and goodness; but unlike the baby in *Tess*, the babies in these novels do not die, and the mothers must go on to build a life for themselves.

In some novels – such as *Tony Unregenerate* (1912) by Janet Dodge, and *The Woman Alone* (1914) by Marie Harrison – a single woman purposely chooses to bear a child and raise it on her own; in others – such as L. Parry Truscott's *Motherhood* (1904) and Anne Douglas Sedgwick's *Amabel Channice* (1908) – the heroine's pregnancy is unplanned, and initially the source of much distress. In Sedgewick's novel the situation is complicated by the fact that the heroine is married, but the child she bears and raises on her own is not her husband's. What all these novels have in common, however, is that the mothers eventually come to the same satisfying realization as the unmarried heroine of Ethel Hill's *The Unloved* (1909) – that her child is 'the true harvest of womanhood'. With some exceptions – such as Maud Churton Braby's novel *Downward* (1910), in which Braby rewards her heroine's travails by giving her a good man who promises to marry her and be a father to her child – a surprising number of these novels allowed the heroine to remain self-sufficient to the very end.

The critic Edmund Gosse was horrified by this trend in fiction, as he indicated in a letter written in December 1910:

> I should like to know what you think of the new craze for introducing into fiction the high-bred maiden who has a baby? . . . I have read *three* new English novels this autumn of which it is the *motif*. . . . I think it is a mark of feminisation . . . I do not know how an Englishman can calmly write of such a disgusting thing, with such *sang-froid*.[21]

It is interesting that fifteen years after the crisis over the new fiction, Gosse was still fearful that the depiction of irregular sexual behavior by women would deprive British fiction (and by inference, the British nation) of its masculinity. But undeniably, many of the novels about unwed mothers were antagonistic toward men, and Gosse's uneasiness was somewhat justifiable. The particular novel he was writing about – *Howards End* – does in fact depict two women, one of whom is an unwed mother, acquiring autonomy and happiness through the often violent defeat of the men in their lives. For Gosse – as for Lawrence, and presumably for many Edwardian men – such an image of female power and self-sufficiency was disorientating and threatening. But for feminists and others who were dissatisfied with traditional narratives of women's lives, novels in which unwed mothers prevail provided satisfying wish-fulfillment. Despite their veneer of social realism, these novels created an imaginary world in which a woman could have the satisfaction of motherhood without any of the troublesome complications of men, sex or marriage. In fact, most of them carefully elide the sexual act that leads to the heroine's pregnancy; they seem to envision, as the radical feminist Frances Swiney did, an ideal state of virgin motherhood.[22] The ultimate expression of this kind of fantasy may be found in Mrs Henry Dudeney's *Rachel Lorian* (1909), in which the widow of a man the heroine once loved gives her their child to raise; Rachel is thus able to satisfy her desire for motherhood and retain a connection to her former lover while preserving her independence and her chastity.

What Gosse did not see was the conservative side of this trend in fiction, which also surely had something to do with its popularity. Although Forster scrupulously avoided sentimentality about mother-hood in *Howards End*, the majority of novels about unwed mothers emphasized the sacredness of motherhood, and presented it as the ultimate achievement in a woman's life. Also, these novels, for the most part, presented a highly sentimentalized picture of the life of an unwed mother; the heroines do not refer to the discomfort of pregnancy, or express any distress at their loss of autonomy, or feel any resentment toward the baby – maternity makes them saintly. Thus the authors of these novels were able to criticize conventional sexual morality regarding illegitimacy and marriage, while never threatening basic gender defini-tions or basic ideas about women's essential nature or role in society. Like the anti-courtship novels, the novels about unwed mothers ack-nowledged the importance of the social advances women had made, yet offered the comforting reassurance that such external changes do not alter women's 'natural' destiny. These independent new women were not killing women like Helena, on holiday with a married man, but nurturing women, safe at home with their babies.

Arnold Bennett and Violet Hunt, along with Forster, were exceptional in that they chose to write about unwed motherhood realistically instead of with sentiment or idealism. Both Bennett, in *Hilda Lessways* (1911), and Hunt, in *White Rose of Weary Leaf*, managed to avoid the ideology of motherhood altogether by focusing upon the sexual experience and pregnancy of their heroine rather than narrating her life after the birth of her baby. These two authors examine closely the ways in which society shapes the desires and expectations of women; in particular, they look at how sexual intimacy, pregnancy, and the cessation of independence are inextricably linked in women's minds, and how that link affects their relationships with men.

Bennett's Hilda is in many ways the quintessential Edwardian heroine, and as such she exemplifies the ways in which that heroine differs from the New Woman heroines of the 1890s. Like the young women in the Findlater novels, like Lucy Honeychurch, she is intelligent and spirited, but otherwise supremely ordinary, unexceptional in either her abilities or her appearance, fallible, at times even dislikable, certainly never ideal. And like those other Edwardian heroines, Hilda is passionately discon-tented with her life, yet unable to formulate exactly what it is she misses or wants; she knows only that she despises the life of 'sheer vacuous idleness' coupled with 'the monotonous simple machinery of physical existence' that her mother lives (5–6). Like most Edwardian heroines, Hilda is not an articulate, crusading feminist, yet her very normalcy is a revealing indication of how much feminism had permeated English society. Dissatisfaction with traditional feminine roles and the desire for autonomy were no longer seen as the purview of New Women, but as almost obligatory rites of passage for all young women.

We are told in the second sentence of the novel that 'Hilda hated domestic work', and it is this hatred which separates her from her mother and conventional ideas about a woman's destiny, and leads her into a new kind of life. When she looks at the immaculate white wristbands of Mr Cannon, the businessman she will eventually marry, all she can think of is

> the washing and the ironing of those wristbands, and a slatternly woman or two sighing and grumbling amid wreaths of steam, and a background of cinders and suds and sloppiness. . . . All that, so that the grand creature might have a rim of pure white to his coat-sleeves for a day! It was inevitable. But the grand creature must never know. The shame necessary to his splendour must be concealed from him, lest he might be offended. And this was woman's loyalty! (55–6)

For Hilda, housework becomes the symbol of the difference between men's lives and women's lives: men are of the world, grand, public, their work important; women are imprisoned in houses, trivial, subservient, their work like some dirty secret that somehow makes them dirty as well. But Hilda, unlike most other dissatisfied Edwardian heroines, actively seeks another life outside 'domestic dailiness', and after taking a course in shorthand writing she gets a job on a newspaper. The novel is very unusual in that Bennett shows in specific, realistic detail what Hilda's working life is like, and makes it clear that her work is completely satisfying to her; her desire is to be useful, successful, even powerful in the world of business, and it has nothing to do with romance or the rejection of romance. Bennett never suggests that Hilda is unnatural or unfeminine, although she herself sometimes has fleeting fears along those lines. Instead, he indicates that Hilda has somehow remained untouched by all the usual social conditioning that girls undergo, and her ambitions have emerged naturally, even unconsciously, out of her strong and unfettered sense of self.

All this changes, however, when Hilda realizes her sexual feelings for Cannon. In the section entitled 'Her Fall', she decides to give up all her dreams and ambitions for the comfortable stasis of marriage; but although her relationship with Cannon is blatantly carnal, Bennett does not imply that she falls in any conventionally moral way. Instead, she 'falls', because she chooses the easy route of acquiring power through sex and marriage over the far more difficult path of attaining power 'such as no woman to her knowledge had ever had' through her own work (415). But Hilda views her failure as inevitable:

> She had been in the male world, but not of it, as though encircled in a glass ball which neither she nor the males could shatter. She had had money, freedom, and ambition, and somehow, through ignorance or through lack of imagination or opportunity, had been unable to employ them. She had never known what she wanted. The vision had never been clear. (415–16)

Like other ambitious and independent Edwardian heroines, Hilda finds it exceedingly difficult to imagine new goals and construct new narratives.

By the end of her honeymoon Hilda is already disillusioned with Cannon, bored with her sexual power over him, and regretful about the new limitations in her life. But in a convenient plot twist she discovers that he is already married, and he departs for Canada to escape prosecution for bigamy. Although Hilda, in her typically resilient manner, immediately begins fashioning new plans for her future, she soon discovers that she is pregnant, and she is left socially and financially tied to her old life in Cannon's Brighton boarding house. Whereas Hilda had previously always prided herself on her agency in the world, she now realizes that her body – the physical fact of her sex – has determined her fate.

There are two other women in the novel whose fates are also determined by their sex, and they shadow Hilda throughout the narrative as signs of what awaits her. The maid Florrie is traditionally feminine, clothes-conscious, flirtatious – she represents all the aspects of womanhood that Hilda loathes. Yet Hilda, despite all her efforts, shares Florrie's fate: at the end of the novel they pass one another on the street, both of them pregnant and unmarried. Cannon's half-sister, Sarah Gailey, is a spinster, like Mayor's Miss Symons in the utter emptiness of her life, but further cursed with lack of money and ill health. Hilda's decision to marry is partially motivated by her desire to escape Sarah's fate, which she views 'with horror and scorn'. But Hilda comes to share in that fate as well, for Cannon's departure makes her responsible for Sarah. The final irony is that Hilda's work as the proprietress of the boarding house is not only the housework she detests, but housework multiplied several times over. The end of the novel leaves her, ill from her pregnancy and subject to the demands of her guests and the increasingly querulous Sarah, trapped in a nightmare world of domesticity and self-sacrifice.

Hilda Lessways was written as the second volume of Bennett's *Clayhanger* trilogy; his particular intention was to tell, from a woman's point of view, the story of the woman Edwin Clayhanger meets in the first volume, *Clayhanger* (1910), and will eventually marry in the third volume, *These Twain* (1916). The structural requirements of Bennett's project, however, leave Hilda in limbo, and as a result the novel's final impression is a disproportionately pessimistic one. There are also drawbacks to Bennett's limitation of the narrative point of view to Hilda's perspective. While it does produce some interesting results, particularly when Bennett is rendering her sexual awakening, the reader is deprived of other people's impressions of Hilda, and of any extended analysis of her by the narrator; there is a strange, flat quality to her, as if Bennett cannot quite get at what makes her unique.[23] Nevertheless, the novel provides a rare and fascinating exploration of the ways in which women are caught in narrow, conventional lives not only through socialization but by their sex; in a sense, Hilda is betrayed by her body – both when she succumbs to her sexual attraction to Cannon, and when she becomes pregnant. She protests that pregnancy is 'a tremendous punishment for so transient a weakness!' (532), but it remains unclear whether Bennett thinks women will ever be able to determine their fate better than Hilda, Florrie, and Sarah are able to. Bennett raises many challenging questions about feminine nature, female sexuality, and women's status in society, but he leaves them provocatively unanswered.

Amy Stephens, the heroine of Hunt's *White Rose of Weary Leaf*, is, like Hilda, a modern working woman; she wanders from job to job, working as a shopgirl, a typewriter girl, a secretary, a companion, an actress, and finally as a governess. It is in that position that she forms a relationship with her married employer. The novel is modelled, in some respects, on *Jane Eyre* (clearly an important book for Edwardian feminist novelists), but Amy, unlike Jane, is a consciously liberated woman who talks incessantly and with bold frankness about love, sex and marriage, and what they mean to women. The novel's volubility and polemics place it in the tradition of the New Woman novel of the 1890s (which is underscored by the fact that the epigraph to the second half is from Grant Allen's *The Woman Who Did*), and like most New Woman novels, *White Rose of Weary Leaf* is more interesting as a record of feminist ideas than it is as a work of fiction.

But Amy is also a typically Edwardian heroine, owing to Hunt's psychologically complex and realistic characterization of her. She is often nervous and unsure of herself, and at times her behavior borders on the neurotic. Amy's wide experience of life has made her cynical and, as Hunt points out with careful realism, the demands of her household work make her perpetually tired. Also characteristically Edwardian is the conflict between Amy's feminist theories and her actions and feelings. Although she confidently asserts that sex, love and marriage are three very distinct things, she is constantly confusing them, uncertain whether she loves her employer, Jeremy Dand, or if she is just sexually attracted to him. She talks knowingly about sex, but remains a virgin, and her adamant rejection of romance seems motivated less by her feminist principles than by her fear of a sexual relationship. Most significantly, the only thing she is unreservedly passionate about is her love for Mr Dand's child; but Hunt implies that Amy's idealization of maternal love is not exemplary but unhealthy and obsessive, a way of escaping from the difficulties of a mature relationship with another adult. Amy finally does have sex with Dand (thinking, mistakenly, that his wife has died), and instead of veiling the experience, as other authors of unwed mother novels did, Hunt devotes an entire chapter to Amy's very candid post-coital musings. Amy is naïvely amazed that losing her virginity does not change her in any obvious way, but her experience does make her realize that sex entails a loss of freedom just as much as love and marriage do. She concludes that while sex might make her sleep well, it gives her little peace, and she decides to end the affair.

But Amy soon discovers that she is pregnant, and like so many other unwed mothers in Edwardian fiction, she ultimately seems relieved to have accomplished her dream of motherhood without the burden of marriage and with a minimum of sex; she accepts Dand's financial assistance but refuses his offer of marriage, and goes off to raise her child on her own. But instead of allowing Amy to endure, like Bennett's Hilda or Forster's Helen, Hunt decided to elevate her to martyr status, and opted for an ending right out of a New Woman novel: Amy dies from childbirth complications, with the doctor's wife proclaiming her to be her ideal of 'the Best Woman – the really newest woman' (430); Dand subsequently kills himself. As Hunt explained in her diary, she originally intended Amy to die in an accident, but her publishers said 'the B P [British Public] won't tolerate a woman being killed with an unborn child in her – so I have to add all the details of Amy's accouchement and kill her neatly afterward'.[24] Why Hunt felt that Amy had to die is unclear; in all her weariness and cynicism, Amy never blames men or society for the circumstances of her life, but it seems that Hunt wished to do exactly that with her tragic ending.

Apart from its interesting feminist polemics, the value of *White Rose of Weary Leaf* lies in its psychologically astute depictions of the sexual dynamics between men and women, and its astonishingly frank and realistic observations about modern life. The novel is perhaps most distinctive in Hunt's refusal to be romantic – not only in traditional ways, but in terms of idealizing feminism. Amy's feminist theories do not make her life easier, or her relationships less difficult; nor can they entirely obliterate the disillusionment and insecurity that at times threaten to paralyze her. In the end, however, the most powerful statement of the confusions and contradictions inherent in being a feminist in the early twentieth century is made by the confusing and contradictory nature of the novel itself. Blending pieces of narratives borrowed from Brontë and New Woman novels and contemporary works, *White Rose of Weary Leaf* is profoundly irresolute about what it wants to do with its rebellious heroine.

There was yet another story about women which appeared in fiction for the first time during the Edwardian years, and that was the narrative of girlhood and adolescence. While this period of a woman's life had been depicted in some nineteenth-century novels, it inevitably formed only a small part of a larger narrative. But as feminists and conservatives alike began to analyze the ways in which traditional ideas about gender roles and female nature were perpetuated through female socialization, the lives of girls and adolescents took on a new significance.

Whereas children's books had previously been intended generally for both boys and girls (although the characters were predominately boys), children's books written exclusively for and about girls began to appear in the late nineteenth century, and were quite numerous and popular by the Edwardian period.[25] For the most part they were conservative texts, written in reaction to the rise of feminism; they were fairly obvious in their intentions to instil traditional values in girls and young women. School stories were particularly popular, although their authors were always careful to indicate that the purpose of education for girls was to make them better wives and mothers, not to prepare them for careers.[26] Girls who wished to read about rebellious and unconventional heroines had to turn to *Jane Eyre* and *The Mill on the Floss* or, if they could get their hands on them, *The Story of an African Farm* and New Woman novels; with the exception of a few short stories by Evelyn Sharp, nothing being written at the time could be categorized as feminist fiction for girls.[27]

What *was* being written was feminist fiction about girls for adults. These novels about female adolescence concentrated on the time between childhood and adult life which had previously been dismissed as not interesting enough to be a fictional subject, for it was assumed that all teenage girls did was wait passively for courtship to begin. Some of these novels are peripherally involved with romance, but they are innovative in that their dominant focus is on the personal and social development of the heroine during this time. These novels of adolescence are in fact *Bildungsromane*, and their appearance during this period is a striking indication of how social changes related to feminism had an important impact on British fiction.

During the nineteenth century, women's position in society made a female *Bildungsroman* an impossibility, according to its classic definition. The *Bildungsroman* is predicated upon the protagonist's growth to maturity; it involves both a search for personal identity and aspiration, and a struggle to find a satisfying form of social integration. The period of adolescence in the *Bildungsroman* is a time of relative freedom and exploration, and the way the protagonist responds to the challenges and choices of this time determines the shape of his character and the course of his life. But such concepts of adolescence and maturity were not applicable to women in the nineteenth century. There was no time in their lives when they had opportunities for freedom and exploration, and their range of options for the future was extremely limited. Women in the nineteenth century did not really attain maturity, as it was defined for men; rather than becoming economically independent and self-determining, maturity for women meant marriage, and thus merely moving from one state of dependence to another. It was only when women began to have actual options in their lives, when economic and social independence became a real possibility, that there could be female *Bildungsromane*.[28]

Sybylla, the heroine and narrator of Miles Franklin's novel *My Brilliant Career* (1901), lives in poverty in rural Australia; she is fervently independent, bluntly honest, wilfully unconventional. At sixteen she has become a financial burden to her parents, who want her to marry; instead Sybylla longs for a career and 'Action! Action!', but no one takes her seriously. She is disdainful of the romantic endings of novels that most young women model their dreams upon, and does all she can to avoid the behavior and vanity that are considered naturally feminine, and to sabotage any romantic opportunities that present themselves. Though it is very funny at times, *My Brilliant Career* is a raw and heartfelt account of a feminist's coming of age; Sybylla is angry and rough and bitter, and as such she stunningly subverts the nineteenth-century feminine ideal.

My Brilliant Career was Franklin's first novel, written when she was sixteen, and it certainly reads like that: there is an emotional immediacy to it that is both powerful and disconcerting, and makes it unclear whether the book is fiction or autobiography or personal fantasy. It is actually a combination of all three, although the suggestion that the novel was autobiographical infuriated Franklin, for she believed that a novel by a man would never be criticized in such a fashion. As a result she wrote a sequel, *My Career Goes Bung*, in 1902, to justify herself as an artist and clear up the autobiographical confusion (although it actually makes matters even more muddled, and was not published until 1946); she then refused to let *My Brilliant Career* be reprinted until after her death.

But lost in the controversy was the fact that the novel is remarkably unique, fresh and new in its language and its form; it is never imitative except when Franklin wishes to usurp situations or language from other genres, such as romance novels, in order to parody them. The language of the novel is a crazy mixture of Australian slang and calculatedly high-flown literary prose, punctuated with ejaculations, digressions, and self-conscious references to the process of writing. The heroine/narrator not only explicitly rejects the romance plot on the first page, but then adds:

> There is no plot in this story, because there has been none in my life or in any other life which has come under my notice. I am one of a class, the individuals of which have not time for plots in their life, but have all they can do to get their work done without indulging in such a luxury. (xviii)

Throughout the novel, Sybylla explores the ways in which fictional narratives shape and distort young women's sense of possibilities in life. Tradition, in fiction and in life, is the enemy, for the plot it offers Sybylla is linear and limiting, tending in only one direction: that of marriage.

The chapter structure of the novel is broken up by letters, diary entries, poetry, and interludes that are announced by bold-face headings; one, entitled 'Self-Analysis', is followed by a note from the 'author', Sybylla, who warns: 'This is dull and egotistical. Better skip it. That's my advice' (39). *My Brilliant Career* not only tells the story of a feminist rebellion but serves as an illustration of a formal rebellion against literary tradition; Sybylla rejects convention, authority and marriage, while Franklin, as novelist, rejects conventional narratives of courtship and marriage, and purposely breaks the rules through her use of multiple and blended genres. Despite Franklin's subsequent protestations, the confusion in the novel between author and character, and fact and fiction, seems artful and intentional.

In that the major conflict in the narrative is whether or not Sybylla will escape the fate of marriage, which she dismisses as a degrading financial arrangement, *My Brilliant Career* is an anti-courtship novel; Sybylla particularly resembles other Edwardian heroines such as Lucy Honeychurch or Nadine or Max in her fear of sex. Yet Sybylla's rejection of physical affection is not depicted as unnatural; rather, it is shown to be an aspect of her tremendous egotism, which is in itself a necessary self-defense. To retain the modicum of independence she has achieved, she must think only of herself, and never lose control through passion. Franklin's astute psychological analyses of Sybylla's motivations in this instance, and in many others, constitute her major achievement. She always goes beneath the qualities which are characteristic of the Edwardian heroine, and shows the conflicts, doubts and guilt which inform them. Sybylla is not conventionally beautiful, and in the familiar Brontë tradition she clings to her plainness as a badge of superiority, and uses her looks to exempt her from the marriage market. But Franklin then goes one step further to show how much Sybylla has internalized society's standards of beauty, and reveals that behind her bravado is a strong sense of inadequacy. Similarly, Sybylla also makes herself exempt from social expectations by her markedly outrageous and unfeminine behavior, particularly with regard to Harry Beecham, whom she describes as 'my first, my last, my only *real* sweetheart' (86). She tells herself that she is acting in this way to indicate that she is not marriageable; but part of Sybylla's rejection of marriage stems from her fear that no one will ask her to marry him, and her obnoxious conduct often seems like a test to see if Harry really loves her. In this case, Franklin shows how Sybylla's unconventional behavior in the name of feminist liberation comes quite close to the worst kind of feminine wiles.

My Brilliant Career often brings to mind Olive Schreiner's influential feminist novel *The Story of an African Farm* (1883), for both are singular narratives about a feminist rebel emerging from the midst of a wild and hostile country. Like Schreiner, Franklin purposely rejected the predictable and satisfying 'stage method' of narration in favor of something more realistic and troubling. But there is nothing of Schreiner's philosophical resignation in Franklin's novel, no acknowledgement that 'we of this generation are not destined to eat and be satisfied . . . we must be content to go hungry' (172–3). Instead, Franklin, through her angry, contradictory and defensive heroine, emphasizes how painful it is to reject tradition, how traumatic it is to choose the unknown, and how frustrating it is to live in a time of transition. She refuses to simplify Sybylla's decision to remain single in order to make it a triumph of feminism; neither does she sublimate the emotional toll of such a decision, as the Findlaters do in their novels:

> I think I was not fully aware how near I had been to loving Harry Beecham until experiencing the loss which stole over me on holding in my hand the acceptance of his dismissal. . . . Our greatest heart-treasure is a knowledge that there is in creation an individual to whom our existence is necessary – some one who is part of our life as we are part of theirs, some one in whose life we feel assured our death would leave a gap for a day or two. . . . And I had thrown behind me this chance . . . (238–9)

In a society where a young woman's value in the marriage market rapidly declined after her early twenties, Sybylla's decision to refuse a proposal of marriage from one of the few eligible bachelors of her acquaintance is a profound one. By rejecting the conventional closure of marriage, she also denies herself the sense of stability and coherence that accompanies it. The life she chooses for herself, like the novel she writes, is unpredictable, messy, and open-ended.

To a certain extent, Sybylla's dream of a 'brilliant career' as a writer is as romantically delusive as other women's dreams of marriage; her talent, like her feminist ideals, is as yet untried. Thus it is essential that the ending of the novel not be triumphant but, rather, ambiguous and unresolved; it remains unclear whether Sybylla has made the right decision, or if her career and her feminist independence will ever bring her happiness. She is a pioneer, not just because she is an Australian but because, as a woman and a writer, she chooses the lonely freedom of the new over the familiar comfort of the old. In its freshness and innovation, but also in its purposeful and radical destabilization – of gender roles, of genre boundaries, of narrative expectations – *My Brilliant Career* is an early modernist novel.

Of all the narratives about single women written in the Edwardian period, the most original is another Australian novel, *The Getting of Wisdom* (1910) by Henry Handel Richardson (the pen name of Ethel Richardson): it is perhaps the first novel written in English to tell the story of the development of a young girl in the classic mode of the *Bildungsroman*. There are many nineteenth-century novels about young women – such as *Jane Eyre, The Mill on the Floss,* and *The Beth Book* – which employ aspects of the *Bildungsroman,* but their narratives inevitably become dominated by romance plots in their latter sections; self-realization and social integration are unavoidably linked with courtship and marriage. *The Getting of Wisdom* stands out from these nineteenth-century novels, and other Edwardian novels about women, in that it does not rely upon romance or marriage in its narrative, neither is it written in opposition to such plots.

Even though the novel is about schoolgirls – it tells the story of Laura Rambotham's education at an elite Melbourne boarding school from the age of twelve to the age of sixteen – it is not intended *for* schoolgirls; it is an adult novel that looks at the ways in which a woman is formed, as an individual and as a member of society, just as the traditional *Bildungsroman* examines that process in men. Romance and sex are present as an undercurrent to the narrative – there are passionate schoolgirl crushes, secret discussions of sex, and dreams of marriage – but Laura is a late bloomer who violently resists the coming of sexual maturity, and is supremely uninterested in boys or the prospect of matrimony. While the goal of all the other girls is to marry after leaving school, Laura feels that 'it [is] impossible to limit your hopes to one single event, which, though it saved you from derision, would put an end, for ever, to all possible, exciting contingencies' (130). The traditional *Bildungsroman* narrative is intentionally fragmentary in that it ends as the hero embarks upon his adult life. In following that tradition, Richardson makes a significant break with another tradition which dictates that female characters must somehow be accounted for and contained by a narrative's end: she dares to leave Laura undefined, unattached and unrestricted at the end of *The Getting of Wisdom,* on the verge of all those 'exciting contingencies' of life.

The 'wisdom' that Laura gets is acquired not through her formal education but through her interactions with her schoolmates and her teachers. From her first day at school to the day of her departure, Laura is faced with an unrelenting onslaught of condescension, cruelty, and demands for conformity. She discovers almost immediately that any divergence from the norm is either mocked or punished, and soon comes to believe 'that the unpardonable sin is to vary from the common mould' (84). Laura, who is naturally enthusiastic, imaginative and sincere, learns not only that those qualities are not valued but also that they are dangerous liabilities, and she strives to suppress them. Although there are echoes of *Jane Eyre* in the novel, there are – more importantly, significant departures from that model. Like Mayor in *The Third Miss Symons,* Richardson makes absolutely no concessions to readerly expectations or sentiment: thus there are no saving graces, no exceptions to the banality and hostility, no single girl or teacher, such as Helen Burns or

Miss Temple in *Jane Eyre*, who can redeem the suffering and inspire the heroine. The novel is unrelentingly realistic, and at times excruciatingly painful to read. Laura is never told that she is worthwhile, as she is, and she is more than willing to sacrifice what is best in her, and become a hypocrite, a liar or a cheat, in order simply to feel that she belongs, to feel some affirmation that she is of value to someone; throughout the novel, she is always precariously close to becoming a truly awful person.

Laura, like so many Edwardian heroines, realizes that she is different from the others, and feels vague yearnings for something more in her life. But she is ashamed of her difference, not empowered by it; in desperation, she realizes that

> you might regulate your outward habit to the last button of what you were
> expected to wear . . . you might, in brief, march in the strictest order along the
> narrow road laid down for you by these young lawgivers, keeping perfect step
> and time with them: yet of what use were all your pains, if you could not
> marshal your thoughts and feelings – the very realest part of you – in rank and
> file as well? (100)

Like Sybylla, Laura cannot help but see through others' pretensions, and she continually says and does things which make her an outcast; in Laura's case these acts are inadvertent, but nevertheless they save her, and that 'very realest part' of her remains intact. The development that *The Getting of Wisdom* charts is a distinctly modern one: Laura's failure at school, and her inability to integrate herself into society, is what guarantees her future growth as an individual and her success in life. Although conflicts between the individual's desires and the demands of society traditionally play a part in the *Bildungsroman* narrative, *The Getting of Wisdom* marks a new kind of 'negative' *Bildungsroman* – one which anticipates those written by modernist writers. Like Laura, the protagonists in both Joyce's *A Portrait of the Artist as a Young Man* and Lawrence's *Sons and Lovers* are misfits who attain personal fulfillment only when they free themselves from familial and social ties; rebellion and exile, not integration, are celebrated in these novels.

In an unusual passage at the end of *The Getting of Wisdom*, the narrator foretells Laura's future and that of the two stars of the school, and reveals that Laura will have an interesting and fulfilling life. It is the only moment of reassurance and hope in the novel, and the only time the narrator allows the reader to step outside the oppressive value system of the school and see Laura on her own terms. Laura's future success is contrasted with the failed lives of her classmates: M.P., who boasts of all the advanced degrees she will earn, is married within six months of graduation; Cupid, who plans to become a journalist, is doomed instead to work as a governess all her life. After witnessing M.P. and Cupid's contributions to Laura's humiliations and failures, it is momentarily pleasurable to contemplate such poetic justice. But that feeling soon yields to one of sympathetic sadness, for it is clear that the conformity that makes M.P. and Cupid successful in school is exactly what makes it impossible for them to escape from the narrow paths their society offers them. The reader can see, as they cannot, that all their academic training is actually a ruse, a way to fill the time until they are old enough to marry or become teachers.

The Getting of Wisdom resembles Mayor's *The Third Miss Symons* in its concentrated style, its cool objectivity and its powerful simplicity. And like Mayor's novel, *The Getting of Wisdom* purposely belies the notion that a small canvas necessarily entails a corresponding limitation in relevance or importance. The story of an insignificant girl in an Australian boarding school provides a surprisingly rich basis for an exploration of the ways in which society exerts pressure upon all its members to conform, and of the price individuals must pay in order to belong. But the fact that this painful process occurs in a girls' school gives the novel an added resonance; not only does the savage cruelty of Laura's socialization seem all the more shocking in that its perpetrators are young girls and spinster school-teachers, but it is also made clear that the homogeneity and submission that are forced upon the girls will necessarily be a more inescapable part of their future lives than they would be for boys.

In the end, Laura, despite all her pathetic attempts to conform, fails to become like the others, but it is only when she literally steps off the school grounds on graduation day that she is able to realize that her failure has freed her. Handing her bag and hat to her sister, she begins to run:

> Right down the central avenue ran Laura, growing smaller and smaller in the distance, the area of her movements decreasing as she ran, till she appeared to be almost motionless, and not much larger than a figure in the background of a picture. Then came a sudden bend in the long, straight path. She shot round it, and was lost to sight. (233)

These are final words of the novel, and what they offer is perhaps the most fitting and poignant image of modern woman in all of Edwardian fiction. After a difficult struggle, Laura has thrown off the social conventions that have imprisoned her and, unfettered, rushes into the public world, unconcerned with the opinions of others; but exactly what will happen to her must for the time being remain unknown, lost to the reader's sight. Richardson ends her novel in a way that would not have been possible in the nineteenth century: her heroine is not only triumphantly alone, completely free from any familial or romantic attachments, but she is out in the world and in motion – an active symbol of progress and of hope.

Even the most conservative Edwardian novels about unmarried women were innovative in terms of the women they depicted; spinsters, unwed mothers, adolescents, and other women who had been invisible in British culture and society alike, were made visible through these novels, and the particular difficulties of their situations were rendered palpable and significant. The appearance of these outcasts of society in Edwardian fiction marks an important transition from the idealization of characters (particularly women) in nineteenth-century fiction to the emphasis in modernist fiction on prosaic, imperfect or unexceptional people. The specific ways in which these unmarried women are portrayed indicates a break with traditional ideas about characterization as well; their anger and dissatisfaction, their fallibility and even unpleasantness, were unprecedented for female protagonists in British fiction. Social ideals of femininity are called into question in many of these novels, for what becomes of value are not those qualities which fit the heroines for marriage and motherhood but, rather, those which prepare them for life in a more general, ungendered sense. Gender definitions, social norms of behavior – even the very idea of conformity – are all unsettled by these novels, for they suggest that difference is a strength, not a liability. These heroines not only tend to be unconventional in both looks and behavior, but in many instances they triumph because of, not in spite of, their deviance from the norm. For all their unconventionality, however, these women are not radical feminists or exceptional New Women; rather, they are recognizable and ordinary; they serve as illustrations of how the lives of even average women were being profoundly influenced by feminism.

But by opening up the novel to new protagonists and new experiences, authors of Edwardian novels about unmarried women were confronted with the inadequacies of the novelistic structures and conventions which had been used to tell stories about women in the past. Traditional narratives were grounded in gender polarization; they figured female desire in terms of romance, and female success in terms of marriage and motherhood. Thus, to tell the story of women who rebel against gender norms and social conventions, it was necessary not only to thematize their rebellion (as the authors of anti-courtship novels did) but to formalize it as well. Novelists themselves had to rebel – against gender stereotypes in their characterizations of women, against the dominance of romance and marriage in the plots they constructed, and against normative narratives which reinforce social conventions as they move toward closure and the reinstatement of the status quo. In challenging the dominant social order, these writers were compelled to challenge the dominant order of fiction. Only a few Edwardian novels about unmarried women were fully successful in their formal rebellions – most notably *The Third Miss Symons, My Brilliant Career* and *The Getting of Wisdom*. But in the provocative innovation of their themes and styles and narrative forms these novels reveal how closely the breaking and making of feminism – the breaking with the past and the making of the new – are aligned with the breaking and making of literary modernism.

Edwardian novels about independent women are representative of the breaking stage of both feminism and modernism. The fundamental movement of these novels is that of breaking free from the tyranny of romance and marriage plots. As a result, Edwardian novels about single women, no matter what their ideological agenda, reinforce the traditional opposition between love and vocation. Novelists such as the Findlaters or Franklin or Richardson saw marriage as such an oppressive institution that it had to be rejected absolutely in order for their heroines to discover a life of autonomy and independent purpose. But having rejected marriage, their rebellious heroines are not left at an impasse, as the women in marriage problem novels tend to be; they are left on the threshold of unarticulated but exciting possibilities. Although many Edwardian women were attending universities, establishing careers for themselves, and even trying to combine romance and vocation, these experiences are rarely treated in Edwardian fiction. That project was left for the next generation – the beneficiaries of the breaking done by the Edwardians.

The breaks with tradition within Edwardian fiction, along with those in the new fiction of the 1890s, set the stage for the more radical breaks of modernist fiction. The new kinds of heroines and new experiences that had been introduced in the 1890s and developed during the Edwardian years had prompted an important shift in valuation. Women in and of themselves, the contours of their daily lives, and their psychological, sexual and material realities, had gained acceptance as legitimate subjects for fictional exploration. The consequences of this shift are most evident in the modernist fiction of Lawrence, Virginia Woolf, Dorothy Richardson, and May Sinclair (whose Edwardian fiction is discussed in Chapter 5). In Lawrence's *The Rainbow* (1915) and *Women in Love* (1921); in Woolf's first two novels, *The Voyage Out* (1915) and *Night and Day* (1919), as well as in her subsequent fiction; in Richardson's *Pointed Roofs* (1915) and the rest of *Pilgrimage*; and in Sinclair's *Mary Olivier: A Life* (1919) and *Life and Death of Harriett Frean* (1922), one can see Edwardian rebel women and their descendants rejecting the marriage plot, and striving to define themselves and their ambitions outside of the limits imposed by gender norms. But one can also see the dramatic ways in which these authors reject traditional novel content and traditional narrative forms, and strive to communicate the reality of their heroines' experiences through innovative representations of consciousness, sexuality and material reality.

These modernist writers fulfill the promise of the Edwardian writers who broke with tradition in their narratives of unmarried women; they are able to complement their breaking with making, and thus to create new kinds of narratives with which to tell the stories of women's lives.

CHAPTER FOUR

Suffragette Stories

You have such a field as never writers had before. An almost virgin field. You are, in respect of life described fearlessly from the woman's standpoint – you are in that position for which Chaucer has been so envied by his brother-poets, when they say he found the English language with the dew upon it. You find woman at the dawn. . . . *Your* Great Adventure is to report her faithfully. So that her children's children reading her story shall be lifted up – proud and full of hope. 'Of such stuff,' they shall say, 'our mothers were! Sweethearts and wives – yes, and other things besides: leaders, discoverers, militants, fighting every form of wrong.'

(ELIZABETH ROBINS [1910])

Deeds not Words!

(MOTTO OF THE WOMEN'S SOCIAL AND POLITICAL UNION)

On the evening of 13 October 1905, at a major Liberal Party meeting at the Free Trade Hall in Manchester, a young woman named Annie Kenney stood up on her chair and shouted 'Will the Liberal Government give women the vote?' Amid the commotion that ensued, she was forcibly removed from the meeting, along with her companion, Christabel Pankhurst; the two women continued their struggle with the police in the anteroom, where Christabel reportedly spat at and struck two of them. The women were found guilty of disorderly behavior and other offenses and, refusing to pay any fines, were imprisoned in Strangeways Gaol for two days. The publicity and interest generated by the incident was overwhelming; membership of the Women's Social and Political Union (WSPU), the suffrage organization headed by Christabel, increased; and thus the militant suffrage movement was born.[1]

Women and men had been organizing for women's suffrage since the nineteenth century, but the movement was given new life in the Edwardian period with the founding of the WSPU in 1903, by Emmeline Pankhurst and her daughters, Christabel and Sylvia. Before that date, the main suffrage organization had been the National Union of Women's Suffrage Societies (NUWSS), which was established in 1897 and led by Millicent Garrett Fawcett. The members of the NUWSS were known as suffragists or Constitutionals, because they sought the enfranchisement of women through entirely legal methods. But the Pankhursts believed that the NUWSS was moving too slowly, and that their conventional tactics were incapable of attracting the kind of publicity needed to garner wide support for women's suffrage. Their previous involvement with the Independent Labour Party (ILP) had shown the Pankhursts the effectiveness of protest demonstrations and intentionally sought imprisonments, and they soon made those kinds of militant tactics the foundation of their campaign. The members of the WSPU were called suffragettes, a term first applied with derision by the *Daily Mail* in 1906, but soon adopted by the militants to distinguish themselves from the suffragists.

There was a third major suffrage organization – the Women's Freedom League (WFL) – which was formed in 1907 by members of the WSPU who were dissatisfied with the autocratic leadership of Emmeline and Christabel Pankhurst, and wished to maintain the ties with the ILP and the working classes that the Pankhursts were gradually dissolving. The WFL, led by Charlotte Despard, considered itself a militant organization, although it never adopted the extreme tactics of the WSPU's final years.

In the early years of the movement, until mid-1909, all three major suffrage organizations focused primarily upon large public demonstrations and processions (often in concert with one another) in order to publicize their cause and gain new recruits.[2] Each of the three published its own newspaper, which members sold on street corners, and numerous specialized suffrage groups sprang up all over England. The militant strategy of the WSPU during this period was predominantly disrupting political meetings; the disrupters would then be imprisoned and heralded as martyrs to the cause, thus gaining publicity and increasing the visibility and the membership of the WSPU.[3]

For thousands of Edwardian women, the suffrage movement provided them with a goal and a community, moved them out of their homes into an activist and public sphere, and allowed them to express their unhappiness with women's unequal status as well as with their own particular lot. As the writer and suffragette Evelyn Sharp noted, 'some women welcomed the militant movement because it enabled them to express their discontent publicly without appearing to reproach any individual man in the home'.[4] Although suffragists and suffragettes recognized that a wide range of social, political, economic and legal changes were needed to improve the position of women in British society, they saw the vote as both a symbol of equal rights and the necessary first step toward attaining the power to institute reforms.

The discontent that fueled the suffrage movement had been surfacing in British fiction for quite some time, but most attempts to break free from the tyranny of romance and wedlock plots had been impeded by the lack of any actual alternatives in women's lives. The New Woman heroines of the 1890s were anomalies in their society; they were isolated and frustrated, and most of the novels that depicted them ended unhappily or in compromise. This pattern continued in Edwardian fiction. The rebellious wives in the marriage problem novels rebelled privately, domestically: because they had no one to turn to and nowhere to go, they usually returned home to their husbands. The defiant spinsters and mutinous young women who populate Edwardian novels are also, for the most part, lonely rebels, like the New Women before them; they have few, if any, role models, and no similarly emancipated friends with whom to ally themselves. While they are proud of their distinctiveness, they also suffer for it. Like their married counterparts, the single women in Edwardian fiction are restricted in their rebellion in that they are unable to formulate any concrete goal to pursue; they know what they don't want, but do not know what it is they want. There are no careers available to them, no sympathetic communities for them to join; the autonomous and happy female community with which Mary Findlater ends her novel *The Rose of Joy* is unusual.[5] Only in fantasy fiction were writers able to imagine lives of public activity and power for women, or a society which encouraged female communities.[6]

The advent of the suffrage movement changed all this: it allowed women to focus upon a specific goal in their rebellion, gave them a sustaining community of like-minded women (and occasionally men), and permitted them to assert themselves in the public world, and take significant actions to alter the social and political organization of England. Correspondingly, the suffrage campaign provided novelists with a new narrative desire for women (the vote), a new arena of activity (the public sphere of political meetings and demonstrations), and a new cast of characters (female comrades in the movement). In theory, these developments had enormous implications for fiction, for they gave writers their best chance yet to break free of the restraints of novelistic conventions and the gender stereotypes which underlay them. But in practice, writing fiction without the safety nets of traditional narratives and modes of characterization presented numerous difficulties, of both a formal and an ideological nature.

In 1908, the playwright and novelist Cicely Hamilton and Bessie Hatton, a journalist, formed the Women Writers' Suffrage League (WWSL), one of the many specialized suffrage groups that served as auxiliaries to the three main suffrage organizations. The object of the League was 'to obtain the Parliamentary Franchise for women on the same terms as it is, or may be granted to men. Its methods are the methods proper to writers – the use of the pen.' The WWSL was a professional organization, the qualification for membership being the publication of 'a book, article, story, poem, or play for which the author has received payment'. The leaflet announcing the formation of the League urged women writers to join, because 'a body of writers working for a common object cannot fail to influence public opinion'.[7]

Many well-known novelists were members of the WWSL, including Marie Belloc Lowndes, Sarah Grand, Beatrice Harraden, Violet Hunt, Elizabeth Robins, Olive Schreiner, May Sinclair, Evelyn Sharp, Flora Annie Steel and Margaret Woods. They regularly supplied newspapers with letters to the editor and accounts of suffrage meetings, wrote plays and poems, and published pamphlets and articles, as well as organizing benefits and public meetings. Because their members were affiliated to all three major suffrage organizations, they did not participate in active political protests; but they did march in several major suffrage processions, carrying their distinctive black and white Writers' banner, as well as banners commemorating women writers such as Jane Austen, the Brontës, and Elizabeth Barrett Browning.[8]

The suffrage movement was supported by many other writers, both male and female. John Galsworthy and his wife were sympathetic to the cause, and attended suffrage meetings; Violet Hunt recalled that once, when she and May Sinclair were soliciting contributions at the High Street Station, 'Galsworthy sauntered along and tipped us immeasurably and gallantly'.[9] Ford Madox Ford (then Hueffer) was enthusiastic about women's suffrage, and wrote a pamphlet in support of it entitled *This Monstrous Regiment of Women*.[10] The poet John Masefield and the novelist Israel Zangwill were associated with the WWSL and the WSPU. H.G. Wells and George Bernard Shaw were also supporters of the general cause of women's suffrage, although their self-styled feminism made their support controversial. Rebecca West was a follower of the Pankhursts (until she became disillusioned with their leadership and their sexual puritanism in 1913), and wrote numerous impassioned articles on women's suffrage for *The Clarion* and other papers. Amber Reeves was a suffragist, as was Florence Farr; F.M. Mayor, though restricted to her rural home by ill health, was also intensely interested in the movement.

But very few of these writers were inclined to deal with the issue of suffrage in their fiction, apart from occasional peripheral references. Although the social problem novel was the pre-eminent genre of the day, the suffrage question was not a popular topic, perhaps because of its explicitly political nature. In Masefield's novel *Multitude and Solitude* (1909), when a suffragette asks the writer-hero why he doesn't write a play or novel about the movement, he replies:

> Because I don't believe in mixing art with propaganda. My province is to induce emotion. I am not going to use such talent as I have upon intellectual puzzles proper to this time. This is the work of a reformer or leader-writer. (148)[11]

On a practical level, many members of the WWSL supported themselves with their writing, and popular novelists like Belloc Lowndes, Harraden, Steel and Woods would have risked alienating their large reading public if they had infused their romance novels with controversial politics. Even the 'Votes for Women' novel series, inaugurated by the suffragist Annesley Kenealy with her novel *The Poodle Woman* (1913), was promoted warily as consisting of 'strong, popular, and non-political love stories'.

In the case of novelists who were suffragettes, they were often too involved in the numerous activities of the movement to have either the time or the inclination to write fiction. In her memoir *Unfinished Adventure*, Evelyn Sharp explains that once she became involved in the suffrage campaign, she earned her living 'almost entirely by journalism, since the writing of books demands a free mind that was rarely mine' (136). In addition, the events of the suffrage campaign were so startlingly fresh and dramatic, and eventually so shockingly violent, that there was no apparent need to transform them into fiction. Most felt that the events spoke for themselves, and that all that was necessary to convey the righteousness of the cause and the unjustness of its opponents was sympathetic reportage.

There was also, perhaps, a sense that to fictionalize the events of this important movement might trivialize them, or at least give ammunition to those who believed that the movement was not a serious one. The strategy of the suffragists – and, in the early years, the suffragettes – was to demonstrate their political acumen and their suitability to be voting citizens through their knowledge of history, statistics, and parliamentary procedure; sharply reasoned arguments and analyses, not popular fiction, seemed the logical way to gain respect from the male establishment. Although all three major suffrage organizations were involved in publishing ventures, most of what they published was non-fiction; predominantly interested in material that could further their cause, they were obviously not persuaded that fiction could have as much efficacy as writing that was clearly propaganda. It is probable that the majority of those who chose to write suffrage fiction were women, and that they had difficulty finding publishers. The woman novelist continued to be restricted by the fact that – as the novelist, playwright and suffragette Elizabeth Robins put it – 'Her publishers are not women. Even the professional readers and advisers of publishers are men. The critics in the world outside, men. Money, reputation – these are vested in men.'[12]

Robins, who was the first president of the WWSL, felt strongly that literature, especially literature written by women, could be just as powerful as propaganda in furthering the cause. In her essay 'Woman's Secret', she discussed the various ways in which women's thoughts, ideas and experiences have been suppressed throughout the ages. She argued that it was imperative that women utilize their 'access to a rich and as yet unrifled storehouse', and bring an end to 'the conspiracy of silence about the things that matter'.[13] In a speech given to the WWSL in 1910 she talked about the power of suggestion in literature, and emphasized how important it was for girls and young women to be able to read fiction about 'significant lives lived by women'. She concluded her speech by calling on her fellow writers to write about all the varieties of experience and action that await women in the modern world, to show that women can be 'Sweethearts and wives – yes, and other things besides: leaders, discoverers, militants, fighting every form of wrong'.[14]

The suffrage movement provided exactly the kind of stirring narratives and brave heroines that Robins protested were lacking in fiction; it also gave women a chance to write about experiences that were uniquely their own in their own way, without having 'to play the man's game', as Robins put it. Since there was no precedent for the women's suffrage movement in British history and fiction, those women novelists who chose to write about it were not compelled to imitate or accede authority to male models. But the uniqueness of the situation also presented these novelists with numerous narrative difficulties. How does one portray women whose aspiration is to attain political representation in a form which traditionally represents romance as women's dominant desire and marriage as women's supreme goal? How is a female protagonist to be validated if she is not the object of romantic desire? How can a form which privileges individual experience be used to depict communal experience and group action? Perhaps the ultimate question that writers of suffrage fiction had to face was whether or not the principal forms of British fiction, with their linear constructions of desire, conflict and closure, were, at the most basic level of narrative dynamics, inimical to the representation of an ongoing movement of feminist rebellion, for they inevitably moved toward stasis, and thus privileged not change, but the status quo.

Several novelists who were involved in the suffrage movement turned their attention to the theater in order to deal with (or, perhaps, avoid) these questions. Certainly the communal and public aspects of drama made it a more appropriate art form for the suffrage movement than the solitary activity of novel writing. The Edwardian period was a time of growing power for women in theater, as actresses began to organize as professionals, and some of them also began to work as actress-managers or actress-playwrights.[15] Cicely Hamilton was an actress and a playwright, and Florence Farr worked as an actress-manager, besides co-authoring two plays with Olivia Shakespear. Elizabeth Robins (who was American) first became famous in England as an actress who both produced and starred in several of Ibsen's dramas; she later wrote two plays.

In 1908, Hamilton and Robins formed the Actresses' Franchise League (AFL); one of the goals of the League was to work for the enfranchisement of women through 'propaganda plays', which would 'illustrate the speeches and pamphlets of the earlier suffrage societies in dramatic form'.[16] But the plays produced under the aegis of the AFL (most of which were presented at suffrage society meetings or at benefit matinées in West End theaters) tended to be comedies or farces, with the 'Antis' bearing the brunt of the humor. Hamilton and the playwright Christopher St. John (the pen name of Christabel Marshall) collaborated on two such works – a one-act comedy about anti-suffragists entitled *The Pot and the Kettle* (1909), and a one-act farce about a women's General Strike entitled *How the Vote was Won* (1909) – both of which were immensely popular with suffrage audiences.[17] Hamilton then went on to write the *Pageant of Great Women* (1909), which depicted women's history through the achievements of fifty-two great women, and was performed by suffrage groups throughout England. By concentrating on pageants, and one-act comedies and fantasies, Hamilton and other suffragist playwrights avoided the narrative difficulties inherent in writing realistic 'propaganda plays' about an ongoing and complex rebellion; instead, they focused upon entertaining and creating a sense of solidarity among their already converted audiences.

In this context, it is interesting to look at the problems Hamilton encountered when she wrote traditional full-length plays for the general public, in which she attempted to reconcile her feminist message with the requirements of popular drama. In *Diana of Dobson's* (first produced in 1908) Hamilton exposed the demeaning conditions under which shopgirls had to work; the play was considered shocking for its depiction, in the first act, of a group of shopgirls preparing for bed in their dormitory room. But Hamilton's criticism of the British economic system is muffled, for the most part, by the light comedy form in which it is presented, and by the play's very conventional (in terms of both romance and economics) happy ending. Similarly, *Just to Get Married* (first produced in 1910, and based upon Hamilton's polemic *Marriage as a Trade*) is a critique of the institution of marriage which nevertheless ends with the heroine running off to be happily wed. Hamilton was clearly attempting to reach a wide audience, purposely couching her feminist ideas in popularly appealing forms (she also later published both plays as novels), and her strategy worked, for the plays were very successful. But especially in the case of *Just to Get Married*, her theatrical compromises became ideological contradictions, which feminists and theater critics alike deplored.

Elizabeth Robins also struggled to achieve a balance between popular appeal and a feminist agenda, and was extremely successful in doing so with her play *Votes for Women!*, which was produced at the London Court Theater by Harley Granville Barker in 1907. It was one of the first, and certainly the most commercially popular, of all the suffrage plays. Robins herself insisted that it was a 'tract', not a play, thus insulating herself from criticism about its polemics and freeing herself from traditional aesthetic criteria. Like Hamilton, Robins went on to broaden the influence of her work by transforming the play into a novel, *The Convert*, which was published later in the same year.[18]

The Convert tells the story of Vida Levering, an attractive thirty-two-year-old woman who becomes radicalized after casually attending several suffrage demonstrations. It is revealed that many years before she had an affair with Geoffrey Stonor, now a prominent MP, and had an abortion when he refused to risk his inheritance by marrying her. They are brought together again after Stonor falls in love with the young and wealthy Jean Dunbarton, who is very impressed with Vida's cause. The novel ends with Vida forcing Stonor to support the suffrage bill by threatening to convert Jean and turn her into the Joan of Arc of the movement.

The novel alternates between public and private scenes, between vivid documentary-like re-creations of suffrage rallies and conventional scenes of drawing-room dialogue. Strategically, this alternation works as a bridge, orientating readers with a recognizable novelistic milieu and easing them into the unfamiliar and potentially alienating world of suffrage demonstrations. The alternation also represents formally the oppositional paradigm of private and public spheres which served so powerfully to restrict women's activities and ambitions. To move from the protection of the private realm into the dangers of the public arena was the single biggest hurdle that suffrage activists had to face, yet as Robins demonstrates, that personal leap was necessary in order to collapse the private/public opposition and other related oppositions which held women to a secondary status.

Robins avoids placing her heroine within a traditional romance or marriage plot by structuring the novel around the drama of Vida's conversion (and Jean's potential conversion) instead. The personal conflict between Vida and Stonor provides an additional narrative thread which links the suffrage scenes and provides dramatic tension, but it is significant that the object of their struggle is power, not love; Vida's desire is not for marriage, but for political and social change. The only romantic relationship in the novel – between Jean and Stonor – is portrayed critically as unequal and exploitive.

Robins is quite candid about what she sees as the relationship between political power and sexual power. Like most women involved with the suffrage campaign, she discovered that the British ideal of chivalry existed only when women remained in their proper place (both physically and politically). As soon as women stepped into the public spaces of men, and began to demand political power, the 'brutishness' of the male power structure – and in particular, its sexual basis – was revealed. Robins reports, for instance, that Members of Parliament routinely and maliciously derided women in general during their sessions, and that suffragettes were often sexually assaulted (by policemen and bystanders) while being arrested. The men in the audience of a suffrage rally admire the beauty of a woman who is seated on the speaker's platform as long as she is silent, but then ridicule her mercilessly when she dares to speak. Vida experiences some of this brutishness personally, when she puts on an old gown and ventures into 'the Underworld' – a poor district of London. There she is shocked to discover 'the bold free look of a man at a woman he believes to be destitute'; she goes on to declare: 'You must *feel* that look on you before you can understand – a good half of history' (224).

For Vida (as well as for Robins and a great many suffragettes), this vision of the hostility and contempt underlying men's ostensible reverence for womankind made the prospect of marriage, or even a relationship with a man, untenable. Vida is unabashed in her recognition of 'Sex-Antagonism' in British society, and does not hesitate to blame men for it. She argues that woman's 'idea of romance and her hope of motherhood' are 'the strongest things in life until man kills them' (239). Robins suggests that until women are given the vote, and British social and political organization is altered, romance and marriage are possible only for those who have a 'fairy-tale view of life'. Although in her political writings and speeches she took great care to emphasize that the movement did not wish to blame men, a great deal of anger and bitterness is directed against men in *The Convert*, prefiguring the man-hatred that was characteristic of the WSPU (of which Robins was a member) in the final years of its militant campaign.[19]

Its sexual frankness and unrestrained social criticism place *The Convert* in the tradition of the realist novels of the 1890s, but it is also realistic in a different way, for it is a documentary novel; by basing her story on actual people and demonstrations, Robins gives her readers a very real sense of what it was like to be involved with the suffrage movement in 1906 and 1907. But *The Convert* is explicitly propaganda, not objective reportage. In presenting the speeches of the suffragettes and the remarks of their hecklers in their entirety, Robins attempts to do the work of a demonstration – to convert the audience to the cause. Theoretically, Vida is the figure with whom the reader is to identify, for prior to her conversion she is shown to be skeptical about the suffragettes' commitment and intelligence, and she mocks 'this suffrage nonsense' along with all the other upper-class characters she associates with at dinner parties, teas, and country house weekends. But Vida's physical beauty, her self-righteousness, and the swiftness and depth of her conversion give her a kind of unreality that jars with the realism of the demonstration scenes. She is not a fallible, realistic Edwardian heroine but, rather, a throwback to the New Woman heroines of the 1890s.

Like the New Woman authors before her, Robins seems to be torn between revealing the reality of women's lives and creating an ideal and inspirational heroine; as a result, her authorial practice comes into conflict with Vida's feminist theories. Vida is an unconventional heroine – a sexually experienced single woman in her thirties who has no interest in romance and is harshly critical of other women's obsessions with physical appearance, fashion, and pleasing men. Yet Robins uses Vida's taste in clothes, her beauty and, most especially, her appeal to men, as indicators of her superior worth. This was certainly strategic, in part; the Pankhursts insisted that the members of the WSPU should be attired in a feminine fashion so as to repudiate the stereotype of the dowdy, 'unsexed' suffragette. But Robins's privileging of Vida's femininity (and of her strong maternal instincts as well) remains contradictory and, as such, underscores the contradictions inherent in the various feminist philosophies which formed the basis for the suffrage movement.

During the nineteenth century two philosophies dominated British feminism, although they were certainly not mutually exclusive. One held that because of their common humanity, women should naturally have the same rights as men. The other argued that women had particular qualities and abilities which were biologically determined, and were essential to society as well as to the government of the nation. This latter position quite often slipped into an argument that women were morally and spiritually superior to men, particularly with regard to sexual behavior.[20] Although all three major suffrage organizations were influenced by both strains of thought, the argument for women's special characteristics had more obvious strategic benefits. It offered the public the reassurance that at the most fundamental level, social organization, family structure, and gender roles would not be altered by the vote; it placed the suffrage movement in the light of reform, not revolution. But even while Mrs Fawcett promised women that in voting they would not give up 'one jot or tittle of your womanliness', and the WFL's paper *The Vote* ran a series called 'Suffragettes at Home', showing various suffragettes happily engaged in domestic chores, the fact that women were organizing and speaking at public demonstrations in an attempt to gain political power was in itself proof that women were able and willing to move beyond the domestic sphere and traditional gender roles.[21]

The tensions between these two philosophies are evident throughout *The Convert*, but they are most obvious in the way in which Robins explains Vida's political commitment through her personal loss. Hecklers at suffrage rallies were fond of reducing the suffragettes' grievances to personal problems, especially of a romantic nature; Vida shakes her head at the ignorance of the typical 'Hyde Park loafer' who asks the speakers why they aren't married or if they have been jilted. Yet Robins makes it clear that Vida's loss of her child and frustrated maternal passion are responsible for her dedication to the cause. Vida explains to Stonor that 'since men have tried, and failed, to make a decent world for the little children to live in, it's as well some of us are childless. Yes . . . *we* are the ones who have no excuse for standing aloof from the fight!' (304). In this way, an opposition between motherhood and feminist activism is constructed, and later confirmed, when Vida placates Stonor by telling him that Jean will lose her feminist ardor after she has borne a child. Not only is the opposition illogical, for Robins depicts a suffragette speaker who has six children (although she is, significantly, a working-class woman); it also indicates a failure of vision on Robins's part. By emphasizing the impact of childlessness upon Vida, Robins remains limited by a traditional conception of the female role in society, and ends up privileging women's biological function as the primary impetus of their being. Vida disparages 'that old pretence . . . that to marry *at all costs* is every woman's dearest ambition', yet she never doubts that all women wish to be mothers (287).

Because Robins was writing early in the suffrage movement, she was able to end the novel with a kind of optimistic indeterminacy. The Liberal Party had just come into power, the suffrage campaign had not yet become violent, and there was not the sense of beleagueredness and desperation that would characterize the movement in later years. Thus Stonor's promise of support provides a satisfyingly hopeful, though tentative, ending. But the particular mechanics of the ending are problematic, for Vida explicitly uses Jean as a pawn, and knowingly dooms her to a mediocre marriage and an unenlightened existence; in the context of the vital potentiality of the suffrage campaign, the stasis of marriage represents not a happy ending but spiritual death. One could perhaps view Jean as a martyr to the cause, except for the fact that she has no say in the matter; it is Vida who sacrifices the unwitting Jean for the sake of all the women who will be helped by Stonor's influence.

The ending is just one instance among many in the novel where women come close to some kind of personal rapport, only to have it swallowed up in the larger cause. On several occasions Vida tries to develop a friendship with Ernestine Blunt, one of the leaders of the movement, but Ernestine is interested only in how Vida can benefit the movement in practical terms. Although Vida speaks with noble rhetoric about the necessity for women to work together, the novel as a whole reveals, inadvertently, how difficult it is to subsume one's individual needs in a mass political movement. Sisterhood, in *The Convert*, is a stirring possibility rather than a reality.

Considering Vida's glamor and the melodrama of her conversion to the cause, it is appropriate that *Votes for Women!* (the dramatic version of *The Convert*) was published by Mills and Boon, a publishing house that would come to be best known for its romance novels. Mills and Boon also published a feminist novel during this first stage of the Edwardian suffrage movement – *Elisabeth Davenay* (1909) by Claire De Pratz – which, like *The Convert*, illustrates how twentieth-century feminists manipulated nineteenth-century feminine ideals to suit their own ends. But unlike *The Convert*, *Elisabeth Davenay* is written in the style of popular romantic fiction; thus, in its excesses, it blatantly reveals the anxieties and contradictions behind the strategies of Edwardian feminists.

The glorious perfection of the titular heroine is emphasized at every opportunity, and in extraordinary detail: every aspect of her toilette, her clothing, her diet, the decoration of her apartment, and her style of entertaining is described for the reader. On the basest level, these details offer an appeal similar to that of a ladies' magazine, and are calculated to attract those who might not otherwise read feminist fiction. But all this information about Elisabeth also serves to emphasize the fact that one can be both extremely feminine and a committed feminist; it offers reassurance to those who are worried that feminism might 'unsex' women.

Elisabeth offers a blunt explanation of the importance of her feminine beauty:

> It is an understood thing that a woman's first duty is to please, and as I want to tell men unkind truths, I must, at least, be attractive, if only to obtain their hearing. The mistake the first pioneers made was that they despised their womanly charm. There they were most unwise. Until we have trained men not only to see our better inner selves, and to seek for and to love them, we must – to a certain extent – make our appeal firstly with our outward selves. . . .
> Charm with us is power. (24)

Elisabeth's philosophy here was a common one for turn-of-the-century feminists: straightforward and equitable relations between the sexes are relegated to an ideal and distant future; the present is figured as a time of war in which all strategies that lead to victory are acceptable. Like Vida, Elisabeth sees nothing incongruous about using her sexual appeal to get what she wants from powerful men in the government, as long as it is in the service of feminism. But as in *The Convert*, the stereotypes of femininity that are manipulated by the heroine (and by the author to validate the heroine) are also used in a very traditional fashion to devalue women. Those women in the novel who dislike Elisabeth, or are distrustful of feminism, inevitably have 'sallow skin . . . hollow eyes . . . lustreless hair', and are unable to attract male interest. Yet if they allow themselves to be converted by Elisabeth, they miraculously become physically attractive and sexually appealing. Although De Pratz gives a new interpretation to social standards of feminine value, those standards remain superficial and restrictive, and perpetuate what Cicely Hamilton called 'the custom of regarding one half of the race as sent into the world to excite desire in the other half'.[22]

Elisabeth lives an impossibly ideal life: she works as a teacher, lectures and writes indefatigably for the feminist cause, solves the personal problems of all her friends, establishes a feminist newspaper, and nobly rejects a marriage proposal from the man she loves, explaining that she is 'an intermediate type', a 'pioneer' who must sacrifice herself for the sake of humanity. But what saves *Elisabeth Davenay* from being just an amusingly silly cultural artifact is that De Pratz also depicts in the novel several women who successfully combine marriage, motherhood and feminism (and, in some instances, a career), and criticize, both explicitly and implicitly, Elisabeth's attempt to create an opposition between marriage and feminism. De Pratz includes many other female characters who are neither perfect nor martyrs, and their stories are embedded within and offer contrasts to the larger story of Elisabeth (without, however, ever challenging her supremacy).

Thus the present-day narrative of Elisabeth's feminist activities is halted at regular intervals by brief histories of other women who have struggled against restrictions and found new lives through feminism. The style of detailed minutiae that is so tedious in the case of Elisabeth becomes fascinating realism as the particulars of the experiences of women who are usually silenced or forgotten – a courtesan, an urban working woman, a rural unwed mother, a society wife, and a woman doctor – are told. Through this device of multiple narratives, De Pratz is able to emphasize the variety of backgrounds and classes that feminists come from, while she represents the unity of all these women through their friendship with Elisabeth and their commitment to feminism. Although this novel is not specifically about suffrage, both the feminist newspaper (whose staff are all women) and the network of female friends Elisabeth establishes are offered as proof that women can successfully organize and sustain one another without the involvement of men.[23]

Robins and De Pratz were transitional feminists; writing in the early years of the Edwardian suffrage movement, they manipulated nineteenth-century values to inspire and convert their twentieth-century audiences.

They roused their readers through realistic depictions of the oppression and suffering of women, yet they ensured that their social criticism would not be too disconcerting by centering their novels upon upper-middle-class heroines who were traditionally feminine and appealing. But as the suffrage movement grew in numbers, as its members became more visible and active, fiction depicting the movement inevitably changed. Idealized, self-sacrificing heroines like Vida and Elisabeth were replaced by realistic and recognizable characters who reflected the large number of ordinary, unexceptional women who chose to join the movement (a development which parallels the broader shift in Edwardian feminist fiction away from the idealized New Woman character). In order for the suffrage movement to gain broad support, suffragists and suffragettes felt it was important that the public understand that they were not elite groups of unusual women but, rather, for the most part, average women who represented a variety of classes and backgrounds.[24]

The plight of the working classes had been a significant concern of the suffrage movement since its inception. Although the NUWSS, the oldest and largest of the three suffrage organizations, had several prominent members who were aristocrats and conservatives, and was largely made up of middle-class women, it had always had strong ties with the Labour movement and continued to strengthen them in the Edwardian period. The WFL was also firmly committed to the needs of working women – this was the main reason why its members broke away from the WSPU in 1907. Initially, the WSPU had worked closely with the ILP and other organizations allied with the working classes and socialism, but Christabel and Mrs Pankhurst eventually broke with the ILP when they moved their headquarters to London in order to attract middle- and upper-class women to their movement. This split was due in part to the ILP's disapproval of the WSPU's militant tactics, and in part to Christabel's growing suspicion of all men, including those in the ILP. But it also marked the paradoxically conservative, elitist bent of the WSPU; Mrs Pankhurst remarked that although the vote would benefit all women, it was 'the fortunate ones . . . the happy women, the women who have drawn prizes in the lucky bag of life' who should do the fighting for it.[25]

This attitude is evident in *The Convert*, for although Robins demonstrates her sensitivity to the ways in which working-class women are doubly oppressed (as in the scene where Vida disguises herself as one), she is often condescending, even contemptuous, when she characterizes members of the working classes in the demonstration scenes. In addition, Robins's traditional privileging of a single heroine prevented her from effectively communicating the multiplicity of the movement. It was understandably difficult for women who had had little contact with the working classes (except servants) to accept them as colleagues, or to write about them in depth. But suffrage writers after Robins obviously felt that it was imperative to represent their working-class sisters, and this shift in content led to formal innovation. Several writers of suffrage fiction turned to multiple narratives – either in the form of multi-plot novels or interconnected short stories; in their inherent collectivity and relativity, these forms were well suited to convey, thematically and structurally, the variety as well as the unity of the suffrage movement.[26]

Both Annie S. Swan in *Margaret Holroyd, or The Pioneers* (1910) and Evelyn Sharp in *Rebel Women* (1910) chose to write about the suffrage movement through collections of interconnecting short stories. Not only did this form permit them to focus on numerous and diverse women instead of a single heroine, it also gave them a way of writing about an ongoing situation without having to come to any comprehensive conclusion. Individual stories might depict a small victory or a personal conclusion, but they remain merely episodes of a larger work (and of a larger movement). It was part of the philosophy of the suffrage movement that women had to retain faith that each small act, each gesture, would have a cumulative effect, even if the immediate rewards were not apparent. In these two collections there are no major resolutions, no battles clearly won, but the various experiences of women in the suffrage movement gradually accumulate significance as one story follows another. This in turn expresses the collectivism of the movement – the belief that only by working together can women attain the power they need to effect political change.

The Margaret Holroyd of Swan's title is a wealthy, unmarried, middle-aged woman who is converted at a suffrage rally near her rural home, and moves to London to work actively for the movement. But after these events are depicted in the first two stories, the focus shifts to other women's conversions and activities. Margaret Holroyd returns in two later stories, and the woman who inspired her conversion, Cecil Field, also provides a link in several; but the main link between the stories is the common cause of women's suffrage. The characters range from a young factory worker to a suburban wife to a dressmaker's assistant to an elderly spinster; one of the conversion stories involves an elderly male scholar whose life is transformed when he falls in love with a suffragist.

Although Swan, like De Pratz and Robins, carefully emphasizes the beauty and 'womanliness' of her suffragist heroines, she is most concerned with the particular difficulties women confront when they move from a domestic to a public sphere, and from private relations to membership of a large movement. Her stories touch upon the common dilemmas suffragists had to face: the disapproval of family and friends, the terror of speaking in public, the physical exhaustion and psychological doubts that resulted from being part of a rebellious and increasingly militant movement. But what is surprising about this collection is Swan's solution to these dilemmas. Although several women are depicted as admirably successful suffragists, at least half of the women in these stories withdraw from active engagement in the movement (while retaining their commitment to the ideal of women's suffrage) and return to private, domestic lives.

The contradictory messages in Swan's stories reflect the conflicts that surfaced within the movement at this time. The first step of conversion was exhilarating for most women (in the case of Margaret Holroyd, it is called an 'awakening'), but the realities of suffrage work, in particular its public and militant nature, proved quite discouraging for many. In addition, after the initial thrill wore away, women began to realize the cost of their rebellion, and for some the loss of family and friends was too high a price to pay. Thus, even in suffrage fiction, the familiar Edwardian pattern of rebellion and retreat surfaces. Swan attempts to soften the retreat by emphasizing the other, more conventional ways that women can work for suffrage, such as through education or through feminine influence upon men; but the retreats clearly represent a regression, for each involves a movement away from London and a female community, and into a rural patriarchal tradition – the irony of which clearly eludes Swan.

The other irony of this collection is that Swan conveys the excitement and righteousness of the cause so effectively that when the daughter of a widower with a large family must give up her suffrage work to run her father's household, or when Cecil Field agrees to end her career as a suffrage speaker in order to move to her father-in-law's country estate and secure her son's patrimony, these decisions, despite all Swan's glowing rhetoric about 'duty', seem more like tragic failures than noble sacrifices. As Robins did in *The Convert*, Swan frames her heroines' choices as either/or decisions, usually in the form of ultimatums given by the patriarch of the family. In story after story, women must choose between their families and their suffrage activities – the two narratives cannot coexist. Margaret Holroyd advises the daughter of the widower: 'it is no part of our creed to break up family life . . . in your case there would be too much to lose'; she goes on to explain that the cause would be best served by the daughter's 'faithful adherence to the duties that lie to your hand in a motherless household' (137–8). Swan's stories ultimately (and inadvertently) reveal the essential contradiction in the suffragists' veneration for the traditional family structure: the very qualities she uses to define that structure – patriarchal dominance, isolation of the private sphere from the public, and strict polarization of gender roles – are antithetical to the ideals of feminism and the suffrage movement.

Swan's 'pioneers' go only so far in their trailblazing; they opt for the familiar 'peace and rest' that conventional narratives offer women, over the open-ended narrative of the suffrage movement. In contrast, the women in Sharp's collection of stories are repeatedly called 'rebels', and there is no inkling of retreat; it is clear from the first story in *Rebel Women* that they are involved not in a tentative exploration, but in fighting a war. In 'The Women at the Gate', a veteran who is watching a confrontation between suffragettes and police makes the association explicit:

'This is the kind of thing you get on a bigger scale in war.... Same mud and slush, same grit, same cowardice, same stupidity and beastliness all round. The women here are fighting for something big; that's the only difference. Oh, there's another, of course; they're taking all the kicks themselves and giving none of 'em back. I suppose it has to be that way round when you're fighting for your souls and not your bodies.' (13)

But very few of Sharp's stories deal with actual physical confrontations between suffragettes and an antagonistic public or police force. Rather than focus on their already obvious capacity for rebellion, Sharp strives to humanize the suffragettes, to show that they are nice, ordinary women who, although dedicated to the battle they are fighting, are sometimes confused, even embarrassed, by the strange situations they find themselves in. In 'Shaking Hands with the Middle Ages', the organizers of a political meeting scrutinize the women in the audience to see if there might be 'one of them' waiting to disrupt the speaker. But they mistakenly believe that suffragettes look like the caricatures in *Punch*, and thus fail to identify the quiet young woman in black as the rebel in their midst. Sharp's purpose in this and other stories is to show that 'one of them' is really not so different from 'one of us'.

A central concern of the stories in *Rebel Women* is the personal difficulties faced by women who are involved in a public movement. Violet Hunt recalled her feeling when she first stood on a public sidewalk to collect money for the cause: it was as if she 'had suddenly been stripped naked, with a cross-sensation of being drowned in a tank and gasping for breath' (52). Sharp's suffragettes feel similarly exposed: as one stands on a sugar box at a street corner, trying to attract a crowd, she thinks 'regretfully of a happy past in which the chief aim of a well-ordered life had been to avoid doing anything that would attract attention' (60). It is these psychological battles, not the physical ones, that intrigue Sharp, for no matter how committed they were, the suffragettes had to struggle to surmount the formidable female tradition of retirement and reticence in order to fulfill the requirements of an increasingly militant movement. Sharp depicts the full range of those requirements: she portrays suffragettes demonstrating, being arrested and sentenced to prison, disrupting (and being thrown out of) a political meeting, collecting money, selling newspapers, and working in a suffrage shop. But although Sharp is sympathetic to the qualms of these women, she is also able to see the humor in the bizarre situations they find themselves in, as when suffragettes who have donned sandwich boards in order to advertise a rally keep knocking things over, yet cannot bend down to pick them up. The deadly serious and the absurd were always side by side during the suffrage campaign, but Sharp was one of the few writers at the time to perceive it and communicate it with compassion.

Swan's focus was on the ways personal relations pulled women away from public activity; correspondingly, most of her stories take place in private, domestic settings. Sharp, on the other hand, was concerned with the challenge of public activity in and of itself, and almost all her stories are set in a public milieu. In that and other ways, her collection is unlike any other fiction about women written at the turn of the century. Adopting a strategem that was as uncompromising as it was unprecedented, Sharp completely subordinates the personal to the political. The reader is told absolutely nothing about what the women in the stories look like, what their family background is, or the details of their personal life. There are no references to romantic love or marriage, and there is not a single reference to 'womanliness'. The women in these stories are already committed feminists, so there are no accounts of conversions or awakenings. Sharp sweeps away the domestic and the feminine, and forces the reader to accept these suffragettes simply as human beings who have been denied their basic rights and are fighting in a variety of ways to attain those rights; the reader must judge them strictly on the basis of their words and their actions. In addition, the absence of romantic or familial ties, in concert with the lack of closure in individual stories and the collection as a whole, allows Sharp to leave her female characters at large, out in the streets, their rebelliousness untamed.

In most of the stories, Sharp accomplishes this depersonalization through the use of an anonymous first-person narrator. Although she presumably experienced much of what the 'I' of the stories experiences (she was an active member of the WSPU), no indication is given that the narrator is Sharp, or that she even resembles her in any particular way. The narrative 'I' is a carefully neutral voice, an uncharacterized observer/participant who allows the reader to enter into the activities of the suffragette. The narrative voice exemplifies the unity of the movement: in that she is unparticularized, it is impossible to know if there is more than one narrator; the narrative voice speaks for all suffragettes, and her experiences are those they all have in common. Also, in that she has no past or future (beyond the goal of gaining the vote), the narrator of most of these stories conveys a vivid sense of being in the present; the intensity of the moment is what Sharp offers in place of traditional narrative satisfactions.

There are three stories, however, in which Sharp uses a third-person narrative voice, and significantly, two of those ('The Women at the Gate' and 'Shaking Hands with the Middle Ages') are the only stories in the collection in which violent encounters between suffragettes and men are depicted. By dropping the narrative 'I', Sharp is able to distinguish these stories from her other more cheerful stories and stress the dangers suffragettes faced when they interrupted political meetings or broke through police lines. But by shifting to the third person, Sharp also backed off, ever so slightly, from conveying the intimate reality of the militant tactics which were the most controversial aspect of the suffrage campaign.

There is another disadvantage to Sharp's narrative strategy. In *Unfinished Adventure* she refers to the special type of friendship she formed with other suffragettes, 'the sort of relationship, even when it is not an intimate relationship, that grows between people who are comrades in work or a cause' (130–31). But she does not take advantage of this rare opportunity to write about women as they are, among themselves, without men. Although she depicts groups of women working together, she never gives the reader any sense of how they feel about one another, or what being part of a group means to them. In emphasizing the political and the public in her stories, not only romantic and familial relationships but all personal relationships disappear.

In only two stories does Sharp turn her focus away from the suffragettes: in 'The Person who cannot Escape' and 'The Game that wasn't Cricket', she looks at two unusual rebels – a working-class mother and a working-class girl, respectively. The overworked, exhausted mother angrily confesses to the narrator that she regrets her baby is a girl, for she does not want to bring another woman into the world. In response, the narrator allows herself a brief dream of the future that her work will bring about – a time, she believes, when the mother will be glad she has daughter. In the second story, a young girl revolts against custom by playing alleyway cricket with the boys while her brother minds the baby; both children enjoy great success in their unfamiliar positions, prompting the narrator to speculate about gender roles and 'sex-antagonism'. Although the girl's 'one instant of wild rebellion' is quickly quashed by the boys, it inspires the narrator with hope, for it demonstrates that what she calls the 'sharp line between the sexes' is not natural, but constructed and controlled by family and society.

The year before *Margaret Holroyd* and *Rebel Women* were published – 1909 – marked a significant shift in the tone and tactics of the suffrage campaign, even though there is little evidence of it in these works, with the exception of two of Sharp's stories which are about the arrests of suffragettes, and an obscure reference by Swan's titular heroine to her disgust with her organization's new methods. The suffrage campaign was moving beyond processions, demonstrations, and the disruption of political meetings to far more militant and dangerous tactics. The rallies and marches, and the occasional arrests, had made women and their cause visible, but the movement was now faced with the problem of how actually to force political action. In June 1909, after a deputation consisting of Mrs Pankhurst and eight other women was refused admittance to Parliament, a protest involving the breaking of government office windows ensued, and over a hundred women were arrested. One of those women went on hunger strike to protest the court's refusal to treat her as a political prisoner; by August 1909, hunger strike had become the standard strategy of imprisoned suffragettes. In response, the government began a program of forcible feeding of hunger strikers, which led to more protests and more arrests.

Most of the suffrage activity in 1910 was of a peaceful nature, owing to hopes that the government would seriously consider and pass the Conciliation Bill, which granted limited women's suffrage. When it became evident that Parliament was going to postpone consideration, however, a militant demonstration was staged outside the House of Commons on 18 November. That day became known as Black Friday, for many policemen brutally and sexually assaulted the suffragettes in their attempt to hold them back; by the end of the six-hour conflict, 115 women and four men had been arrested.[27] This day had an important effect on the subsequent actions of the WSPU; it heightened the suffragettes' sense of a 'sex war', and led them to place less emphasis on demonstrations involving physical confrontations in favor of the destruction of property, for which they would be quickly arrested. Although there would be a truce during much of 1911 – due to the coronation celebration and because the Conciliation Bill was again under consideration – by the end of the year the WSPU had embarked upon a systematic campaign of window-breaking that would continue until the outbreak of World War I. And with the resumption of the militant campaign, the pattern of arrests, hunger strikes, and forcible feedings also resumed.

In 1911, two novels were published which dealt with these violent developments in the suffrage movement: *No Surrender* by Constance Maud and *Suffragette Sally* by G. (Gertrude) Colmore. Like *Rebel Women*, these novels have a dual agenda: to provide an intimate, eyewitness account of the activities of the militant suffragettes and, in so doing, to gain sympathy for the cause by demonstrating that these women, despite their extreme actions, are normal, rational, and well intentioned. These novels are propaganda, in that they strive to counteract negative press coverage and public antipathy; but they also function as investigative journalism, for they expose, in documentary detail, the horrors of imprisonment and forcible feeding.

Both novels mark a departure from previous suffrage fiction in that they feature working-class heroines. Although Swan had made a factory worker the focus of one of her stories, the character is never given any interiority, and is seen mainly through the eyes of a male doctor who befriends her. Sharp's interest in the connections between class oppression and sexual oppression is obvious in almost every one of her stories, yet the first-person narrator and her fellow suffragettes are all educated, upper-middle-class women like the author herself. But Maud devotes over half of her novel to Jenny Clegg, a mill-worker, and Colmore names her novel after Sally Simmonds, a housemaid. Both women are treated without condescension or stereotyping, the details of their work are not elided, and they are given credence as significant members of the campaign.

The novels have many similarities. Both novelists recognized the impossibility of telling the story of the movement through the single narrative of one individual woman; thus they opted for several heroines. The multiple, intertwining narratives of these novels convey the unity as well as the variety of the movement, particularly with regard to class. Both purposely transgress the line between fiction and non-fiction, using actual events to determine the structure and time frame of their narratives, and mingling the lives of their characters with those of real people;[28] both focus in particular on incidents which shed light on the sufferings of working-class women. They both retell the story of Lady Constance Lytton, an upper-class woman who, distressed by the preferential treatment she had received in prison, disguised herself as a working woman called Jane Warton. She was arrested, sentenced to prison, and began a hunger strike. But instead of being exempted from forcible feeding because of a heart condition (as Lady Lytton had been), Jane Warton was forcibly fed several times, resulting in permanent damage to her health, and extreme embarrassment for the government when her true identity was revealed.[29]

The most significant innovation of *No Surrender* and *Suffragette Sally* is that they depict women enjoying romance or marriage *and* work outside the home: both novels have a romance narrative that coexists rather than competes with the main narrative about the militant suffrage campaign. Marriage and feminism are not presented as mutually exclusive, as they are in *The Convert* or *Margaret Holroyd*, or in most Edwardian fiction; Maud and Colmore argue that feminist beliefs and feminist activism are conducive, not antagonistic, to marital harmony. Romance and marriage do not dissipate the suffragettes' convictions (as Robins had suggested) but, rather, strengthen their resolve to help all women to have the opportunity to enjoy equitable, sympathetic relations with men.

Both novelists also make it clear that the ultimate fulfillment for their heroines is their suffrage work, not their personal relationships, and this is underscored by the fact that romantic resolutions are not placed at the end of these novels, but occur in the penultimate chapter. In *No Surrender*, for example, Joe, Jenny's working-class boyfriend, must demonstrate his commitment to the movement before she will agree to marry him; the final scene shows him marching in the procession (separately from Jenny) carrying a banner representing John Stuart Mill. In each of the successful romantic relationships in these novels, it is the men who enter into the female world and make adjustments to conform to its demands, rather than the other way round. Whereas in traditional narratives, marriage leads to the isolation of the woman in a domestic world, in Maud's and Colmore's radically new narrative pattern marriage brings the man into the woman's public sphere of political activity.

Maud was affiliated to the WFL and Colmore to the WSPU, but both took quite a moderate attitude toward men. While the WSPU increasingly strove to shock the public, novelists, even those who supported the militants, could not afford to alienate their readers. These two novelists do describe the ways in which women are legally and physically abused by men, particularly emphasizing the apparent relish with which men turned against those women who dared to venture into public places to promote their political agenda. Nevertheless, there is no sex war in these novels; the rhetoric of man-hatred promulgated by Christabel Pankhurst and the more extreme members of the WSPU is nowhere in evidence. Although they do not criticize the suffragettes who do not wish to marry, these authors explicitly use their heroines' heterosexual relationships to affirm that suffragettes are healthy, normal and attractive women (though the latter quality is not stressed, as it is in Robins), and that they want to reform the structure of British society, not destroy it. How much of this was strategic and how much reflected the authors' own beliefs is impossible to tell; but certainly the tactic of condemning only particular men and their particular actions instead of the entire sex made their arguments more persuasive and palatable.

Maud and Colmore also avoid presenting the personal and the political in either/or terms, as previous suffrage writers had done. In *The Convert*, Robins was clearly anxious about the relationship between the two; she vigorously tried to show that the suffragettes were not inspired by personal grudges, yet her heroine is apparently motivated by the ill treatment she received from her lover. In *Rebel Women*, Sharp tries to distance her suffragettes from personal motives by completely omitting any personal information about them or their backgrounds. But in *No Surrender*, for example, Maud purposely confronts the issue: in a chapter entitled 'Canterbury Tales', she depicts 'five women of widely different type, age, class, and education' sharing a prison cell, and taking turns telling 'what made me a Suffragette' (103). None of them has been jilted, and none of them hates men, but all of them have witnessed or experienced injustices which they refused to tolerate.

For the women in these two novels, the personal basis for their political commitment is important; their interest in suffrage is not theoretical or objective, and their personal passion is contrasted positively with the aloof male political establishment. By refusing to draw neat boundaries between personal experience and political commitment, or between romance and suffrage activism, both Maud and Colmore (and the actual women they based their novels upon) were working to break down the ideology of separate spheres which had limited women's lives for so long.

For all their similarities, however, *No Surrender* and *Suffragette Sally* are very different in terms of tone and mood, and the differences between them illustrate some of the limitations involved in writing propagandistic fiction. Despite its formal and ideological innovations, and its historical interest, *No Surrender* is, for the most part, a tedious book, for it never alters its relentlessly upbeat and inspirational tone. The suffragettes depicted never waver in their conviction, never feel depressed or discouraged. Even when they are faced with forcible feeding, they retain their positive outlook and their self-control: the co-heroine, Mary O'Neil, gently forgives the doctor who jams a tube down her throat, saying: 'Never forget all we women share the same sex as your mother' (295). Jenny's delight in interrupting political meetings and private parties in various disguises makes her seem more like a madcap heroine in a comic novel than a determined suffragette risking imprisonment. Maud was obviously trying to demonstrate that suffragettes were normal, likable women, and to inspire other women to join the movement. But the positive tone of the novel often jars with the horrible and violent facts of the movement, in a way that calls to mind the 'Who's Who' section of *The Suffrage Annual*, a directory of the suffrage movement published in 1913. In each woman's biographical entry in the *Annual*, information about windows she has broken or the number of arrests or hunger strikes she has endured is followed by an innocuous list of her 'recreations', such as cycling, gardening, or reading.[30] The contrast is bizarre, and seemingly irreconcilable. Surely some kind of enormous wrench occurred when an average Edwardian woman decided to spend her afternoons breaking windows instead of reading, but Maud's polemical purpose prevents her from giving the reader any insight into the enormity or the price of such a transformation.

Colmore's *Suffragette Sally* is a remarkable achievement because its author chose to focus on that transformation from private to political woman, and specifically, on the problems and risks involved. Like *No Surrender*, *Suffragette Sally* is part propaganda, part documentary realism. But it is also a sensitive and complex investigation of the personal toll of the militant suffrage movement upon three women: Sally, a working-class woman with a fiancé; Edith, a middle-class woman who thinks she must choose between love and the suffrage movement; and Lady Geraldine, a married upper-class woman who is devoted to the cause.

Through these characters, Colmore pays particular attention to the ways in which the militant suffrage movement forced women to reevaluate and redefine their own concepts of 'womanliness' – not in terms of nineteenth-century ideals, but in terms of the realities of the modern world. She also uses the interconnected narratives of these three women to examine the different ways women from different social classes responded to the movement and its demands, and to depict the friendships that developed across classes. Colmore's use of multiple plots is more methodical than that of other suffrage writers, however, in that she has her three heroines serve as emblems not only of different classes but of the three arenas in which women struggled when they joined the movement: Lady Geraldine represents the spirit, Edith the intellect, and Sally the body.

Lady Geraldine is the character who is most like the ideal heroines of early suffrage fiction; she is physically striking, calmly resolved, well read, articulate and brave. Her life of privilege has given her the freedom and the sense of entitlement that allow her to campaign actively for votes for women. She realizes that it is working women, not women like herself, who are in greatest need of the vote, and to better understand their experience she disguises herself as one (as did Lady Lytton). Her commitment to the cause is thus depicted as selfless and pure, and she remains spiritually strong throughout her imprisonment and forcible feedings. She represents the movement at its best: she is the unifying link between the various women of all classes in the novel as well as their spiritual guide, and her militant actions are always carefully calculated and ideologically defensible.

But for all her inspirational qualities, Lady Geraldine is neither a saint nor a martyr. Although she loves her suffrage work, she must also take periodic breaks from it: she seeks out 'wide lonely places – for a time, for a change', in order to cleanse her soul of all the conflicts she engages in; in her prison cell she feels relieved to be alone, to experience 'a comparative peace' after the tumult of her arrest and sentencing. At the celebratory breakfast for newly released prisoners, Geraldine enjoys the new spirit of comradeship she feels as each woman tells of her prison experience, yet at the same time she cannot help longing to get home to her husband. Through Lady Geraldine, Colmore speculates on how one's sense of individuality and privacy can be threatened by being part of a mass movement, even when it is conceived of as a supportive, feminist community. Colmore offers the rich and complex life of Lady Geraldine as a model for a middle ground for women between selfish seclusion and fanatical self-effacement; her individual narrative ends when her husband becomes an active proponent of women's suffrage, and she is finally able to achieve a workable balance between her private life and her political activism.

Middle-class Edith, in contrast, must struggle simply to get out of her house. She is so enslaved by social conventions that her activity is predominantly intellectual: she constantly debates various feminist philosophies and suffrage tactics with herself and others, but her social conditioning prevents her from taking any significant action. Through Edith, Colmore examines how the training in femininity that girls receive almost ensures that they will be hampered in public life. In adhering to the rules and regulations of her gender, Edith is quiet and submissive, eager to please, terrified of criticism. When she collects signatures in the town square and later, when she is assigned to interrupt a political meeting, she becomes literally paralyzed; in her mind the public world is linked with physical and sexual danger, so she finds it almost impossible to call attention to herself in a public place. Even though Edith believes that women should have the vote, the demands of the suffrage movement make her feel dangerously exposed, not exhilaratingly free. Her fears and failures demonstrate how women's lives are restricted by many other impediments besides the lack of political representation.

Edith's narrative is a variation on the two-suitor plot. Her first suitor, Cyril Race, is an MP whose traditional ideas about womanliness and marriage are initially a source of comfort to Edith. She believes that she can work for the vote by influencing him, thereby avoiding any public activity or personal sacrifice. But whereas in early suffrage novels, such as *The Convert* or *Elisabeth Davenay*, the manipulation of powerful men to further the cause was acceptable, in *Suffragette Sally* Edith comes to realize that such a strategy is based on an ideology which grants women only sexual power, and is thus regressive and hypocritical. Unlike the usual two-suitor plot Cyril is eclipsed not by another suitor but by a woman – Lady Geraldine – and by the suffrage movement. Edith is soon taught by Geraldine, however, that it is wrong to place female friendship and political commitment in opposition to romantic love; Geraldine's own life proves to Edith that the neat separations between private life and political beliefs, and between womanliness and militancy, to which Cyril subscribes are false.

Edith's second and proper suitor is Robbie Colquhoun, who, in traditional fashion, is a childhood friend who is present but unappreciated throughout most of the narrative. The contrast between the two suitors is figured in political, not romantic terms; Robbie's fitness to be Edith's husband becomes evident when he votes for the Conciliation Bill and Cyril does not. But Robbie goes even further to prove his devotion to the cause: he strikes Cyril for his betrayal of the Bill, and goes to jail for it. Robbie, like Lady Geraldine, challenges Edith's desire to fit everything into discrete categories; he acts both constitutionally and militantly, and unlike Cyril, he offers Edith a life that is both personally fulfilling and politically meaningful. Edith never becomes a militant activist, but the ending of her narrative can be seen as a testament to the private rewards of feminism; their commitment to the cause is what brings Edith and Robbie together, and the reader is led to assume that their marriage will be a happy one, for it is based on feminist principles.

Sally, the housemaid, is not concerned with principles, or philosophies, or even social conventions. From the moment she is introduced, rushing home late from her first suffrage rally, it is clear that she is interested in women's emancipation on a far more personal and immediate level than Edith or Geraldine. Worrying about the reproaches of her mistress, she finds her master instead waiting for her at the back door:

> That was worse in a way, though better in another. The mistress scolded, but the master kissed. . . . The master's arm was round her waist and the master's hard, bristly moustache scraped her cheek. She did not want that encircling arm, and she greatly disliked that particular moustache, yet she accepted the embrace almost without resistance. It was in a day's work, so to speak; most men were like that; most masters, at any rate . . . (11)

It is not Colmore's sexual frankness but, rather, Sally's resigned acceptance of her master's behavior that makes this passage so radical for its time; throughout the novel, Colmore employs a bluntly realistic style to shock her readers into a recognition of how the economic oppression of working-class women often led to their sexual oppression. For women like Sally, there were no tidy divisions between public and private; subsequently, it was not difficult for them to recognize the personal implications of women's lack of political power. The standard arguments against equal rights for women were usually predicated upon ideas about feminine weakness and naturally separate spheres, but Sally's life illustrates the fallacies of those arguments. She has never had any privacy, and has always been expected to work; thus she willingly accepts the public duties of the suffrage movement – speaking, marching, and selling the paper *Votes for Women*. The suffragettes soon convince Sally that she can indeed fight her subjugation, and her first militant act is to hurl a sausage at her employer's face when he derides Lady Geraldine; immediately afterwards she goes to the WSPU offices to find a new job, and declares herself 'a full-blown suffragette'.

But the differences between Sally's experiences with imprisonment and forcible feeding, and Lady Geraldine's, demonstrate how difficult it was for working women to participate in the militant movement. Not only does time in prison mean a loss of income for Sally, but it is also far too much like her daily life to function as an ennobling, spiritual experience. Lady Geraldine and other educated women might speculate on the symbolic resonance of the male establishment taking women out of the public eye and locking them in tiny rooms; such women might appreciate the irony that the one activity of the suffragettes that men cannot call 'unwomanly' is that of starving themselves. But for Sally, her jail cell is just another cramped, uncomfortable room, not unlike other rooms she has lived in. And starvation is something she has been battling all her life; her decision to go on a hunger strike is thus quite different from that of Lady Geraldine, who knows she will return to her upper-class life upon release from prison. The horrible paradox of Sally's experience is that she seeks out the suffrage movement as her salvation, only to have it lead to the further abuse of her body – by policemen, prison matrons and doctors. Sally's health is broken by her imprisonment and forcible feeding, and she dies a few months after her release. Colmore uses Sally as a reminder of the crucial differences that underlie the suffrage movement's ideal of unity: while suffrage is predominantly a matter of principle for women like Lady Geraldine and Edith, for working-class women it can be a matter of life or death.

Class differences also account for the fact that Sally is the only one of the three heroines who is unable to mesh her private and political lives. Her boyfriend Joe is an average working man who tries very hard to sympathize with her commitment, but impatient for a home and family of his own, he gives Sally an ultimatum. She cannot accept him, for as a working-class wife she would not have the freedom that the childless Lady Geraldine has in her marriage. But after Joe leaves her, Sally wonders if the suffrage campaign is worth such a loss:

> It all seemed far away, unreal, a sort of dream, and not a pleasant one. The
> reality was Joe, and Joe's arms and kisses, and the home she might have had.
> Somehow she had thought that he would wait for her, till she was ready, till
> the vote was won, and she was free to settle down. . . . But he didn't care
> enough, for her or for the Cause; he wouldn't wait. (212)

Sally, more than the other two women, feels as if she is at war: she is stuck at the front, with no private, domestic realm to retreat to, and she is unable to make plans beyond the next battle. She is grateful for the sense of solidarity and purpose she has gained from the movement, but she clings to 'visions of golden days ahead . . . when the vote would be won, and there would be no suffrage question to stand between a girl and her lover' (243). For Sally, her female community does not make up for the absence of a husband and family; her political commitment is no substitute for private happiness.

Both Colmore in *Suffragette Sally* and Maud in *No Surrender* recognized the need to avoid conventional closure for their novels. Because they were demanding social and legal change through their narratives, it was imperative that they should not impart a sense of quiescence to their readers. In addition, they had to ensure that their principal subject – the burgeoning female energy of the movement – would not be subdued through narrative resolution. Maud ends her novel with a description of a large suffrage procession in London, thus embodying in a single image the unity, strength, and continuing forward motion of the suffrage campaign. Colmore ends hers in several layers, some of which offer a kind of narrative satisfaction, but cumulatively they leave the reader unsettled. Lady Geraldine gains her husband's support and Edith finds love with Robbie, but the mounting violence of the suffrage campaign overshadows any personal happiness they feel. Sally's narrative ends when she experiences the 'thorough change' she had been searching for in death, but Colmore does not allow death to be the final image of her novel. The entire final chapter is comprised of a verse from Julia Ward Howe's 'The Battle Hymn of the Republic' which ends with 'OUR GOD IS MARCHING ON'; like the ending of *No Surrender*, its purpose is to stress that action will continue even after the narrative has ended.

But Colmore makes her novel even more inconclusive by adding yet another layer at the end: an author's note which rejects the idea of closure and denies the reader any feeling of stasis:

> This is a story which cannot be finished now. The happenings in it, in so far as they have to do with matters political, with prisons and public meetings and turmoil in the streets, are true happenings; and the end has not happened yet. . . . [The tide] is bound to come in, since the forces of evolution are stronger even than the force which draws the material tide; it may not pause in its coming; but, till it has reached its appointed place, the end of this book cannot be written. (320)

Colmore dates her note precisely (23 February 1911), as she also dates all the major fact-based events in the novel. The dates and the note serve as clear signals that she is not interested in any sort of traditional literary timelessness or universality; her novel is a message which she is explicitly sending out into the world she lives in. But strangely, this odd combination of immediacy and indeterminacy remains compelling even when the eventual ending of the story is known.

Suffragette Sally is unique among Edwardian suffrage fiction in its detailed and realistic emphasis on the particular plight of working-class women and their role in the movement. It is also exceptional in its frank presentation of the conflicts many women felt when they were faced with the difficult demands of the suffrage movement; although the novel is clearly intended as propaganda, Colmore does not restrict herself to the ideal, the uncomplicated or the upbeat. But there are other important ways in which she cautiously tempers her story; specifically, she is reticent about the violence, the anger and the sexual tensions that were important and controversial components of the militant suffrage movement.

Colmore's engagement with the question of militancy most often takes the form of philosophical discussion, and through the measured arguments of Lady Geraldine she makes a very persuasive case for the necessity of violent protest. But like all other suffrage fiction *Suffragette Sally*, despite its rhetoric and imagery of war, rarely deals with actual battles, and focuses instead on private trials and moments of solidarity. Colmore's descriptions of suffragettes destroying property are always brief, and they offer no insight into the emotions of the women involved. On the few occasions when she describes violent confrontations between men and the suffragettes, as in the following description of Black Friday, Colmore moves into an impassive, generalized style that does not focus on particular women:

> Deputation after deputation came up from Clement's Inn, and was broken up and dispersed; and here was a wild turmoil of struggling men and women; and there a woman lay upon the ground; and there again were women hurled by the police into the crowd, and back from the crowd against the line of police.... Women who had been told they must not have the vote because they could not fight, showed they could fight that day; there was nothing to be done but fight, since all around was warfare; since well-dressed men and youths amused themselves by striking women; since a man appealed to for help, turned on the girl who appealed to him and hit her again and again.
>
> And all this because a man in power refused to receive twelve women who had none. (303)

By not giving these women any individuality or interiority, Colmore avoids having to consider how it feels to fight or be fought; she does not have to deal with the personal or irrational side of violence, or with the anger that the suffragettes must have felt. Despite the fact that women did fight back, Colmore strives to depict them as pure victims, martyrs to their cause.

Colmore describes the sexual assaults that occurred on Black Friday, but again her distanced style precludes her dealing with any complicated feelings of sexual violation or hatred. She also never considers the ways in which forcible feeding was a physically violent expression of sex antagonism, tantamount to a rape, although it was recognized as such by the suffragettes and others at the time. In *The Emancipation of English Women* (1910), the historian W. Lyon Blease made the connection between forcible feeding and rape explicit: 'The mental condition which was produced [by the feeding] was even more horrible than the physical, and if women had been violated in their cells by order of the Government,

they could hardly have been filled with a deeper sense of degradation'
(261). But Colmore adopts her aloof style when she describes a forcible
feeding, with an anonymous woman standing for all who go through the
experience:

> Very wide the doctors open her mouth, just as wide as the jaws will stretch,
> and the gag is fixed so that the teeth cannot close. Then down the throat goes
> an indiarubber tube, not too small.
>
> She is choking now, or feels as if she were; all the agony and the horror of
> suffocation is upon her. It seems as if it would never stop, the passing of that
> tube; the delicate mucous membrane is hurt and irritated; the choking, the
> sensation of not being able to breathe, grow worse and worse. (205)

As with the public confrontation scenes, Colmore's description of a
forcible feeding neutralizes any sexual tension, and precludes the
expression of personal response. Surely there was anger, surely there
was hatred, surely there was sex-antagonism – on both sides. But
Colmore declined to wade into these murky waters. The men who fight
with the suffragettes are simply stupid brutes – their emotions are never
explored; the suffragettes are free from anger, free from personal
resentments, free from sexual anxieties; their militant actions are
calculated and well intentioned, never fueled by ignoble emotions.
Colmore dwells on the spiritual struggles the suffragettes go through
before their public protests or during their imprisonments, but their
actual acts of violence are quickly skimmed over. Although *Suffragette
Sally* gives a far more honest and complex picture of the movement than
any other suffrage fiction of the period, it still leaves many questions
unanswered. What did it feel like to commit a public act of violence – to
break a window, destroy property, strike a policeman? What was it like to
fight with men? Did the suffragettes feel anger or exhilaration? Was there
a sense of power, or perhaps of freedom? What were the ramifications in
their subsequent lives for the militant suffragettes? Did their militant
actions alter their relationships with men, or their sense of themselves as
women?

These questions were never answered in Edwardian fiction. No other
novels were written in support of women's suffrage between 1911, when
the campaign of property destruction became systematic, and 1914, when
the movement itself was effectively brought to a halt by World War I.
Thus there are no sympathetic or even objective fictional representations
of the most controversial, sensational and violent stage of the suffrage
movement. The motto of those who were intimately involved with the
violence – the WSPU – was 'Deeds not Words', and clearly its members
did not find novels useful weapons of war. Instead they chose to break
windows, destroy golf greens, burn letterboxes, slash paintings and,

ultimately, embark on a campaign of arson which resulted in thousands of pounds' worth of damage. In the final years of the militant suffrage movement the public was continually faced with women expressing anger, women acting with violence, women claiming physical power in the world. That no novelist chose to write about this aspect of the movement demonstrates the antipathy of most pro-suffrage writers to the WSPU's violent tactics. But it also underscores the fact that the ultimate taboo for women in British society was not the expression of sexuality, but the expression of anger and power.

Women who broke with convention through their sexual behavior nevertheless remained within their ordained realm of personal feelings, defined by their physical attractiveness and their relations with men, circumscribed by their biological role. But the violent and public actions of the suffragettes transgressed society's most essential ideas about women, and made a complete break with social conventions as well as laws: they were destroyers, not nurturers; they were physically violent, rather than pacific and passive; they acted collectively and publicly, rather than individually and domestically. The suffragettes' actions seemed to be a fulfillment of the worst nightmares of the doomsayers of the 1890s; their actions shattered gender definitions, and threw the public's ideas about femininity and masculinity into confusion.[31] In response, the male government acted in ways that increasingly seemed, at the very least, unchivalrous, and at their most extreme, violent and sadistic. Forcible feedings continued to be the answer to the suffragettes' hunger strikes, until the infamous Cat and Mouse Act was instituted, which allowed ailing prisoners to be released, while claiming the right to rearrest them when their health was restored. During the years 1913 and 1914, a war between the sexes truly was being waged in England.

An organized anti-suffrage campaign had begun in 1908, founded by the novelist Mrs Humphry Ward, among others, and many supporters of women's suffrage hailed it as proof of the growing power of the suffrage movement. Another proof of that power – or, at least, of the level of anxiety and confusion generated by the militants – was the numerous negative depictions of suffragettes which began to appear in Edwardian fiction in the years before the war. The stereotype these depictions promulgated – that of the ugly, sexless and neurotic spinster/suffragette – was well known to readers of *Punch* and daily newspapers. In the early years of the militant movement the Pankhursts, and novelists like Robins and De Pratz, had worked to counteract such stereotypes by emphasizing the suffragettes' traditional femininity, despite the evident ideological contradictions of such tactics. But the negative stereotypes persisted, in part because they offered comfort to those who simply could not believe that an attractive, 'feminine' woman would want to break windows or burn down a house in order to get the vote. These stereotypes reasserted

traditional gender definitions, and reassured the public that the suffragettes were not *real* women but social misfits – mannish, abnormal and
obsessed.

Most of these negative depictions in fiction are quite brief;[32] the
suffragette character is always presented as an outsider, and usually
humor is derived from her fanaticism and her 'unsexed' appearance. The
suffragettes in E.V. Lucas's *Mr. Ingleside* (1910) compare their bruises and
wail when they hear of a comrade's marriage; their leader, Miss Custer,
hates men and craves power more than the vote. The heroine of Compton
Mackenzie's *Carnival* (1912) turns to the suffrage movement when she is
jilted, in order to get 'revenge upon the opposite sex', but she is repulsed
by the ugly clothes and bad complexions of the suffragettes, 'whose
antipathy towards men seemed to be founded on an inability to attract the
hated male'; she soon abandons this 'ineffectual aggregation of Plain
Janes'. One of the most antagonistic treatments of the movement occurs
in a short story by Saki: it presents 'an unrecorded episode in Roman
history', in which the Emperor is gleefully entertained when a menagerie
of wild beasts set upon the protesting 'Suffragetae' who have invaded the
Imperial Circus.

But it was not only male writers who promoted stereotypes and
criticized the suffrage movement. The popular romance novelist, Marie
Corelli, was moved to write an anti-suffrage pamphlet, *Woman or
Suffragette: A Question of Rational Choice* (1907), in which she condemned
the 'loose conduct and coarse speech' of the suffragettes, and warned of
the dangers of women giving up 'the birthright of their simple
womanliness'.[33] Julia Frankau, a well-respected novelist who wrote under
the name Frank Danby, portrayed the suffrage movement as a pernicious
enemy of domestic happiness in her novel *Joseph in Jeopardy* (1912).

The best-known anti-suffrage work of fiction was Mrs Ward's *Delia
Blanchflower* (1914). Most famous for her religious novel *Robert Elsmere*
(1888), she was a well-respected and popular novelist as well as an ardent
anti-suffragist. Mrs Humphry Ward wrote numerous articles attacking
the idea of women's suffrage until 1918, the year the vote was given to
women over the age of thirty. She opposed women's suffrage in her
novels as well, although in a far more moderate tone than her non-fiction
pieces; like the suffrage writers, Ward strove to attract the reading public,
not to alienate them, and in *Delia Blanchflower* she allows her characters to
voice a fairly wide range of opinion concerning women's suffrage.[34] But
unlike the suffrage novelists, Ward's conservative agenda allowed her to
work with rather than against traditional narrative patterns and modes of
characterization; she strives to persuade her readers not by articulating
anti-suffrage arguments but by satisfying their narrative expectations
through the domestication of her suffragette heroine.

Delia Blanchflower is the story of a beautiful twenty-two-year-old woman who is caught up in the suffragette movement through the influence of her tutor, Gertrude Marvell. She eventually becomes torn between her devotion to Gertrude and the cause, and her growing feelings for Mark Winnington, the executor of her late father's estate and her legal guardian. The narrative is basically that of an anti-courtship novel, and Ward employs that genre's typical rhetoric of the natural and the unnatural when she analyzes her heroine's choice of allegiances. Delia runs away from Mark when she realizes she has fallen in love with him, only to see later that she has turned from a 'natural' impulse toward life in order to ally herself with 'unnatural' forces of destruction and death. This realization is confirmed when Gertrude is killed in the act of burning down the ancient English manor house of an anti-suffrage MP.

In the traditional fashion of a Victorian novel, the bad woman is punished by death and the good woman is rewarded with marriage, for Delia subsequently decides to marry Mark. Although she declares that she is now a 'Suffragist' instead of a 'Suffragette', there is no indication that her new life will allow for political activism, and the whole issue of suffrage is reduced to an abstract idea which cannot compete with Delia's 'thirst for individual happiness, personal joy': Ward confidently asserts that Delia, by choosing marriage, 'was thereby best serving her sex and her race in the fore-ordained ways of destiny' (362).

Ward's manipulation of traditional ideas of essential womanliness to prove her anti-suffrage case demonstrates how antagonistic that ideology is to feminism, even though it was advocated by suffragettes and suffragists alike. Women are praised for their special abilities and characteristics, but always with an eye on the limits of those abilities and 'nature's intentions in endowing women with them:

> [Mark's] admiration for women was mingled indeed often with profound pity; pity for the sorrows and burdens that nature laid upon them, for their physical weakness, for their passive role in life. That beings so hampered could yet play such tender and heroic parts was to him perennially wonderful . . . (35)

Through the development of Delia's attraction to Mark, and through a curious interlude in which her natural nurturing abilities are aroused through the illness of her faithful maid, Delia comes to realize her female 'destiny'.[35] It is Delia's physical beauty which marks her as a good and womanly woman; Ward emphasizes that for Delia to use her beauty to attract followers to the suffrage movement rather than to continue her race is perverted and wrong. Influence and social work are offered as acceptable outlets for women with an impulse toward reform, but Ward argues that to do anything more of a public or political nature would entail neglecting those very abilities and functions for which women are specially intended.

To further her point, Ward must demonstrate that the suffragettes are 'unnatural' and 'unwomanly'. She does so in the usual fashion: by depicting them as unattractive, straight-figured, and plainly dressed; one is physically crippled, another is mannish, all lack Delia's beauty and fullness of form. Ward also demonstrates the unnaturalness of the suffragettes by using their personal backgrounds to undermine their commitment instead of to justify it: because of her family or her looks or her social class, each one is bitter about her lot in life. Ward depicts their communality as abnormal and pathetic; they are together only because no one else will have them. Although she is never explicit, Ward also hints that the absence of men leads to the development of passionate relationships between the suffragettes.

Whereas feminist suffrage writers worked to blur the lines between domestic and public spheres, and between personal and political actions, Ward's strategy is to emphasize the necessity of such divisions. Delia longs to redecorate her country home, but Gertrude, who has littered it with telegrams, papers and suffrage pamphlets, criticizes Delia's desire for domestic comfort and beauty as a stereotypically feminine waste of time. The suffragettes also take over Delia's London apartment, and Ward offers the fact that they make it indistinguishable from an office and leave Delia with no private living quarters as the ultimate indictment of the depraved nature of the suffragettes. Ward links this confusion of private and public with the suffragettes' confusion about gender roles, and condemns their refusal to respect socially ordained boundaries.

Ward makes her sympathies most pervasively evident by allying the narrative voice of *Delia Blanchflower*, in tone and philosophy, with the main character in the novel – who is Mark, not Delia. As an older man, as the legal representative of Delia's father, and as a lover of 'all that was ancient and deep-rooted', Mark is the patriarchy incarnate and idealized; it is interesting that as Delia's love for him grows, Ward's descriptions of her increasingly focus on the 'childlike' nature of her features and attitudes. Along with the emergence of Delia's 'softness' and vulnerability comes her recognition that patriarchal politics and social arrangements are not only naturally right, but are necessary for the health and stability of the nation.

This latter point is most blatantly made at the climax of the novel, when a little girl (who also happens to be crippled and working-class) in search of her father enters the house set ablaze by Gertrude, and is killed. Gertrude's last words are 'The child! – the child!', which Ward describes as 'that wail of a fierce and childless woman – that last cry of nature in one who had defied Nature – of womanhood in one who had renounced the ways of womanhood' (410). The symbolic implications of the scene are overwhelmingly obvious: the unnatural woman, in destroying the house of the patriarchal tradition, also destroys the future of the child, who, as a representative of all the weak members of society – women, the handicapped, the poor – is clearly in need of the patriarch's help. But in the final pages of the novel, the narrator offers reassurance that such destructive behavior will have no permanent effects: Delia and Mark will have their own children, and although the militant suffrage movement continues, it will ultimately be seen as 'but a backward ripple on the vast and ceaseless tide of human efforts toward a new and nobler order' (411).

Delia Blanchflower is the only Edwardian novel that depicts the final and most violent stage of the militant suffrage movement, when the WSPU had evolved into a desperate guerrilla group committed to arson and other illegal activities. For an insider's view of those activities, or for any sympathetic insight into women like Gertrude Marvell, one must turn to memoirs written many years later; but those memoirs, for the most part, tend to depict militant actions of the suffragettes in a briskly impersonal fashion, and they certainly never address Mrs Ward's insinuations about lesbian relationships among them.[36] In the first issue of his avant-garde journal *Blast*, published in June 1914, Wyndham Lewis issued a boldly printed message to the militant suffragettes: 'WE ADMIRE YOUR ENERGY. YOU AND ARTISTS ARE THE ONLY THINGS (YOU DON'T MIND BEING CALLED THINGS?) LEFT IN ENGLAND WITH A LITTLE LIFE IN THEM.' But unfortunately, the militants' life and energy were never translated into fiction during the Edwardian age.

The militant suffrage movement came to an abrupt halt in August 1914, when World War I broke out. The images of the movement which have endured come almost exclusively from its sensational final years, and consist for the most part of variations on the negative stereotypes of 'unsexed' and hysterical spinster-suffragettes which were promoted in fiction and in the popular press by writers opposed to women's suffrage.[37] The reluctance or inability of pro-suffrage writers to depict the suffragettes' violent actions left a large part of the story of the suffrage movement untold, and it is difficult not to speculate on the numerous missed opportunities of the period. Because writers downplayed personal relationships in order to fight the dominance of the romance plot, they rarely had a chance to develop their depictions of female friendships and female communities. With the exception of Colmore's *Suffragette Sally*, the complexities of negotiating between political commitment and personal relations were also not examined in fiction. Finally, the radical subject of women's desire for power, and women's potential for violent and destructive behavior in their quest for that power, was never seriously explored. Elizabeth Robins's vision of a new, heroic body of literature written from a woman's standpoint remained unfulfilled.

There were many Edwardian feminists, most notably Rebecca West and other contributors to *The Freewoman*, who supported the idea of women's suffrage but criticized the focus and the tactics of the militant movement. They wrote numerous articles which analyzed the roots of women's subjugation and emphasized the importance of looking at other, more pervasive social and political changes that were needed as much as, if not more than, women's suffrage. They were particularly critical of the suffragettes' manipulation of an outmoded and restrictive ideology of essential femininity and sexual purity. But suffrage fiction declined to partake of these debates. Just as the suffrage movement tended to fixate on the single goal of the vote, so suffrage fiction was seldom able to deviate from its explicit purpose into critiques of gender, sexuality or marriage. These topics were relegated to other Edwardian fictional genres such as the marriage problem novel or the spinster novel.

Only rarely did writers look at the particular impact of the suffrage movement upon sexual relations between men and women, or upon a woman's or a man's own sense of their sexuality or personal power. In West's short story 'Indissoluble Matrimony', published in the first issue of *Blast*, the burgeoning political power of women is seen from a man's point of view. With dark humor, West depicts the terror and loathing of a husband who thinks that his wife is growing in physical size and sexual voraciousness as she gains prominence as a political speaker. In *Sons and Lovers* (1913) Lawrence considers the connection between feminism and marital discord through the character of Clara Dawes, who is a suffragette. But for the most part, Edwardian suffrage fiction avoided subjects which would complicate the public's perception of an already controversial movement.

It is important to keep in mind, however, that it was not the intention of suffrage writers to explore the complexities or conflicts of the suffrage movement, nor did they set out to be formally innovative. Their fiction had a purpose, an explicit function in the world – to record, to persuade, to convert, and ultimately to effect social and political change. Good and bad had to be clearly delineated, and the message had to be made palatable, without betraying the basic aims of the movement; ambiguity and intricacy were antithetical to the project of the suffrage writer. Although most of these writers probably considered themselves artists, they were concerned with art not for its own sake but in terms of how it would help them to promote their cause.

By focusing outward toward social and political problems which could be addressed actively, suffrage writers were able to turn away from the self-blame and guilt that characterized (and paralyzed) the New Woman characters of the 1890s. But in their avoidance of introspective or psychological fiction they remained distanced from important literary developments concerning subjectivity, consciousness, and point of view that would soon be essential components of modernist fiction. The suffrage writers' commitment to documentary reportage also limited the temporal range of their narratives, and precluded any extended development of characters or relationships. In a way, they can be seen as martyrs to their cause: they sacrificed themselves as writers for what they saw as a larger purpose. They were limited by the topicality of their subject matter, and guided by the needs of the movement rather than the literary developments of their age. When the movement died, their fiction died with it.

But it is necessary to look beyond the limitations of the suffrage writers and the sense of unfulfilled promise that pervades their fiction in order to appreciate the significance of their accomplishments. Their writings are, first of all, valuable historical documents. In a way that is unparalleled by newspaper reports or memoirs, suffrage fiction communicates a sense of what it was actually like to be part of the movement in its early years – how it felt to march in demonstrations, to speak at rallies, to be arrested, to be imprisoned, to feel a growing sense of sisterhood and empowerment and purpose. Although it is only a partial picture, these writers did, as Robins urged them to, record the suffragettes' 'Great Adventure' for future generations.

The work of the suffrage writers is also important for its revelation of the ways in which it is possible to write about women apart from traditional narratives of romance and marriage. Although they were not interested in formal experimentation in and of itself, these writers found that the traditional narrative structures and modes of characterization they had inherited were based upon and perpetuated the very social structures they wished to change. As a result, they were forced to be formally innovative in order to tell their stories about suffragettes and the suffrage movement. Their most essential battle was against the tyranny of the romance plot; in its place, suffrage writers substituted a type of quest narrative, and romantic desire was either omitted entirely or made subordinate to the desire to win the vote. By basing their narratives on actual events, the suffrage writers created episodic, non-linear narratives; each event perhaps allowed the suffragettes to circle in closer to their goal, but the achievement of that goal remained profoundly indeterminate. Because of their link with an actual movement which was still in progress, the narratives of suffrage fiction had to remain inconclusive. But in a more pervasive way, it was necessary for these novels to be openended because conventional closure would entail privileging stasis over change, or reinforcing the status quo, and would thus undermine the aims of the movement. The suffrage writers refused to give narrative satisfaction where there was none in real life.

In order to convey the multiplicity of the movement, the suffrage writers employed multiple narratives, through either short-story collections or multi-plot novels. In order to convey the collectivity of the movement they interconnected their various narratives, using the movement in general, and demonstrations and prison cells in particular, to bring their disparate heroines together. These interconnections between various narratives also allowed some suffrage writers to defy the ideology of separate spheres, both formally and thematically. By declining to give their heroines either/or choices between feminist activism and marriage, by placing political discussions in private contexts, by giving personal motives to public actions, both Colmore in *Suffragette Sally* and Maud in *No Surrender* worked to break down the traditional divisions that reinforce gender polarization and keep women subordinate. Boundaries of class are also challenged in these works, for women of different classes serve as heroines and work together for a common cause.

By refusing to make romance or marriage the heroine's primary desire, by refusing to characterize a woman by her physical attributes, by refusing linear narrative development leading to resolution, stasis, and the reinstatement of the status quo, by refusing to isolate fiction from the realities of political struggles, by refusing traditional gender roles and class divisions, and by refusing sexual reticence, suffrage writers made a significant break with literary traditions and the prevailing ideologies of British society. Thus, ironically, suffrage fiction, which of all Edwardian fiction is the least conscious of its place in literary history (as opposed to social and political history), prefigures some of the most important formal and ideological innovations of modernist fiction.

CHAPTER FIVE

New Wine, New Bottles: H.G. Wells and May Sinclair

All through the early 'nineties, . . . there was a rebel undertow of earnest and aggressive writing and reading, supported chiefly by women and supplied very largely by women, which gave the lie to the prevailing trivial estimate of fiction. Among readers, women and girls and young men at least will insist upon having their novels significant and real, and it is to these perpetually renewed elements in the public that the novelist must look for his continuing emancipation from the wearier and more massive influences at work in contemporary British life.

(H.G. WELLS, 'The Contemporary Novel' [1914])

And it seems to me that the first step toward life is to throw off the philosophic cant of the nineteenth century. I don't mean that there is no philosophy of Art, or that if there has been there is to be no more of it; I mean that it is absurd to go on talking about realism and idealism, or objective or subjective art, as if the philosophies were sticking where they stood in the eighties . . . criticism up until now has been content to think in *clichés*, missing the new trend of the philosophies of the twentieth century. All that we know of reality at first-hand is given to us through contacts in which those interesting distinctions are lost. Reality is thick and deep, too thick and too deep, and at the same time too fluid to be cut with any convenient carving knife. The novelist who would be close to reality must confine himself to this knowledge at first-hand.

(MAY SINCLAIR, 'The Novels of Dorothy Richardson' [1918])

Two of the best-known feminist novelists of the Edwardian age were H.G. Wells and May Sinclair. Despite the enormous differences in their fiction, they are linked by their common interest in feminism and their self-conscious modernity. Both Wells and Sinclair were highly attuned to the social, political and literary developments of their age, and responded to them in their fiction. Wells was an active member of the Fabian Society, while Sinclair was a supporter of the suffrage movement. Both wrote many works of non-fiction – Wells on political and social reform, Sinclair on philosophy and psychoanalysis. As bestselling novelists they were part of the literary establishment, but they also had numerous friends among the literary avant-garde. Both Wells and Sinclair were absorbed by the need to break with Victorian values and traditions and they wrote novels that were aggressively modern in their subject matter, their attitudes and their morality. In particular, in their Edwardian novels they were consistently concerned with the most controversial issues associated with women and feminism: they wrote about female sexuality, the marriage problem, adultery, pregnancy and contraception, and did so with a degree of frankness that made them notorious, albeit in quite different ways.

In the fiction of both Wells and Sinclair one can see a growing awareness of the ideological implications of fictional form, and a subsequent effort to find a form that is appropriate to their subject matter. Nowhere in Edwardian fiction are the pressures which modern content and feminist ideology exerted on traditional fictional forms and the concomitant restrictions imposed on fictional content by formal conventions more evident than in their novels. Both authors engaged in the quintessential Edwardian struggle of trying to put new wine into old bottles; but ultimately, only Sinclair recognized the inevitable necessity of creating new bottles.

Wells praised the modern novel as 'the only medium through which we can discuss the great majority of the problems which are being raised . . . by our contemporary social development'. It was the content of his fiction that mattered to Wells, and he often emulated 'the lax freedom of form, the rambling discursiveness, the right to roam' of early English novels in order to express his ideas to the fullest.[1] At times, Wells demonstrated his awareness of the limitations of conventional narrative structures by commenting on them self-consciously within his fiction, as he does in *Tono-Bungay* (1909) and *The Wife of Sir Isaac Harman* (1914) (both of which, significantly, have unconventional, indeterminate endings). But more often than not, he would plunge into the writing of a novel with little consideration for questions of form.

Sinclair, in contrast, was highly aware of the structure of her fiction, and was constantly trying out new narrative forms and prose styles, assimilating the innovations of other novelists, and adapting them to suit her needs. She has been criticized for following trends and not developing her own organic style, but such complaints ignore the fact that Sinclair was one of the few Edwardian novelists who responded to the pressures being exerted upon the novel with formal experimentation.[2] She moved beyond the modern content she shared with Wells, and sought new narrative structures and styles with which to express it.

NEW WINE: H.G. WELLS

Wells's *Ann Veronica* (1909) is perhaps the best-known and certainly the most notorious of all Edwardian novels written about feminism's impact on modern women. This story of a young woman who leaves her father's home to live on her own in London, and subsequently runs off with her married biology professor, was banned by circulating libraries, censured from pulpits, and condemned by critics. The extremely negative and often hysterical reviews which the novel received recalled the critical denunciations of the New Woman novels of the 1890s, especially in terms of the personal nature of the condemnations.[3] In general, the critics' distress stemmed from the fact that not only did Wells depict Ann Veronica as having sexual desires, but that he characterized those desires as healthy and natural; departing from nineteenth-century novelistic tradition, Wells declined to make Ann Veronica 'pay' for her sexuality, or for her adulterous relationship with her professor, Capes. But as Wells explained in his *Experiment in Autobiography*:

> the particular offense was that Ann Veronica was a virgin who fell in love and showed it, instead of waiting, as all popular heroines had hitherto done, for someone to make love to her. It was held to be an unspeakable offence that an adolescent female should be sex-conscious before the thing was forced upon her attention. But Ann Veronica wanted a particular man who excited her and she pursued him and got him. With gusto. (395)

Despite Wells's claim to originality, *Ann Veronica* clearly followed in the tradition of the New Woman novels of the 1890s, and critics were quick to use such an association to deride the book. Ironically, Wells himself had written a harshly critical review of Grant Allen's *The Woman Who Did* in 1895, although he focused his attack on its aesthetic failings, particularly with regard to the characterization of the heroine. But the majority of Allen's critics, and subsequently Wells's, centered their criticisms upon what they saw as the immorality of the novels; in 1909, as in 1895, many critics wrote with the assumption that fiction influenced life, and novels which depicted rebellion and female sexuality threatened social stability.

One critic went so far as to assert that *Ann Veronica* was 'capable of poisoning the minds of those who read it'.[4]

In the case of Wells, however, critics had good reason to make such associations between fiction and life. In 1908 Wells had embarked on an affair with the novelist Amber Reeves, who was a student at Cambridge at the time; she became pregnant, and since Wells was unwilling to leave his wife, Catherine, Reeves entered into a marriage of convenience with a college friend. The affair in itself was profoundly shocking to Wells's friends and fellow members of the Fabian Society (Reeves was the daughter of two prominent members); but to make the affair public by writing a novel based upon it was for many a breach of decorum never to be forgiven.[5] Incredibly, Wells persisted in this mode, and in 1910 he published *The New Machiavelli*, a novel which also made use of the Reeves affair and contained thinly veiled caricatures of Sidney and Beatrice Webb, two of the founders of the Fabian Society who greatly disapproved of his sexual conduct.

Although the sexual frankness of *Ann Veronica* can be traced to the influence of New Woman novels, the novel is grounded firmly in the Edwardian era – not only in its historical setting, but in its feminist heroine and its narrative structure. The story of a well-educated young woman who is wary of the limitations of romance and marriage, and seeks a wider, more exciting sphere, *Ann Veronica* has much in common with the anti-courtship novels and feminist *Bildungsromane* which were emerging at the time; in particular, it resembles Forster's *A Room with a View*, which had been published the preceding year. Like Forster's heroine Lucy Honeychurch – but also like Sybylla in *My Brilliant Career*, or Hilda Lessways – Ann Veronica is a young woman who is impatient with what she calls her 'wrappered life' in a suburban home with her father and aunt: 'she was wildly discontented and eager for freedom and life . . . she wanted to live. She was vehemently impatient – she did not clearly know for what – to do, to be, to experience' (3–4). Like those other Edwardian heroines, Ann Veronica is an attractive woman, but far from idealized or stereotypically feminine. She is impulsive, skeptical and fallible; she plays field hockey and practices jujitsu, she loves to dissect things in the laboratory, and her speech is peppered with phrases like 'Ye gods' and 'Oh, damn'.

Like other Edwardian anti-courtship novels and *Bildungsromane*, *Ann Veronica* focuses on the years between adolescence and marriage. The trend at the turn of the century toward marrying later in life left young women with a significant period of time in which they lived, like Ann Veronica, 'a functionless existence varied by calls, tennis, selected novels, and dusting in her father's house' (5). The conventional expectation was that this 'state of suspended animation' would end when the right man came along and proposed (28). But not only did this situation prompt young women to seek more satisfying ways to spend their time, through higher education or social activism, but it also precipitated a questioning of marriage itself. Ann Veronica is thoroughly unimpressed with marriage as experienced by her two older sisters, and early in the novel she rejects two proposals. But Wells deviates from the usual pattern of the anti-courtship novel by making it clear that Ann Veronica does not reject marriage because she is unnatural or fearful of sexuality; she simply has other more interesting things to do. And unlike most other Edwardian heroines, when Ann Veronica finally does rebel, she does so with a very specific goal in mind which she is determined to achieve – she wants to study biology at Imperial College at Westminster.

Thus the narrative of *Ann Veronica* is not based upon the oppositional impetus typical of the anti-courtship novel, in which the heroine tries to escape from romance; rather, it is centered upon a positive search for knowledge and independence, characteristic of the *Bildungsroman*. Wells curbs his tendency to make polemical authorial statements by allowing his characters to make his points for him, and he allows the reader to experience Ann Veronica's intellectual and emotional growth by giving her extended interior monologues. Until the end of the novel, Wells's primary focus is on Ann Veronica as an individual, not as part of a romantic relationship, and the result is a remarkably lively character who is articulate about her rebellion and self-conscious about her feminism in a fashion unlike any other Edwardian heroine, with the exception of Franklin's Sybylla.

Although Ann Veronica does get to attend classes at Imperial College, most of her education occurs outside the classroom, and much of it has to do with sex. As befits a biologist, Ann Veronica's attitude toward sex is one of frank curiosity. She refuses to accept the Victorian morality of her father and aunt, which values sexual ignorance, and turns to modern literature and her anatomy textbook for information. But when Ann Veronica moves to London, she discovers that what seems so interesting and liberating in theory can in reality be restrictive. On her first afternoon in the city she wanders through the streets feeling wonderfully liberated, imagining herself to be Shaw's Vivie Warren. But her idyll is destroyed by a middle-aged man who propositions her, and then follows her: 'now no longer dreaming and appreciative, but disturbed and unwillingly observant', Ann Veronica realizes that she can no longer enjoy 'that delightful sense of free, unembarrassed movement' (81). Similarly, she is pleased by the friendship (as well as the financial assistance) that Mr Ramage, an older, married man, offers her, only to discover that he expects to be repaid with sex. Ann Veronica quickly learns that her personal sense of autonomy does not significantly alter her position in the world, or how she is perceived by others; in the eyes of men, she remains an object, to be desired and owned.

Ann Veronica's quest for independence is impeded in other ways: she has great difficulty finding an apartment that she can afford and which will accept single women, and she is unable to find work, having been left utterly unqualified for any job by her education. Not surprisingly, she turns to the suffrage movement in her indignation about her treatment in the wider world, but is quickly put off by the narrowness of its scope. In response to Ann Veronica's queries about dealing with the issues of economic inequities and personal prejudice, the suffrage leader Miss Brett replies, 'with bright contagious hopefulness, "Everything will follow"' (189). But an even greater source of disillusionment for Ann Veronica is the feeling of sex-antagonism she encounters in the suffragettes. This aspect of the movement is embodied in her friend, Miss Miniver, who cites outrageous biological theories of female supremacy and finds men repulsive. Miss Miniver tells Ann Veronica: 'maternity has been our undoing', and when she is asked if she desires the love of a man, she goes on at length about 'the horrible coarseness':

> 'Bodies! Horrible things! We are souls. Love lives on a higher plane. We are not animals. . . . We do not want the men . . . with their sneers and loud laughter. . . . Brutes! . . . Science some day may teach us a way to do without them. It is only the women matter.' (144)

But Ann Veronica has her own biological theories – theories which support her liking of men, despite the bad experiences she has had: she feels that '[bodies] are the most beautiful things in the world'. Wells sets up a dichotomy between the unnatural, life-denying sex-antagonism of the suffragettes and the natural, life-affirming sexual desire that Ann Veronica has begun to feel for her professor, Capes, and there is little doubt what choice healthy, well-adjusted Ann Veronica will make. While she is in prison after being arrested during a raid on Parliament, she makes the decision to let biology rather than feminism be her guide:

> 'A woman wants a proper alliance with a man, a man who is better stuff than herself. She wants that and needs it more than anything else in the world. It may not be just, it may not be fair, but things are so. It isn't law, nor custom, nor masculine violence settled that. It's just how things happen to be. She wants to be free – she wants to be legally and economically free, so as not to be subject to the wrong man; but only God, who made the world, can alter things to prevent her being slave to the right one.' (206)

As this speech demonstrates, Wells shifts the direction of the narrative in an astonishing fashion at this point: what had appeared to be a feminist

Bildungsroman is revealed to be a romance narrative after all. The reversal is similar to the one which occurs in Edwardian anti-courtship novels, where the heroine, after spending most of the novel rejecting romance, comes to realize that romance and marriage are the rightful, the natural – indeed, the only – narratives for her. In *Ann Veronica*, romantic love, which the heroine previously considered merely a possible component of a multifaceted life, is elevated to 'the supreme affair in life ... woman's one event and crisis that makes up for all her other restrictions' (142). However, just as Forster did in *A Room with a View*, Wells characterizes his heroine's decision to accept her natural destiny as a feminist and socially subversive act rather than an embrace of the status quo. Ann Veronica is the one who first declares her love, not Capes, and the fact that he is a married man makes their elopement to the Alps a bold rejection of social and legal conventions. For Ann Veronica, to base one's actions on sexual feelings rather than traditional moral codes or political theories seems the ultimate liberation – one which, in a paradoxical way, accepts the primitive as the supreme expression of the new: looking forward to her future life with Capes, she thinks: 'Modern indeed! She was going to be primordial as chipped flint!' (260).

Ann Veronica and Capes's time together in the Alps supports her view that sexual liberation is the path to feminist fulfillment. As they hike in the mountains, they enjoy an idyll of sexual equality, for they travel as comrades, dressing alike, sharing burdens and physical activity, and ensure Ann Veronica's freedom by practicing contraception; they declare that they are 'equal', each 'the real, identical other' (284). But the 'honeymoon' must end, and the couple must leave the freedom of Europe to establish a life together in England. In *A Room with a View*, Forster avoided the problem of the 'after' by ending his novel with Lucy and George's Italian honeymoon. But Wells, in the final chapter of *Ann Veronica*, depicts the daily domestic life of Ann Veronica and Capes four years after their elopement and, in so doing, exposes the inconsistencies in his narrative and his feminism.

Before the final scene, all Ann Veronica's movements have been away from enclosed spaces toward openness, and in particular toward the natural world. She escapes from her locked bedroom, and from her father's suburban house, to experience the wide-ranging possibilities of London. Other traps await her there: she lives in a tiny rented room; she is nearly raped in a small private dining-room; she travels to a raid on Parliament in a furniture van, which results in her spending time in a prison cell. But all those various enclosures serve to convince her that what she desires is an open, natural place – both literally and spiritually. Throughout most of the novel this is represented by the biology lab: it is described several times as a pleasant, large, open room full of light and air; it is there that she pursues the scientific studies she loves, and it is there that she tells Capes she loves him. Their escape to the Alps provides them with the perfect setting for their free love and their frankness. But the narrative logic of this pattern of enclosure and escape is violated by Wells's conclusion, in which he places Capes and Ann Veronica in a tiny urban apartment. Although the tone of the final chapter indicates that Wells intended the ending to be read as a happy one, it is undermined by its cramped domestic setting.

Ann Veronica and Capes are now married, Capes having got a divorce; Ann Veronica is expecting their first child. Capes has given up science for a successful career as a playwright, but there is no explanation as to why Ann Veronica is no longer involved with science. She is completely absorbed in the realm of domesticity and dusting that she was so wild to escape. But even though it appears that Ann Veronica has run away from her father's home only to find its equivalent, it is clear that for Wells, what transforms this domestic sphere and makes it desirable is sex. Like Forster in *A Room with a View*, Wells is trying to depict a new kind of marriage, based on sexual attraction and equality. Ann Veronica is not 'tied and dull and inelastic' (58), like other married women she has observed; hers is a 'hot-blooded marriage' (49), and that, we are to believe, makes all the difference.

But it is difficult to accept that all Ann Veronica's inchoate yearnings for freedom and fulfillment, all her dreams of education and financial independence, could be so easily transmuted into a simple desire for love and sex. Instead, it seems as if the sexual imperative that once freed her has now limited her for ever; since she has classified herself in purely biological terms, the only role available to her now is the biological one of mother. In Ann Veronica's final happy/sad speech, she looks back over the past four years as if her life is coming to an end, and mourns that

'the great time is over, and I have to go carefully and bear children . . . and when I am done with that I shall be an old woman. The petals have fallen – the red petals we loved so. We're hedged about with discretions – and all this furniture – and successes.' (295)

Despite Wells's efforts to the contrary, when Ann Veronica's father and aunt arrive to have dinner and give their approval to her marriage, it seems that what has ultimately triumphed is not sexual equality and passion, but the status quo.

The awkwardness of the ending was evident to all Wells's contemporary critics, both pro and con, but the general feeling was that the final chapter constituted a 'fairy tale ending to a work that is otherwise a study of reality'.[6] No one commented on the contradictions inherent in Ann Veronica's abrupt limitation of her aspirations, and no one considered that the fairy tale was Capes's (and Wells's) but not Ann Veronica's.

It was certainly daring and new for Wells to equate women's liberation with sexual fulfillment, but most feminists viewed such an equation with skepticism: conservative feminists had no interest in undermining the institution of marriage; radical feminists were suspicious of anything having to do with men, especially sexual intercourse; and in general, Edwardian feminism was far more concerned with specific, practical reforms such as women's suffrage. But Wells, in all his visions of the future and all his plans for social reform, downplayed the political, economic and social (as distinct from sexual) significance of women's liberation.[7] Although his characterization of the predatory Ramage indicates that he was well aware of how men could manipulate feminism for their own ends, he was remarkably unaware of how self-centered his own insistence on the primacy of sexual freedom was. It is telling that the narrative point of view starts to pull away from Ann Veronica after she has achieved her sexual liberation, for as far as Wells was concerned the narrative he was most interested in telling – that of a young woman discovering the joys of sexual love – ended at that point.

Once Ann Veronica declares her love for Capes, Wells subtly shifts his narrative focus to include more and more of him; he does this not by giving him comparable interiority to Ann Veronica, but by allowing him to dominate their dialogues with lengthy speeches. Capes is clearly a figure for Wells, and it is through him, not Ann Veronica, that Wells explicates his theories about sexual relations. Not only does this allow Wells to speak finally in his own voice, more or less (something he was notorious for in his fiction), it also allows him to avoid confronting a woman's perspective on sexual liberation and marriage with any intimacy or specificity. Although Ann Veronica's cheery matter-of-factness about sex is a welcome change from the sexual anxieties of the New Women of the 1890s, she deteriorates, by the end of the novel, into a psychologically flat and dissatisfying character. The reader is given no indication that Ann Veronica feels any fears or doubts about her sexual initiation, and she never questions her decision or thinks back on what she has given up to be with Capes. By distancing the reader from Ann Veronica, Wells tried to circumvent the contradictions involved in her acceptance of the domesticity and economic dependence she once railed against so vehemently. Only in the last chapter does she voice a few feelings of regret and confusion over the situation she has ended up in, but her discontent is written off as a symptom of her pregnancy.

It is ironic that despite Wells's desire to write a novel of feminist rebellion, and despite all the novel's scandalous advocacy of extramarital sex, *Ann Veronica* is just as conservative as Edwardian anti-courtship novels which oppose feminism, such as *Dodo the Second* and *Max*. This conservatism is due not just to the biological imperative of Wells's feminism but also to the traditional form of his fiction. Despite his promise to Henry James – 'I will seek earnestly to make my pen lead a decent life, pull myself together, think of Form' – the formal structure of his fiction tended to be the last thing Wells thought about as he became passionately engaged with his ideas.[8] So, as in many other Edwardian novels, Wells created a lively new kind of female character, an embodiment of modern feminism, and then did not know what to do with her. Rather than try to create a new ending for her that respected her feminist convictions and her scientific interests, or to acknowledge future possibilities by leaving the ending unresolved, Wells adopted without question the traditional either/or dichotomy which insists that women must choose between love and work, and resorted to the most conventional of novelistic endings – a happily-ever-after marriage.

The narrative shift in *Ann Veronica* epitomizes a recurrent moment in Edwardian fiction: the modern content strains the traditional form almost to the breaking point, and the author quickly grabs a convention in order to end the novel, rather than brave the exigencies of a break with tradition. Like Forster – who opted in three of his Edwardian novels for sudden and violent (and rather incredible) deaths in order to end his narratives – Wells's imagination fails him at the moment when he has gone the farthest – when the lovers reject their society's moral code and run away together. Although in *Tono-Bungay*, his pessimistic novel about the decay of the modern world, Wells saw the necessity of leaving the ending ominously indeterminate, in *Ann Veronica* he blithely opts for a traditional ending, seemingly unaware that it is also an ideological retreat.

Another of Wells's Edwardian novels about women – *The Passionate Friends* (1913) – is also troubled by a tension between its modern characters and themes, and its conventional narrative structure. In his famous correspondence with Wells about novels and novel-writing, James had warned him not to indulge in first-person narratives, and this novel confirms the wisdom of such a warning. Through Stephen Stratton, the protagonist of *The Passionate Friends*, Wells expounds at length on his theories of marriage, sexual jealousy, social organization, labor management and a number of other things, and it is thus no wonder that Lady Mary Justin, the married woman he loves, remains a cipher throughout. When she finally speaks in her own words, via a letter, they sound remarkably like Stratton's (and Wells's). At most, Mary is a useful illustration of Wells's ideas about women and marriage, and it is to this purpose that *The Passionate Friends* ends with her suicide, which is motivated ostensibly by her entrapment in a loveless marriage. But as with *Ann Veronica*, Wells apparently chose this retrograde ending without fully considering its implications. In seeking a dramatic conclusion to his discursive novel, he unintentionally reinforced the moral double standard which excuses men for their sexual behavior but insists that the woman must pay; literary tradition imbues Mary's death with unavoidable connotations of guilt and punishment.

The Passionate Friends is one of three novels that Wells wrote in the Edwardian period explicitly to address the issues of feminism and marriage. He referred to them as 'discussion-novels', and later dismissed them as being dated by their topical concerns:

> They had their function in their time but their time has already gone by. . . .
> They helped release a generation from restriction and that is about all they achieved. Aesthetically they have no great value. No one will ever read them for delight. (*Experiment* 392)

But by limiting them to their intended function, Wells failed to appreciate that two of his marriage discussion novels – *Marriage* (1912) and *The Wife of Sir Isaac Harman* – are not only fascinating historical documents that capture the temperament of his times with a unique specificity, but also richly textured and often wonderfully humorous novels whose modern heroines are presented with a degree of sympathy and psychological insight that was rare for the age.

At first glance, *Marriage* promises a richer and more intimate analysis of a woman's experience of marriage than *The Passionate Friends*. The titles of each of the three books of the novel – 'Marjorie Marries', 'Marjorie Married', and 'Marjorie at Lonely Hut' – lead one to assume that the focus will be on Marjorie, and the third-person narrative voice in the first third supports that assumption: it is linked almost exclusively with Marjorie, offering minute descriptions of her physical appearance and her thoughts as she rejects the fiancé endorsed by her parents and elopes with a handsome young scientist. Marjorie resembles Ann Veronica in her vivacity and independence, as well as her choice of husband, and *Marriage* can be seen as a kind of sequel to *Ann Veronica*; it depicts the drama of the problems of a young married couple after their rebellion has been transformed into domesticity. But just as Ann Veronica becomes overshadowed by Capes following her declaration of love for him, the narrative point of view in *Marriage* undergoes a subtle shift when Marjorie marries; titles notwithstanding, Marjorie's story and that of her marriage become subsumed within the story of her husband, Trafford, as he struggles to retain his integrity amidst the demands of modern life and modern marriage.

In *Marriage*, as in *Ann Veronica*, Wells demonstrates a remarkable imaginative sympathy with his heroine; no other male writer of the period created such intelligent, lively and complex female characters. But also as in *Ann Veronica*, a male character (whom Wells clearly identifies with and speaks through) gradually supplants the heroine at the center of the narrative. Certainly one reason for this is that Wells, as in *Ann Veronica*, could not stay away from center stage for an entire novel, and simply had to reassert himself in the figure of Trafford, as he did in that of Capes. But it is also important that Wells's sympathetic identification with Marjorie begins to fade when she becomes a wife, and then diminishes further when she becomes a mother. The scene in which Marjorie and Trafford's first child is born is striking for the fact that the birth is presented entirely through Trafford's reactions; one feels a purposeful resistance on Wells's part to entering into Marjorie's experience or offering her point of view. As with Ann Veronica, Wells finds Marjorie most intriguing when she is a rebel on the verge of sexual liberation; that accomplished, his interest in her fades.

But there is another possible explanation for Wells's retreat from psychological intimacy with Marjorie, and it can be found in *H.G. Wells in Love*, the 'Postscript' to his *Experiment in Autobiography*, in which he details his numerous extramarital love affairs. In it Wells praises his wife highly, and remembers her with great emotion, but there is a disquieting lack of perspective about her role in their unusual marital arrangement; there is virtually no imaginative speculation on what it was like to be the wife of H.G. Wells, particularly with regard to his sexual activities. This avoidance of consideration of Catherine's point of view was clearly necessary in order for Wells to maintain their arrangement without feeling guilty or uncertain. But it is interesting that in the novels which relate most closely to his relationship with his wife, Wells cannot continue his imaginative identification with his heroines into marriage and motherhood; not only was there the danger that he might have to confront Catherine's pain and sacrifice, there was also the chance that he would be forced to scrutinize his own behavior as a husband.

The first section of *Marriage* follows the pattern of a comic courtship plot. Trafford's plane crashes on to the lawn of the summer home Marjorie's family are renting, and he succeeds in rescuing her from her infantile and tyrannical father, and from her suitor, a humor writer named Mr Magnet. Trafford reminds Marjorie that they have met before, when he administered an exam at her school; he tells her that he had thought 'how certain it was that your brightness and eagerness would be swallowed up by some silly ordinariness or other – stuffy marriage or stuffy domestic duties. The old, old story...' (134). Marjorie almost succumbs to that old, old story, because she is in debt and Magnet is wealthy, but Trafford persuades her to choose a marriage based on romantic passion instead. The relationship between Marjorie and Trafford is presented as an ideal love match which contrasts with her stilted relationship with Magnet and the parody of marriage her ill-suited and unhappy parents enact. Trafford and Marjorie run away together, and begin what they believe will be a splendid new story; Trafford asks that Marjorie be 'his mate and equal' (230); he informs her that he is 'half-feminine' (134) and promises to try to understand her perspective.

The comic tone of the first part of the novel gradually fades as Wells turns his attention to the early years of Marjorie and Trafford's marriage. His psychologically acute charting of the subtle developments, adjustments and disillusionments of marriage is unparalleled in Edwardian fiction. Most marriage problem novels of the period criticize marriage by focusing on the dissatisfactions of one partner or the other, but rarely on both. With the exception of Sinclair, no other Edwardian writer besides Wells examined the actual dynamics of the marital relationship, the intimate give-and-take that characterizes daily married life. One of the reasons why Wells was able to do this in *Marriage* is that he completely avoided the subjects of adultery and sexual jealousy. These were his personal fixations, and their appearance in his fiction is always unbalanced and overbearing. But by making sexual compatibility and fidelity moot points in *Marriage*, Wells was able to escape from what Rebecca West called his 'sex obsession' and focus intensively upon the nature of the marital relationship itself, and its effect on the individuals involved.[9]

Before Wells turns his attention to the character of Trafford, he analyzes the responses of both Marjorie and Trafford to 'the most difficult and fatal phase in marriage' (273), when 'the sustaining magic of love' has been exhausted and 'the lovers face each other, disillusioned, stripped of the last shred of excitement – undisguisedly themselves' (274). Their romantic love has fulfilled its 'purpose' – their first child – and they are left to face 'the life-long consequences of their passionate association' (275). Trafford focuses on his scientific research, while Marjorie concentrates on creating a home and a social life; they both begin to feel a 'widening divergence' where there was once 'a complete sympathy of feeling, an almost instinctive identity of outlook' (275).

From Trafford's perspective, one of the greatest problems in their marriage is that Marjorie is always buying things for their home, and spending beyond their budget. Almost from the day they return from their honeymoon, she is envisioning how she wants the rooms in their house to look, and purchasing wall hangings and furniture and countless other items she persuades herself are essential. When Trafford discovers all the bills and the overdrafts Marjorie has hidden from him, he is horrified – not only because of the debt incurred, but also because he sees her spending as an indication of a kind of moral profligacy. But even though Marjorie occasionally seems as blindly irresponsible in her materialism as Emma Bovary or Rosamond Vincy, Wells clearly wants the reader to see her spending from her perspective, and to understand it as a symptom of a larger social imbalance.

For Marjorie, marriage means having 'time on her hands, superabundant imaginative energy, and no clear intimation of any occupation' (281). What seems on the surface to be vulgar consumerism is really an expression of her powerful desire to create beauty. Marjorie's intellectual and artistic abilities have no outlet other than what she can find at home, but even her decorating schemes are hampered by her husband's modest income. Wells uses the example of this frustrating waste of talent and energy to criticize the social and economic organization of England in the early twentieth century. For Trafford and Marjorie, as well as for

> thousands of young couples in London . . . the breadwinner was overworked, and the spending partner's duty was chiefly the negative one of not spending. You cannot consume your energies merely in not spending money. Do what she could, Marjorie could not contrive to make house and child fill her waking hours. (281)

Marjorie, conscious of the impulses behind her spending and frustrated by her economic dependence, is unable to come up with a solution, short of developing some national plan for the 'Endowment of Womanhood' (312).

Wells emphasizes how Marjorie's dilemma is peculiar to the period of transition in which she lives. Bored with domestic labor, most of which is taken care of by a servant anyway, and lacking the skills needed for work outside the home, aware of her uselessness but prevented from doing anything about it, Marjorie is trapped in the middle of a feminist revolution: 'Woman's come out of being a slave, and yet she isn't an equal. . . . We've had a sort of sham emancipation, and we haven't yet come to the real one' (415). Like so many other Edwardian heroines, Marjorie wants to reject the traditional narrative of a woman's life, but finds herself thwarted by the paucity of new narratives.

In search of something to do, Marjorie investigates various Movements which the narrator characterizes as 'absorbents of superfluous female energy' (284), and decides upon the suffrage movement ('one of the less militant sections') by a process of elimination rather than by preference. But after witnessing a meeting in their home, Trafford asks Marjorie to give up it up:

> Marjorie regarded him quietly for a moment. 'I must go on with something,' she said.
>   'Well, not this.'
>   'Then *what?*'
>   'Something sane.'

'Tell me what.'

'It must come out of yourself.'

Marjorie thought sullenly for a moment. 'Nothing comes out of myself,' she said.

'I don't think you realize a bit what my life has become,' she went on; 'how much I'm like some one who's been put in a pleasant, high-class prison. . . . It doesn't give me an hour's mental occupation in the day. It's all very well to say I might do more in it. I can't – without absurdity. Or expenditure. . . . You see, you've got a life – too much of it – *I* haven't got enough. I wish almost I could sleep away half the day. Oh! I want something *Real*, Rag; something more than I've got.' (295–6)

But Trafford never helps Marjorie to find anything real to take the place of the suffrage movement, and neither does Wells; it is at this point in the novel that he virtually abandons Marjorie's narrative in order to focus on Trafford. Having brought her to a difficult breaking point, he leaves her with no resources and little hope.

One of the keys to this strange shift in narrative point of view lies in the very Wellsian speech that Marjorie makes to her suffrage group. In it, she argues that 'the advancement of science, the progress of civilization, and the emancipation of women were nearly synonymous terms' (291). But clearly there is a hierarchy as well as a sequence to these three areas, and in both cases the women's cause ranks last. Wells was skeptical of work which placed the emancipation of women first, such as the suffrage movement; this is evident in his mockery (in all his Edwardian novels) of the suffragettes as a bunch of silly, humorless women in feathery hats, and his bracketing of the movement with such causes as dress reform, the encouragement of garden suburbs, and the prevention of animal food. He did not believe that women could make a difference on their own; and thus he turns from Marjorie's problems to Trafford's scientific work and social theories which, like the theories of Stratton in *The Passionate Friends*, are directed toward sweeping universal solutions which have very little to do with or say about the specific problems of women.

The narratorial bias toward Trafford is evident, however, even before this shift in focus occurs. He is defined predominantly by his educational background and his scientific research, and his dreams and his problems are always taken very seriously. Science is treated with reverence in the novel, and Wells just stops short of depicting Trafford as some kind of holy man. Marjorie, in contrast, has no abiding interest outside her marriage, her home and her children; her concerns are often mocked with gentle humor and condescending exclamations of 'Poor Marjorie!'. She is defined by her appearance and her possessions; we know everything about her, from the shape of her ears to the cost of her luggage, while the only thing we know about Trafford's physical personage is that he is tall.

Wells emphasizes that it is Trafford who suffers more from the disillusionment and compromises of married life: 'it was he who had made the greatest adaptations to the exigencies of their union . . . he had crippled . . . the research work upon which his whole being had once been set' (274). He perceives his life as a battle between the reality of Marjorie and his marriage, and 'this big wider thing' – his research. He believes that Marjorie – and in particular, her material needs – are 'destroying an essential thing in his life' (275). Trafford must give up research and become a corporate scientist in order to support his growing family. And as the babies come, one after another, Marjorie seemingly becomes an embodiment of the Shavian Life Force, destroying her man in her drive to reproduce. But Wells has developed the character of Marjorie too fully for her to dwindle to a mere emblem of the demands of the body and the material world. The glimpses he offers of her in the middle sections of the novel suggest that she too feels beaten and trapped by life; she too feels that the demands of marriage have forced her to prostitute herself. And when Trafford decides to isolate himself from the demands of work, society and family, and spend a year in the wilderness of Labrador in an attempt to save himself, she decides to go too.

Wells had first entertained the idea of retreat and renewal in *A Modern Utopia* (1905), a work of non-fiction in which he imagines that the world of the future will be governed by a group of 'voluntary noblemen' called the Samurai, who practice self-denial, and who,

> for seven consecutive days in the year, at least, . . . must go right out of the life of men into some wild or solitary place. . . . Partly, it is to ensure good training and sturdiness of body and mind, but partly, also, it is to draw [the minds of the Samurai] for a space from the insistent details of life . . . from personal quarrels and personal affections and the things of the heated room. (302–3)

Marjorie and Trafford deviate from the Samurai plan in that they go into solitude together, for they want to save their marriage as well as themselves. 'Personal quarrels' as well as gender distinctions become unimportant as they face the challenges of a winter wilderness together. Like Ann Veronica and Capes in the Alps, Marjorie and Trafford, once they are in Labrador, become equals in their dress, in their personal needs, and in their work; as they struggle to survive, they regain their 'instinctive identity of outlook'. Labrador frees Marjorie from the constraints of her life in London and the burden of her neurotic consumerism, and she thrives; at each camp site she discovers that some personal possession has become inessential, and leaves it behind.

In contrast to Marjorie, Trafford seems somewhat muted by the wilderness, for it distances him from the research and theories which form the core of his existence. But he is also muted because in this final, bizarre section of the novel the narrative focus switches again – temporarily – back to Marjorie. Perhaps Wells wanted to illustrate the shifting balance of power in marriage – how one partner is always dominant, even in the most equitable of relationships. Perhaps this shift is simply an example of how the novel is 'scandalously bad in form', as Wells apologized to James.[10] But it is equally possible that Wells was unable to suppress the fascinating character of Marjorie and, as an experiment of sorts, wanted to test the strength and integrity of a modern woman in a primitive environment – perhaps to see if a woman, too, could be a Samurai.

The test Wells devises for Marjorie is that Trafford is badly wounded by a lynx, far away from their hut; she must rescue him, nurse him back to health, and defend their home and food supply from wolves. Not only does this adventure call for considerable strength and bravery on the part of Marjorie, but the initial success of her rescue effort is almost completely reliant upon her skillful planning of exactly what items she will need in order to tend to Trafford and somehow get him back to the hut. It is through Marjorie's being 'as clear-minded and as self-possessed as a woman in a shop' (461) during the crisis that Trafford's life is saved. It becomes evident that no matter how neurotic Marjorie's affiliation to the material world had seemed in London, it derives in some fundamental way from a practical sense of life and survival. In contrast, Trafford's distance from the basic realities of life is underscored by his physical helplessness and his feverish ravings about how he will regenerate mankind through science. In the harsh environment of Labrador, Marjorie's prosaic concerns achieve transcendence over Trafford's utopian visions.

After three days Marjorie manages to get Trafford back to the hut, where she is surprised to discover that

> she was deeply happy. It was preposterous that she should be so, but those days of almost despairful stress were irradiated now by a new courage. She was doing this thing, against all Labrador . . . she was winning. It was a great discovery to her that hardship and effort almost to the breaking-point could ensue in so deep a satisfaction. She lay and thought how deep and rich life had become for her, as though . . . some unsuspected veil had been torn away.
> (473)

It is Marjorie, not Trafford, who has proved herself a Samurai, and in so doing she finally finds the 'something *Real*' she had searching for. But once again, in a way reminiscent of the conclusion of *Ann Veronica*, Wells turns his back on the exciting implications of Marjorie's new-found strength. Illogically, bewilderingly, Marjorie decides, after Trafford regains his health, that what she has learned from this incident is not independence but dependence; she has come to see that she is rightfully Trafford's 'squaw and body-servant':

> 'What are we women – half savages, half pets, unemployed things of greed and desire – and suddenly we want all the rights and respect of souls! . . . We needn't press upon you; we can save you from the instincts and passions that try to waste you altogether on us . . . . We can't *do* things. We don't bring things off. And you, you Monster! you Dream! you want to stick your hand out of all that is and make something that isn't, begin to be! That's the man –.'
> (488–9)

Initially, Trafford protests that she is going too far and generalizing too much, but before long he is espousing Marjorie's philosophy of the sexes to her as if it were his own: 'The women are the backbone of the race, men are just the individuals' (505). He decides to turn from the study of crystals to the study of men and women, and the final forty pages are dominated by his explanations of his new plan for the future of humanity; once again Marjorie recedes into the background.

Marriage follows the distinctive Edwardian pattern of rebellion and return, even though Wells tries to dress up the final return (that of Marjorie and Trafford to London) as the start of a new life. As in *Ann Veronica*, he links the modern and the new with the primitive, and implies that by escaping the jaded sensibilities of twentieth-century London and facing the challenges of life in the wilderness, Marjorie has gained insight into basic truths about the relations between the sexes. Wells claims, paradoxically, that Marjorie is freed by limiting herself to a distinctly female sphere, the function of which is to support men. Not only is her willing repression of her abilities and desires incredible, but Wells compounds the offense by reintroducing his theme of women's materialism. As Trafford's theories begin to take over the novel again, as well as his conversations with Marjorie, her private thoughts increasingly turn to how she will decorate their home to suit their new lives: she 'naturally' starts envisioning the paperweights and bookshelves and rugs that will provide a suitable environment for Trafford's work. Wells plays this divergence in plans for comedy, and reduces what was once the subject of a sensitive and sympathetic social analysis into the punch line of a sexist joke.

Why was Wells, the man who liked to look into the future and imagine new worlds, unable to imagine new narratives for the new women that he created? Why did he choose to write about women who are unusual and independent and strong, only to stifle all those qualities in the end? The contradictions in Wells are emblematic of the contradictions of the Edwardian period. He was fascinated by the unexplored potential of women, and excited by the women he knew who had escaped Victorian proprieties and restrictions; he even speculated occasionally about the role of the untapped energy and resources of women in the development of his world of the future. But Wells's challenges to the prevailing sexual ideology went only so far; he was clearly apprehensive about the restructuring of power relations and the necessity of personal redefinition that a radical departure from traditional gender roles would entail. In his social theories, in his fiction, and in his personal life, he flirted with the new while clutching the old.

Only in *The Wife of Sir Isaac Harman* was Wells able to solve the problems which trouble his other Edwardian novels about women and marriage; the heroine does not recede into the background, nor does she opt for a regressive marital relationship. For that reason, it is the most interesting and unusual of Wells's novels on the subject; it is also the funniest. It tells the story of Lady Harman, the young wife of a wealthy, elderly bakery and tea-shop magnate, who longs to escape from her marriage and do something meaningful with her life. Lady Harman is Wells's most satisfying feminist character; although her interest in feminism is more intuitive and less intellectual than that of Ann Veronica or Marjorie, she has the determination and the financial means to work actively for women's causes. She also makes the radical personal decision to reject the traditional closure of romance and marriage. The cohesiveness of the character of Lady Harman and the freshness of her narrative can be ascribed in part to the influence upon Wells at this time of two women, both of whom were novelists and both of whom had been his lovers: Amber Reeves and Elizabeth von Arnim.

In his 'Postscript' to *Experiment in Autobiography*, Wells explains that the model for Lady Harman was Amber Reeve's mother, who was forty when he first met her, and 'working out a sort of liberation for herself from the matrimonial flattening she had undergone' (71). Mrs Reeves found 'a curious sublimation of her secret rebellion against her husband' in the suffrage movement, and through her activities she was able to escape her husband's domineering control. Wells adopted this strategy for the heroine of *Wife*: Lady Harman counters her husband's tyranny by working to improve the living conditions of his female employees.

But this plot line raises the possibility that Wells was also influenced by Amber Reeves, for it is remarkably similar to that of her novel *A Lady and Her Husband*, which was published in the same year as *The Wife of Sir Isaac Harman*. Mary, the heroine of Reeves's novel, feels unfulfilled in her marriage, and decides to investigate her husband's teashops and work for reforms. There is insufficient publication and biographical information to trace any specific line of influence, and perhaps the only link is that of the common model of Mrs Reeves.[11] (Although, tellingly, Reeves made her heroine a mature woman with grown-up children – like her own mother at the time – while Wells felt it necessary to transform Mrs Reeves into a twenty-three-year-old.) But it is important to note that *Wife* is the first novel in which Wells treats women's desire to work for economic and political change seriously; like Reeves's Mary, Lady Harman reads and researches and, most importantly, goes to talk to the actual workers themselves – something the men in these novels never think of doing. Amber Reeves herself was a Fabian and an economist, and it seems probable that her serious treatment of the subject of women's involvement in labor reform (as well as the example of her mother) was influential in shifting Wells's attitude to women's ability to facilitate social change.

Elizabeth von Arnim's influence upon *The Wife of Sir Isaac Harman* is more evident and better documented than that of Reeves. Wells and von Arnim first met in 1910, and their affair, which began shortly thereafter, continued until 1913. During the final year of their relationship, von Arnim resurrected the first draft of her novel *The Pastor's Wife*. She had begun the novel in 1896, and it was based in part upon the early years of her marriage to Count von Arnim-Schlagenthin. At the time von Arnim was living in her chalet in the Alps, where Wells was a frequent visitor; her diary and autobiography indicate that she talked with him about the novel.[12] One of von Arnim's revisions in 1913 was the addition of the final section, in which the heroine, Ingeborg, runs off to Italy with the English artist, Ingram; it is generally accepted that Ingram is based upon Wells. But strangely, there have been no concomitant speculations about any influence von Arnim might have had upon Wells's novels, even though there are striking parallels between *The Wife of Sir Isaac Harman* and *The Pastor's Wife*, both of which were published in October 1914.[13] Since von Arnim's book is autobiographical, it is ultimately impossible to determine how much Wells was influenced by it or by von Arnim's own accounts of her marriage (with which she regaled Wells from their first meeting). But what is clear is that in writing *The Wife of Sir Isaac Harman*, Wells drew a significant amount of material from von Arnim.[14]

Wells pays homage to von Arnim in *Wife* by referring to her as 'that little sister of Montaigne', and by having Lady Harman be 'greatly delighted and stimulated' by her book, *Elizabeth and Her German Garden* (125).[15] But despite all the attention paid to gardens in the novel, Wells's debt in *Wife* is not to the whimsical Elizabeth who wrote chatty garden books, but rather to the sharply satirical feminist Elizabeth who wrote *The Pastor's Wife*. The character of Lady Harman is remarkably similar to that of von Arnim's Ingeborg, despite the differences in their situations and backgrounds; and Wells uses Lady Harman, as von Arnim does Ingeborg, to criticize the inequities women face in marriage and society. Both heroines are naïve, unformed young women who, utterly ignorant about sex and reproduction, enter into marriage with an older man. In both novels the husband's repulsive sexual advances are described as 'clutchings'; Lady Harman, like Ingeborg, quickly discovers that sex is *'unpleasant,* abounding indeed in crumpling indignities and horrible nervous stresses' (*Wife* 86). These bewildered heroines soon discover, to their dismay, that they are to be 'that strange, grown-up and pre-occupied thing, a mother'; reluctantly putting all the joys of girlhood behind them, both are subjected to a 'wild career of unbridled motherhood' (*Pastor* 290).

Lady Harman and Ingeborg both eventually arrive at a point of personal crisis when they refuse to have any more children, start to read and think for themselves, and subsequently attempt to fashion a new life; this is where Wells begins his novel. Such a project was unprecedented for him in several respects. Whereas he traditionally lost interest in his heroines when they became wives and mothers, in this instance the heroine is a married mother at the start of the narrative. Equally remarkable is the fact that Wells allows his heroine to desire work and power, rather than love or material things. And not only does he sustain his focus on Lady Harman for the entire novel, but for the first time in his fiction he stays with the heroine's perspective even when he is discussing sex and childbirth.

These changes can be traced in part to von Arnim's influence. On a personal level, her relationship with Wells broke his pattern of affairs with young, unmarried, sexually inexperienced women; his affection for her helped to broaden and complicate his interests and sympathies where women were concerned. (*Wife* has significantly fewer generalizations about women's nature than any of his earlier novels.) Ingeborg's ordeals were von Arnim's as well, and in *The Pastor's Wife* she is astonishingly frank about the horrors of forced sex and uninformed childbirth, and thoroughly unsentimental about maternity. Wells was clearly influenced by von Arnim's candid revelations about her experience of marriage, and he strove to make the physical subjection of Lady Harman explicit and discomfiting. He also followed von Arnim's lead in his refusal to idealize or sentimentalize maternity. The birth of Lady Harman's first child, for example, is described as 'that lurid occasion when she had been the agonized vehicle for the entry of Miss Millicent Harman upon this terrestrial scene' (362). Lady Harman even admits to herself, after realizing that her hated husband's nose has turned up on each of her children's faces, that she really doesn't *like* her children very much. Like von Arnim, Wells tempers the horror of his heroine's situation with humor, but the line between the two is always disconcertingly fine.

As in Wells's other novels about women, the heroine must share the spotlight with a male character; Wells never focused exclusively on a female protagonist, as Bennett and Forster did. But *Wife* marks a significant departure for Wells in that Lady Harman's foil, Mr Brumley, is a comic character whose narrative runs alongside and occasionally intersects with her own, but never dominates it. Although Brumley is a writer, and his name recalls Wells's birthplace (Bromley), and he does talk at length in one chapter about his social theories, he clearly does not represent Wells; he is neither a scientist nor particularly knowledgeable about social reform. Since there is no surrogate for Wells in the novel (except for the embittered and scandalous writer Wilkins, who makes a brief appearance at a dinner party) there is no one to talk too much and overshadow the heroine; the narratives of Lady Harman and Mr Brumley remain balanced from beginning to end.

In fact, Wells uses the character of Brumley to satirize (quite self-consciously) the ways in which women are continually denied the right to their own narratives by men (like Capes or Trafford or Wells himself) who want to cast them in supporting roles. The morning after Mr Brumley first meets Lady Harman, '[his] imagination, trained very largely upon Victorian literature . . . leapt forward to the very ending of this story' – which he envisions as having to do with marriage and himself (32). Brumley cannot get past the fact that Lady Harman is young and beautiful, and he cannot imagine any other narrative but that of a romance for her:

> The only path of escape he could conceive as yet for Lady Harman lay through the chivalry of some other man. That a woman could possibly rebel against one man without the sympathy and moral maintenance of another was still outside the range of Mr. Brumley's understanding. (268)

Completely 'overlook[ing] the absence of any sign of participation on the part of Lady Harman in his own impassioned feelings', as well as disregarding the existence of her husband and their four children, Brumley persists in seeing himself as the knight who will rescue Lady Harman, and show her what 'true marriage' is (266). But Wells's intention in *Wife* is to disappoint Brumley's conventional expectations about women, marriage, and narrative, along with those of the reader.

In his other Edwardian novels about women, Wells seems blithely unaware of how contradictory it is for his unconventional heroines to embrace the conventional narratives he returns them to in the end. But in *Wife*, he scrutinizes how traditional narratives limit women's roles to those of lover, wife or mother, and makes those limitations his subject. From an author's perspective, he criticizes traditional narratives as inadequate responses to and reflections of modern women's lives. But he also considers the powerful ways in which fictional narratives influence and restrict people's ideas, desires and behavior – a topic he had briefly considered in *Ann Veronica*. Mr Brumley's taste for Victorian novels almost ruins his friendship with Lady Harman, for he can think of only romantic solutions to her problems. The views of Sir Isaac, Lady

Harman's husband, about women and marriage have an even more outdated provenance: he pores over *The Taming of the Shrew*, underlining key passages, and makes plans as to how he can best restrain his wife.

Lady Harman, in contrast, reads modern fiction, for she is searching for some vision of new possibilities for women's lives. After reading *Elizabeth and Her German Garden*, she is 'stirred by an imitative passion'; she resolves to be cheerfully optimistic like Elizabeth, and not let Sir Isaac oppress her. When that particular narrative proves untenable, she then turns to Elizabeth Robins, whose novels allow her to witness women living independent and active lives. Robins's novels, and her own growing awareness of feminism and the suffrage movement, inspire Lady Harman to attempt to create a new narrative for her own life, even while all around her resist such an innovation, and try to prevent her from abandoning the traditional narrative in which she began.

Lady Harman's most formidable opponent is her husband, who believes she has no choice in the matter of how to live her life. He insists that the marriage contract makes the wife the property of her husband: 'He on his side had to keep her, dress her, be kind to her, give her the appearances of pride and authority, and in return he had his rights and his privileges and undefined powers of control' (98). Like Soames Forsyte in Galsworthy's *The Man of Property*, Sir Isaac bullies Lady Harman into marrying him, then when they are married he becomes obsessed with jealousy. And also like Forsyte, he imprisons his wife in their home, demands sex from her, comes close to abusing her physically, and finally decides to hide her away in a country home, because in the city, 'she gets ideas'. When those ideas lead Lady Harman to request a modicum of autonomy and an allowance, Sir Isaac immediately assumes she has a lover: ' "If it isn't that . . . why should a woman get restless? . . . You've got everything a woman needs, husband, children, a perfectly splendid home, good jewels . . ." ' (217–18). It is inconceivable to him that she would be interested in feminism and the suffrage movement, for he thinks of feminists as lonely spinsters with 'red noses and spectacles and a masculine style of dress' (108). Like Brumley, he can imagine Lady Harman only within a very limited narrative – one circumscribed by her gender and her beauty.

Lady Harman herself has a difficult time defining what exactly it is that she wants. In a typically Edwardian fashion, her rebellion initially has 'no definite end' – she just wants to go to a luncheon party that Sir Isaac has told her she cannot attend (176). Wells uses this one small incident to demonstrate the ways in which an upper-class woman could actually be a prisoner in her own home. The chauffeur will drive Lady Harman only to places Sir Isaac has approved, and without any spending money or knowledge of pawnbrokers, she cannot even afford to take a bus. But Lady Harman is determined, and in a scene which was a characteristic one in Edwardian fiction about women by 1914, she finds herself walking down a London street alone, feeling exhilarated by her new-found independence and marvelling that she has not partaken of it before.

One thing leads to another, given that 'ideas of insubordination' are simply 'in the air' at the time (107). Lady Harman's feminist sister gives her a subscription to *Votes for Women*, and later Lady Harman meets the suffrage leader Agatha Alimony (an import from *Marriage*). Chafing at her husband's growing tyranny, and finding that Agatha's 'discourse of a general feminine insurrection fell in very closely with the spirit of [her] private revolt' (136), she decides to leave her husband.

As in so many other Edwardian marriage problem novels, the heroine, once the initial rebellious break is made, is at a loss as to where her story goes next. The only new narrative Lady Harman sees awaiting her is that of the suffrage movement, so she goes to Agatha's flat. But to Lady Harman's astonishment, Agatha assumes, as Mr Brumley and Sir Isaac assume, that she must have left her husband for another man. Although Agatha (who is single) imagines all kinds of grand possibilities for herself and the Movement, she dismisses Lady Harman's dreams of autonomy and social responsibility, and in a rigidly conventional fashion she reminds her of her duty to home and children. Lady Harman, however, refuses to return to the narrative of her marriage, and in a final, desperate move, she breaks a window in the Post Office (an action which Agatha quickly claims for the Movement) and is sentenced to a month in prison. But it is a temporary respite, and she is soon back with Sir Isaac.

Most Edwardian marriage problem novels, with their pattern of rebellion and return, would end at this point; in fiction and in life, there were not many options available to unhappily married women. But Wells, like von Arnim in *The Pastor's Wife*, transforms his marriage problem novel into a novel of awakening, a delayed *Bildungsroman* which recognizes that for many married women, as for Lady Harman, 'life had happened . . . before she was ready for it . . . her mind some years after her body was now coming to womanhood, was teeming with curiosity about all she had hitherto accepted' (66).[16] The second half is concerned with that curiosity, with the growth of Lady Harman's feminist and socialist consciousness, and with her plans to establish residence hotels for Sir Isaac's female tea-shop employees. He agrees to build the hotels as a condition of her return to their marriage, but it is not long before her vision of liberality and independence is transformed into Sir Isaac's model of restriction and control. Whereas Wells willingly allowed Capes and Trafford to dominate their wives' narratives, he criticizes Sir Isaac's usurpation of Lady Harman's hotels, and offers it as an example of how men use and abuse their power over women.

Lady Harman finally understands that 'to be a married woman . . . is to be outside justice. It is autocracy' (422). She gives up any hope of freedom or agency as long as she is married. Fortunately – for her and for the novel – Sir Isaac soon dies, and it is telling that one of Lady Harman's first thoughts upon her husband's death is that 'never more could hateful and humiliating demands be made upon her as his right; no more strange distresses of the body nor raw discomfort of the nerves could trouble her – for ever' (432). Lady Harman's sexual slavery is the troubling undercurrent in this comic novel of emancipation; it epitomizes for her the horrors and inequities of the marital relationship, and offers the clearest explanation why she determines never to marry again.

Mr Brumley, who has been a faithful friend to Lady Harman through all her troubles, assumes that she will marry him now that she is free. But she values her new freedom above anything else, and decides that although she likes Brumley very much, 'the person she wanted, the person she had always wanted – was *herself*' (425). In the final scene Brumley, crushed by Lady Harman's rejection of his marriage proposal, stumbles away from her in tears. But she runs after him, and, 'she crouched down upon him and taking his shoulder in her hand, upset him neatly backwards, and, doing nothing by halves, had kissed the astonished Mr. Brumley full upon his mouth' (465). Thus the novel ends, in a delightful reversal of roles. But beyond that, what makes this conclusion so striking is that Lady Harman rejects not only Brumley's marriage plot but also the traditional either/or configuration into which he assumes her choice of life narratives falls. Just as earlier she had seen no reason why she could not work and be married, so now she refuses to accept that being unmarried entails celibacy. Lady Harman, wealthy and independent, escapes from the tyranny of either/or choices and is finally able to write a new narrative for herself – one which she controls, one which includes work and passion and independence. It is a remarkable conclusion for a novel by Wells – the triumph of a mature woman who is powerful, sexual and free.

The Wife of Sir Isaac Harman is a rich and humorous chronicle of its age, and it is no wonder Wells thought that of all his Edwardian marriage discussion novels, it would survive as 'a fragment of social history' ('Postscript' 71). The novel manages to combine successfully feminist wish-fulfillment and realistic social criticism, and it marks an important broadening of Wells's sympathies and vision. In *The Wife of Sir Isaac Harman*, Wells is finally able to get away from what Vida Levering, in Robins's *The Convert*, called his ' "dolly" view of women' (208); for the first time in his fiction, he recognizes that women might have a significant (rather than supporting) role in building the world of the future. *The Wife of Sir Isaac Harman* also marks an interesting point in Wells's development as a novelist, for in it he confronts, thematically and structurally, the conservative ideology underlying traditional narratives about women. Although he was always far more engaged with ideas than with matters of form, his interest in women and feminism ultimately obliged him to acknowledge that the form of his fiction made meaning, and that it could express his ideas as well as his words. In *The Wife of Sir Isaac Harman*, Wells is finally able to give one of his extraordinary heroines a narrative she deserves.

NEW BOTTLES: MAY SINCLAIR

In contrast to Wells, May Sinclair's primary concern throughout the Edwardian period was the form of her fiction. Her novels focused upon many of the same subjects as Wells' – women, feminism, marriage, sex – but she was not satisfied with the genre of the discussion or social problem novel within which he worked. Although she was a feminist and supported the suffrage movement (her pamphlet *Feminism* was published by the Women Writers' Suffrage League in 1912), she was not interested in using her novels as vehicles for social reform. Her feminist concerns were always tempered by her aesthetic interests, and what she strove for during the Edwardian period was a narrative form and style that would allow her to depict the reality of women's lives as truthfully as possible. The reality she focused on was initially an external, social one, but increasingly she turned her attention inward, and sought to represent women through psychological realism.

The 1890s were a formative decade for Sinclair as a writer, and the influence of the new fiction of that period is evident in the psychological complexity and sexual frankness of her fiction, as well as in her emphasis on the previously unexamined or undervalued aspects of women's lives. Her first novel, *Audrey Craven* (1897), the story of a young woman trying desperately to be 'New', was clearly influenced by George Moore's novella 'Mildred Lawson'.[17] In 1901 Sinclair published the novella 'Superseded', which tells the story of an elderly, unmarried schoolteacher who comes to realize that in the eyes of her society she is utterly superfluous. Narrated in a compressed and objective style, and focusing on the forces which unavoidably determine the course of her life, the novella not only recalls Moore but also anticipates the concentrated prose style and objective narrative stance of Mayor's *The Third Miss Symons* and Joyce's *Dubliners*. Sinclair also read Hardy during this period, although his influence would not be evident in her fiction until the middle of the Edwardian age, when her fiction became more psychological and her use of nature more symbolic.

Sinclair changed direction with her next novel, *The Divine Fire* (1904), an allegorical narrative (based upon concepts of philosophical idealism) about the development of a young poet; it became a bestseller in England and America, and established her reputation as a serious novelist. But in typical fashion, Sinclair immediately moved into a new fictional mode, and her next several novels are essentially realistic social problem novels in which she examines the sexual double standard, the marriage problem, and other topics associated with the Woman Question. Her novels of this period – *The Helpmate* (1907), *The Judgment of Eve* (1907) and *Kitty Tailleur* (1908) – were considered shocking for their sexual frankness, but despite all their references to sexual relations, adultery and pregnancy, these are discussion novels, not sensation novels, and their tone is cool and ironic. Sinclair also went on to write a social problem novel in a distinctively Wellsian mode called *The Combined Maze* (1913), in which she depicted a young lower-middle-class man struggling to better his lot in life. But she was beginning to find the presence of explicit argument in fiction aesthetically displeasing; she wrote to Wells that his novel *The New Machiavelli* was marred by the fact that 'the ideas run away with it'.[18] Sinclair was also disappointed by the psychological flatness that resulted when she used her characters predominantly to exemplify the various ideas she was discussing. Out of this dissatisfaction she began to develop her psychological novel.

The Creators (1910) is Sinclair's first novel in which the psychological complexity of the characters takes precedence over the expression of ideas. Once again she turns to the themes of sexuality and marriage, but for the first time her psychological focus allows her to scrutinize gender roles and examine the ways in which gender determines one's sense of self. The structure is basically that of a Victorian multi-plot novel, but the central concern – subjectivity and the difficulty of achieving a sense of wholeness or integration – is an extremely modern one. Sinclair uses this form in order to explore the lives of several characters, and interestingly, the sheer number of plots works to dissipate the conventional linear movement of the narrative; the structuring principle becomes instead the non-linear psychological vicissitudes of the characters.

The novel tells the stories of the relationships and careers of five writers – the 'creators' of the title. Jane Holland and George Tanquerary are the two main characters: she is a bestselling novelist who is also critically acclaimed; he is a hard-edged realist who is contemptuous of Jane's fame, yet secretly desires it. The others are Nina, a modern Emily Brontë; Laura, a writer of short stories; and Prothero, a poet whose work is described as being fifty years ahead of its time. *The Creators* is, in part, an investigation into the nature of creativity, but it is also a marriage problem novel, for Sinclair explores the demands of creative work in order to consider the concomitant demands of sexuality and marriage; whether these competing demands can ever be reconciled is the central question.

The Creators is an unusual novel in that it focuses upon three women who are defined primarily through their work. Jane, Nina and Laura are characterized by and valued for their intellect and their artistic achievements rather than their physical beauty or their relationships with men. Although each woman participates in a romance plot of sorts, the narrative tension arises from the women's desire to write, and from the pressures of publication and critical reception. They all support themselves by their writing, but their commitment to their work goes beyond its practical benefits; Sinclair emphasizes that their creativity is an essential part of their lives, and that it would be unthinkable for them to give it up. She also uses the women's commitment to their art to demonstrate how creativity transcends gender. The 'genius' of all the writers in the novel, male and female, affects them in exactly the same way: when they are writing they are determined and self-absorbed, and crave isolation and freedom from interruption. But as the novel develops, it becomes clear that the writing experiences of the men and the women are vastly different, and that although creativity may not distinguish between genders, gender ultimately determines the circumstances of creativity in important ways.

The male writers suffer at times from a lack of critical or popular support for their writing, but the simple fact of being a writer is never a problem for them. They feel no conflict or guilt when their work pulls them away from family and friends, for not only does their society traditionally identify men by their work, it also tends to encode their specific kind of work – artistic creation – as masculine. But the women writers are not given that kind of affirmation. What defines them as women is utterly opposed to what defines them as artists, and as a result they feel that there is an inherent contradiction in their being writers:

> 'Doesn't it look . . . as if genius were the biggest curse a woman can be saddled with? It's giving you another sex inside you, and a stronger one, to plague you. When we want a thing we can't sit still like a woman and wait till it comes to us, or doesn't come. We go after it like a man; and if we can't get it peaceably, we fight for it, as a man fights. . . .' (105)

These women have been taught that to be a woman is to focus on others, to nurture, to sacrifice; they have been socialized to associate womanliness with attractiveness, softness, acquiescence. But none of those qualities is operative when they are writing: they become careless of their appearance, and equally careless of the needs of others. The powerful drive to create that they feel, and the egotistical focus of that creativity, seem to them to be the result of a masculine force which inhabits their female bodies, and they are left feeling divided, at war with themselves.

The three women writers are aware of this conflict not only in their personal sense of identity, but also in the expectations of others in their lives. Laura suffers the most, for she is required to be both nurturer and creator; her days are spent nursing her ailing father, her nights writing in order to support him. As a result she is continually exhausted by these dual demands, and it is intimated that her work is the slightest of all produced by the group. Nina comes to realize that her work as a writer suffers whenever she becomes romantically involved with a man. Struggling with what she characterizes as a masculine will to create and a feminine desire to be loved, she accedes to the conventional either/or dichotomy that says women must decide between marriage and a career, and chooses celibacy: 'I *believe*, if any woman is to do anything stupendous, it means virginity' (106). Both Laura and Nina advise Jane not to marry, but she refuses to accept that there is an irreconcilable conflict between being a woman and being a writer. Arguing that George has recently married without adversely affecting his writing, she insists that she will be able to combine her career with marriage and motherhood, and marries Brodrick, editor of a prominent literary journal.

At this point the novel shifts from a study of creativity to a marriage problem novel, as Sinclair uses the subsequent careers of Jane and George to comment upon the inequities of the institution of marriage, as well as to scrutinize the inadequacies of gender norms. When George marries, there are no expectations that he will change; there is no conflict in his being a husband and a writer. What George gets from marriage is a wife, whose major function is to provide him with the comfort and solitude he needs in order to create. That society ranks a wife as little more than a privileged servant is underscored by the fact that George marries Rose, a woman who once worked in the boarding house where he lived. He must still struggle for success as a writer, but it finally comes to him, in part because his wife has allowed him to remain focused on his work.

The appalling irony of Jane's situation is not only that does she not get a similarly supportive wife when she marries, but that she is actually expected to *be* a wife herself, with respect to household duties and self-sacrifice. Jane needs solitude and time to write as much as George does, yet her husband assumes that she will run the household and, when children are born, give up her writing altogether. Sinclair uses Jane's utter ineptitude at traditional women's work to demonstrate the absurdity of generalizations like those voiced by Wells about women's 'natural' proclivity for household management; Jane feels as suffocated by the material demands of the domestic world as Wells's male protagonists do. This is further emphasized by the fact that Jane is a mature and independent woman when she marries; her career is established, and she has no desire or need to define herself through the role of a traditional wife.

The Creators differs from other marriage problem novels in that it is not a novel of awakening or of rebellion; instead it depicts a woman who actively chooses marriage and motherhood, but also struggles to redefine them and reconcile them with the demands of her career. *The Creators* is also the only Edwardian novel (and probably the first British novel) which addresses the actual problems of a two-career marriage. Negotiations between husband and wife for time and space, the daily demands of children, financial pressures and sexual tensions – all these concerns are treated with seriousness and specificity.

Like the New Woman novelists before her, and like a great many Edwardian novelists, Sinclair examines domestic relationships as an important source of women's oppression. But like few other novelists of the period, she also scrutinizes the powerful role gender plays in the psychological subjection of women. In particular, she explores the ways in which gender norms shape one's sense of identity, and how challenges to those norms, while they are necessary to a feminist pursuit of social and political change, can result in a tremendous sense of self-division. Although Jane is a feminist, she has internalized her society's gender definitions and has great difficulty escaping them; as a result, her marriage exacerbates the sense of conflict she already feels as a woman writer. She can favor her 'feminine' side, and be a devoted wife and mother, or she can let her 'masculine' talent dominate, and be a successful writer, but she never feels that she can integrate these roles in any way. When she is writing, her husband and child must be out of sight and hearing. When her child falls ill, she is completely unable to work. Jane thinks of her writing self as Jane Holland and her married self as Jane Brodrick, and when it dawns on her one day that they are 'inseparably and indestructibly one', she feels a shock of 'spiritual dislocation' (285–6). The quality of her writing declines, since she is unable to work for any sustained period of time. She begins to envy the now successful (and celibate) Nina, whom she envisions as 'stripped for the race, carrying nothing but her genius' (376). In contrast, Jane feels like a juggler on a tightrope:

> She had so many balls to keep going. There was her novel; and there was Brodrick, and the baby, and Brodrick's family, and her own friends. She couldn't drop one of them. . . . But now she was beginning to feel the trembling of the perfect balance. It was as if, in that marvelous adjustment of relations, she had arrived at the pitch where perfection topples over. She moved with tense nerves on the edge of peril. (342)

There are also external forces which work to unbalance Jane's efforts to restructure her marital and maternal relations. Her own self-doubt is intensified by the weight of patriarchal tradition, represented by Dr Henry Brodrick, her brother-in-law. The doctor brandishes the authority of scientific theory as he argues for strict gender opposition and separate spheres in an attempt to suppress Jane's independence. Constantly hovering in the background, Henry taps into Jane's worst fears by telling her that her desire to work is 'unnatural' and harmful to her health; he even intimates that she has damaged her baby's health by working during her pregnancy.

An even more powerful voice of tradition is Gertrude, Brodrick's former secretary and housekeeper. Jane decides that what she needs is a 'wife' to take over her domestic duties, and asks Gertrude to return to the household.[19] But what Gertrude does is to gradually (and eerily) usurp Jane's place – first caring for the children, then sitting in Jane's place at the table when she is too exhausted from her writing to come to breakfast, finally attempting to seduce Brodrick when Jane goes away to the country to write. As the embodiment of the ideal of the womanly woman – the completely feminine, servile, self-effacing domestic angel – Gertrude is a threat and an admonition to Jane rather than a help. The ideally feminine woman is a recurrent figure in Sinclair's fiction, where she is always the villain, for she is the one who holds women back, and makes it impossible for them to forge new identities and narratives for themselves. Sinclair implies that as long as women like Gertrude exist, living exclusively for and through men, independent women like Jane won't have a chance.

The novel reaches a climax of sorts when Jane returns home from her artistic retreat to break up the developing relationship between Gertrude and her husband, but this ancillary narrative of adultery is quite brief and sketchy. Although it is clear that Gertrude is ousted, the narrative point of view pulls back from Jane and Brodrick in the final chapter, and the reader is left only with the speculations of Jane's friends as to whether she is happy or not. The question remains unanswered, and the main narrative of Jane's life is left unresolved. The gender polarization that Jane and her friends feel is never reconciled in any way. There is no indication that the tension between Jane's creativity and her marriage has diminished. Sinclair was not interested in promoting feminism by giving her heroines happy endings, as writers like the Findlaters did in their fiction. Instead, she strove to portray realistically the difficulties that arise when women try to redefine themselves and their role in society, and in so doing she focused upon the issues which were of the greatest concern to Edwardian feminists, but were ignored by the majority of Edwardian novelists – children, household management, and the conflict between work and marriage. Sinclair saw that there were no easy answers to these problems; thus she offered no satisfying closure.

The Creators is also notable for its frank and psychologically complex exploration of female sexuality. Although the shocking sexual candor of the new realism and the New Woman novels of the 1890s was assimilated to a large extent into Edwardian fiction, that candor was most often exhibited in explorations of male sexuality or of relationships; explicit discussions or representations of female sexuality continued to be stigmatized. Even Wells, who was certainly not intimidated by social conventions, never depicted female sexual desire with any intimacy or specificity. What mattered to him was that women like Ann Veronica and Lady Harman actually *act* upon their sexual desires. But it is all the doubts and dreams and fears that exist behind those actions that intrigued Sinclair, and in that respect she followed in the tradition of the new fiction of the 1890s, particularly that of George Egerton. Besides Sinclair, the only Edwardian writers who dared to confront the reality of female sexuality in their fiction were Lawrence, Bennett and Hunt, and all were criticized for being throwbacks to the 1890s.

The Creators marks the beginning of a shift in Sinclair's work, as she turned her attention from external social circumstances to psychology and sexuality in order to portray what she felt was the truth of women's experience. She saw sexuality and gender as crucial determining forces in women's lives, and she was especially interested in the discrepancies between the gender norms and social roles assigned to women, and their sexual desires. The result of these discrepancies is most often sexual repression, and Sinclair is particularly effective in depicting its existence and its cost. In two striking scenes, she describes women seeking physical pain to stave off the sexual desire they are not supposed to be feeling – 'giving pain for intolerable pain' (259): when Nina breaks off her relationship with the poet Prothero, she purposely burns her arm on a candle in an attempt to find some sort of release; when Gertrude learns that Brodrick is to marry Jane, she violently squeezes her breasts, unable to admit to herself any feelings of desire or jealousy. The power of these scenes derives from Sinclair's ability to represent unconscious desire through a single, forceful and symbolic physical action. Although most of *The Creators* is written in a traditionally realistic and frequently effusive narrative style, the compression and symbolism of these two scenes anticipate the new style Sinclair was to develop in subsequent novels in which she focuses increasingly on sexuality, psychology and the unconscious.

This style emerges first in *The Flaw in the Crystal* (1912), an unusual exploration of paranormal experience and sexual domination, and then in *The Three Sisters* (1914); in both novels, Sinclair moves the 'action' from the outside to the inside. Rather than focus on external reality and the influence of circumstances upon an individual's life, in these novels she emphasizes the interior reality of her characters' psychology as she scrutinizes the roots of identity, gender, and social relations. In stressing individual consciousness and the importance of the unconscious, Sinclair begins to write fiction that is not only modern in content but modernist in form. Although there are romance and marriage plots in *The Three Sisters*, they do not provide the key structure. Instead, the novel is centered around the consciousnesses of three sisters, particularly that of the middle sister, Gwenda; the rhythms of their inner lives determine the rhythms, and ultimately the shape, of the work. By eschewing a traditionally realistic narrative, Sinclair not only escapes the standard requirements of plot – especially the problematic one of closure – but is also able to take as one of the novel's themes the limitations and ideological implications of conventional narratives about women.

Sinclair's shift in emphasis from public to private, and from action to consciousness, anticipates the work of Dorothy Richardson and Virginia Woolf, both of whom were writing their first novels at this time.[20] Although neither Sinclair nor Woolf characterized this new kind of novel of consciousness as a particularly feminine mode, it is obvious from their fiction that it was nevertheless uniquely suited for depicting those whose inner life dominates the outer, which was certainly the case with women like Sinclair's three sisters, who have absolutely no practical function in the world. They live quiet, secluded lives in which (as Sinclair once remarked about Dorothy Richardson's fictional world) 'nothing happens'. Oppressed by their domineering father, cut off from the possibility of acquiring lovers or even friends, theirs are lives of intensely felt moments alternating with monotony; they live on thoughts and feelings and small interactions. There is insufficient material here for a traditional novel which relies upon action; this is one of the reasons why the daily domestic experiences of ordinary women had not hitherto played a significant part in British fiction. But by shifting the terms of valuation, by privileging the inner life, Sinclair revealed what rich material those previously ignored experiences could yield. Like Bennett, von Arnim and Mayor, but also like Woolf, Dorothy Richardson and Joyce, Sinclair celebrates the ordinary and the quotidian.

To be a woman in the Edwardian age, as Edwardian feminists from Maud Churton Braby to Rebecca West knew so well, was to live a double life, one that was alternately (or even simultaneously) Victorian and modern, repressive and liberating, traditional and radically new. Previously, in *The Creators*, Sinclair had represented the self-division that can arise from living in a time of transition as the conflict between a character's expressed desire for autonomy and agency, and her internalization of society's conservative values. She continued that strategy in *The Three Sisters*, but enriched it by focusing upon the desires and motivations which exist on an unconscious level. Here Sinclair conveys the unconscious through the symbolic style she began to develop in *The Creators*, as well as through parenthetical narrative commentary. She eventually dismissed the latter device as awkward and intrusive after encountering Richardson's 'stream-of-consciousness' style in *Pointed Roofs* (1915). But even with parenthetical insertions, the compressed, poetic style that Sinclair created in *The Three Sisters* is effective, for it allowed her to probe beneath the hysterical illnesses and self-destructive sacrifices of her characters to expose their anger, their yearning for power, their sexual desires and the suppression of those desires – all the forces which determine their actions but which they themselves are unable to recognize or articulate.

Sinclair's exploration of the unconscious, sexual desire, repression and sublimation in *The Three Sisters* was clearly influenced by recent developments in psychoanalysis. She was a founding member, in 1913, of the Medico-Psychological Clinic of London, and by the time she wrote *The Three Sisters* she was familiar with the works of Freud and Jung, among others. But although psychoanalysis provided her with a new perspective from which to write, the lives and works of the Brontë sisters were an even more significant influence in terms of their particular engagement with the inner lives of women. Between 1908 and 1914, Sinclair wrote an introduction to a reissue of Mrs Gaskell's biography of Charlotte Brontë, and introductions to reissues of six Brontë novels. In addition, she published a critical biography of the Brontës in 1912 entitled *The Three Brontës*, in which she praised the sisters particularly for their feminism and their psychological insight. Like so many other Edwardian feminist writers, she felt greatly indebted to the Brontës for their innovative depictions of women's lives; she saw in their fiction a prefiguring and an affirmation of her own emerging fictional project, as is evident in her description of *Villette*:

> The book is flung, as it were, from Lucy's beating heart; it is one profound protracted cry of longing and frustration. This was a new note in literature. *Villette* was the unsealing of the sacred secret springs, the revelation of all that proud, decorous mid-Victorian reticence most sedulously sought to hide. There is less overt, audacious passion in *Villette* than in *Jane Eyre*, but there is a surer, a subtler and more intimate psychology.[21]

In *The Three Sisters*, Sinclair looks for those 'sacred secret springs' within three 'types' of women that recur in British fiction; by revealing their true natures and motivations, she also reveals the inaccuracy and inadequacy of conventional ideas about women and femininity.

The distinctions among the sisters are made clear in Chapter Five (quoted in its entirety below), in which they reflect upon Dr Rowcliffe, the only eligible man in their community:

> Their stillness, their immobility were now intense. And not one spoke a word to the other.
> All three of them were thinking.
> Mary thought, 'Wednesday is his day. On Wednesday I will go into the village and see all my sick people. Then I shall see him. And he will see me. He will see that I am kind and sweet and womanly.' She thought, 'That is the sort of woman that a man wants.' But she did not know what she was thinking.
> Gwenda thought, 'I will go out on the moor again. I don't care if I *am* late for

Prayers. He will see me when he drives back and he will wonder who is that wild, strong girl who walks by herself on the moor at night and isn't afraid. He has seen me three times, and every time he has looked at me as if he wondered. In five minutes I shall go.' She thought (for she knew what she was thinking), 'I shall do nothing of the sort. I don't care whether he sees me or not. I don't care if I never see him again. I don't care.'

Alice thought, 'I will make myself ill. So ill that they'll have to send for him. I shall see him that way.' (10)

After establishing these three stereotypes of female nature and behavior, Sinclair proceeds to dismantle and complicate them. The eldest sister, Mary, is a domestic angel, acquiescent to her father, devoted to making the lives of others comfortable. She is so self-effacing that she does not even really know what she is thinking. Yet her complicity in the patriarchal order does not preclude a desire for power; it is just that she achieves power by manipulating others' expectations based upon traditional gender roles. She ruthlessly seduces Dr Rowcliffe away from her sister Gwenda, all the while seeming guileless and innocuous to them both. She is another of Sinclair's dangerous womanly women, like the protagonist of *The Helpmate*, or Gertrude in *The Creators*; by conforming to her society's ideal of womanhood, she staves off healthy change, making new women appear unnatural and dulling men into a stupor through her domestic entrapment. By the time she has finished with Dr Rowcliffe, his passion for Gwenda feels merely like an annoyance, and his grand ambitions have dwindled to a vague plan to work less while earning more money. Through her domestic skills, she perpetuates a status quo of complacency and repression.

On the surface, Alice conforms to the Victorian type of the frail, neurasthenic girl on the sofa – anemic, asexual, able to express herself and exert control over her life only through her illnesses. But her feigned ill health becomes real and life-threatening, as a result of her father's vigorous efforts to cut her off from any opportunity for romantic, and thus sexual, satisfaction. The slight, pale flower of womanhood is revealed to be a frustrated woman who is being driven mad by her powerful sexual drive. She eventually becomes involved in a sexual relationship with a local farmer, and marries him after becoming pregnant, thus escaping the repression and sexual denial of her father's household.

The central focus of the novel is upon the middle sister, Gwenda. She is a typical Edwardian heroine in several ways, not the least of which being that she follows in the tradition of the Brontës' heroines (she is in part modelled after Emily Brontë) and combines their rebelliousness with a modern sensibility. She is independent, physically strong, skeptical of received ideas, and resistant to her father's control. Although she feels attracted to the doctor, she resists confining herself in a relationship. But rather than allow this modern woman to rebel, Sinclair uses her to examine the difficulty of maintaining one's independence and the personal price one must pay when one rejects the status quo. As she did in *The Creators*, Sinclair shows how even when one rejects the patriarchy intellectually, one can still internalize and suffer from its system of values. First in the interests of Alice's health, then in order to nurse her father, Gwenda denies herself and succumbs to the Victorian ideal of feminine self-sacrifice and sexual repression.

Initially, Gwenda is able to sublimate her desires, through vigorous physical exercise and intellectually taxing reading; she strives to exhaust her body through her mind:

> She took to metaphysics as you take to dram-drinking. She must have strong, heavy stuff that drugged her brain. And when she found that she could trust her intellect she set it deliberately to fight her passion. (352)

But her lack of any outlet for sexual expression ultimately begins to break her down, and it is through the frustration and emptiness of Gwenda's life that Sinclair moves from a psychoanalytic study into a social critique. By adhering to her society's gender definitions, by devoting herself to the care of her father, Gwenda has wasted her life utterly. There is no feeling of closure at the end of the novel, only a sense that while nature goes on endlessly renewing itself, Gwenda will only grow older and weaker. The sense of isolation, entrapment and monotony is overwhelming, and functions as a powerful indictment of the patriarchal social order.

But the psychological studies of the protagonists do not constitute the whole of Sinclair's achievement in *The Three Sisters*. One of its most distinctive features is her compressed and poetic prose style; the dream-like mood it sustains is evocative and disturbing. Her attention to the dynamics of intimate exchanges is also remarkable: underneath tense, terse dialogues, emotions swing back and forth between love and hate with startling yet believable rapidity and passion. Although there are scattered details which indicate that the novel has a contemporary setting, what dominates it is the sense that these characters and their struggles exist in some timeless, even mythic, realm; Gwenda implicitly recalls Artemis as she walks alone with only the moon for a companion. Nature is a powerful force here; following Hardy, though with a minimum of description, Sinclair uses the natural world to convey her characters' states of mind, and place their problems in perspective.

The Three Sisters serves as an important link between the innovations of the new fiction of the 1890s and those of the modernist novel.[22] All its characteristic elements – the concentrated poetic style, the narrative comprised of moments, the emphasis on consciousness, the symbolism, the psychology – can be seen in Egerton's short stories as well as in Woolf's novels. A common goal animates their fiction: Egerton, Sinclair and Woolf all strove, for feminist and artistic reasons, to find a new kind of realism – one which would allow them to move behind the surface of external reality to reveal the truth of modern women's inner lives with specificity and honesty. The exigencies of this fictional project forced them to reject traditional narrative forms and prose styles, and to develop new ones – each author, in turn, making a progressively larger break with tradition. They constitute an important line of development in the genealogy of literary modernism, but one which is usually overlooked.[23]

In this context, it is interesting to note the striking stylistic and thematic similarities between *The Three Sisters* and D.H. Lawrence's early fiction. Like Sinclair, Lawrence was strongly influenced by the combination of feminism and realism in the new fiction of the 1890s: he was inspired not only by Hardy but by Schreiner, Gissing and Moore, among others, in his quest to write about women with psychological insight and sexual frankness. And also like Sinclair, Lawrence was an Edwardian, excited by the social and political developments of his age, wanting to write about the lives of modern men and women, but struggling against gender stereotypes, novelistic conventions, and traditional fictional forms to do so. He too strove to shift the focus of his fiction to the unconscious, and he experimented with various methods for conveying it, including symbolism, mythic allusions, and a poetic and repetitive prose style. Lawrence is also aligned with Sinclair in his fascination with the contrast between the sophisticated façades of modern men and women and the primal, especially sexual, forces that motivate their actions. From his letters, it is clear that Lawrence was familiar with Sinclair's work, and interesting comparisons have been made between *The Three Sisters* and his story, 'Daughters of the Vicar', which was revised and published after the publication of Sinclair's novel.[24] But what is significant for this study is not whether one influenced the other but, rather, that the parallels in their developments as writers illuminate a more general development in British fiction which threads from the 1890s through the Edwardian period into the modernist era – a development which is significantly linked to feminism by its sexual frankness, its psychological realism, its serious valuation of the experiences of women, and its critical scrutiny of gender norms and social institutions.[25]

This is not to say, however, that the fiction of Sinclair and Lawrence is the inevitable culmination of the transition which began in the 1890s, or that their innovations solve all the formal problems which confronted Edwardian authors of fiction about women and feminism. Both Sinclair and Lawrence chose to reject the genre of the social problem novel, and focus on the psychological and sexual realities of contemporary life. But in the case of Sinclair, this change brought her into conflict with the feminist ideology which had previously informed her work; this conflict is evident in *The Three Sisters*. In moving the novel away from external realities and into the inner world of subjectivity, Sinclair also moves it, by implication, away from the public world of influence and agency that women had just begun to enter. Similarly, by setting the novel in a timeless, mythic, symbolic realm, she takes her characters out of a historical world of causality and potential social change. One of the most important contributions of Edwardian fiction about women and feminism is its recognition of a variety of women's experiences, and its insistence on chronicling the previously disregarded details of their lives. But it is difficult to say where the recording of the limitations of women's lives leaves off and the perpetuating of them begins. Despite the modernity of Sinclair's narrative structure and prose style, her exclusive focus on her heroines' personal emotions and intimate relationships thrusts them, in effect, back into the nineteenth century.

The depiction of female sexuality in *The Three Sisters* is, paradoxically, also regressive. As Wells did in *Ann Veronica* and *Marriage*, Sinclair posits an ideal of an essential, primal relationship between the sexes which, she suggests, civilization has obfuscated and distorted. The ultimate liberation becomes figured as a return to the primitive and the natural; women can theoretically be freed by recognizing sexual polarities and responding to their sexual desires. The woman who finds the most satisfaction in *The Three Sisters* is Alice, whose love affair and subsequent marriage with the farmer Greatorax fulfills her sexual needs and maternal instincts. Sinclair implies that Greatorax, by virtue of his class and his rural background, is more attuned to the natural rhythms and demands of life than others in the novel; thus he alone is able to restore Alice to physical and psychic health. In the psychological theories that Sinclair embraces there is an implicit biological determinism which can easily be transformed into a biological trap. Like so many of the New Women in the fiction of the 1890s, Gwenda tries to rebel against the circumstances of her life, only to discover that she is actually trapped by her frustrated sexual desires and feelings of feminine inadequacy and guilt. The emphasis on myth and psychology in the novel imparts a sense of inevitability to Gwenda's limitations, and she responds as the New Women did before her – with self-blame, pessimism, and paralysis.[26]

Sinclair continued to develop and experiment with the psychological novel during and after World War I; her two stream-of-consciousness novels, *Mary Olivier: A Life* (1919) and *Life and Death of Harriett Frean* (1920), are generally considered her most significant achievements. She also continued her advocacy of sexual frankness in fiction and her opposition to censorship; she was the only other English writer besides Bennett who denounced the suppression of Lawrence's *The Rainbow* in 1915. She lent her support to a wide variety of new writers; she eagerly welcomed modernist literature, and was particularly active in her support of experimental writers such as H.D., Ezra Pound, Dorothy Richardson, T.S. Eliot and F.S. Flint, all of whom she wrote about with perception and sympathy.[27]

Wells, in contrast, remained essentially an Edwardian all his life; although his writing career continued until his death in 1946, he never experimented in any significant fashion with the form of his fiction. He admired the work of Joyce (writing an enthusiastic review of *A Portrait of the Artist as a Young Man* in 1917) and Dorothy Richardson, but he gradually became disengaged from current trends and developments in literature after the war. For personal and historical reasons, feminism ceased to be of vital interest to Wells in the latter decades of his life, and as he became increasingly absorbed in world affairs, he wrote more non-fiction than novels. His fiction was frequently used by the next generation of writers and critics as a standard against which to define themselves; writers such as Woolf and West justified their own fiction by rejecting Wells's polemics, his conventionally realistic style, and his traditional narrative structures.[28] But it was really Victorian fiction that the modernists were rebelling against, not Edwardian fiction like Wells's. He, like the modernists, was struggling to break with the old and create something new, but he got caught in the transition, between two worlds.

The novels of both Wells and Sinclair elucidate the influence of feminism upon Edwardian fiction and upon the development of literary modernism. The fiction of the 1890s was an important source for both writers, but they progressed along two quite different paths. Wells believed that fiction had 'inseparable moral consequences', and like the New Woman novelists, he wrote in the hope that his fiction would change the world. He was fascinated by 'that extraordinary discontent of women with a woman's lot', and saw it as offering women and men an opportunity to restructure their relations with one another – particularly sexual relations. Sinclair, in contrast to Wells, tried to avoid polemics in her fiction; she emulated the new realists of the 1890s in her search for an objective narrative voice that would allow her characters' consciousnesses to shine through. Her novels are also informed by the new fiction of the 1890s in their sexual frankness, their psychological realism, and their focus upon feminist rebellion.

In Wells's fiction, the discussion of ideas usually takes precedence over formal considerations: thus while Wells often thematized feminist rebellion, he did not realize it formally. For the most part, he resisted acknowledging that the narrative forms he chose and the points of view he adopted had ideological implications which contradicted his declarations of support for feminist rebellion. Sinclair, in contrast, was sensitive to the pressures exerted upon the form of her fiction by its feminist content; she began by eschewing gender stereotypes and traditional narratives of romance and marriage, and went on to create novels structured upon the consciousness of her female protagonists. Following Egerton – and pursuing a path similar to those chosen by Mayor, Franklin, and Henry Handel Richardson – Sinclair sought new fictional forms with which to tell the stories of women's lives; in so doing, she moved from a content-driven modernism to the modernism of form.

The novels Wells and Sinclair published between 1901 and 1914 are quintessential Edwardian novels; distinct from Victorian novels in their rebellious heroines, their sexual frankness and their unconventional morality, hesitating on the brink of modernism in their formal struggles, they are first and foremost novels of transition. As such, they are also valuable historical documents – not just for the social and political developments they chronicle, but for the literary history in which they participate. The Edwardian novels of Wells and Sinclair both depict and exemplify the difficult, sometimes awkward, but ultimately exhilarating drama of the old yielding to the new.

Notes

INTRODUCTION

Epigraph: Edna Kenton, 'A Study of the Old "New Women"', *Bookman* 37 (1913): 155.

1. I have followed standard practice in using the term 'Edwardian' to refer to the years from 1901 to 1914; distinctions between Edwardian and Georgian are not particularly useful for discussions of fiction produced during this period.

2. For example, see Ann Ardis, *New Women, New Novels: Feminism and Early Modernism* (New Brunswick, NJ: Rutgers University Press, 1990); Gerd Bjørhovde, *Rebellious Structures: Women Writers and the Crisis of the Novel 1880–1900* (Oslo: Norwegian University Press, 1987); and Elaine Showalter, *Sexual Anarchy: Gender and Culture at the Fin de Siècle* (New York: Viking, 1990).

3. See John Batchelor, *The Edwardian Novelists* (New York: St. Martin's, 1982); Jefferson Hunter, *Edwardian Fiction* (Cambridge, MA: Harvard University Press, 1982); Jonathan Rose, *The Edwardian Temperament 1895–1919* (Athens, OH: Ohio University Press, 1986). The exceptions are Samuel Hynes, *The Edwardian Turn of Mind* (Princeton, NJ: Princeton University Press, 1968) and Elaine Showalter, *A Literature of Their Own: British Women Novelists from Brontë to Lessing* (Princeton, NJ: Princeton University Press, 1977); each devotes a chapter to Edwardian fiction about women. Patricia Stubbs in *Women and Fiction: Feminism and the Novel 1880–1920* (Sussex: Harvester, 1979) and Peter Keating in *The Haunted Study: A Social History of the English Novel 1875–1914* (London: Secker & Warburg, 1989), discuss Edwardian novels about women and feminism, but Stubbs fails to consider any women

writers while Keating concludes that during this period 'there were no women novelists of a literary stature even remotely comparable to that of James, Conrad, Hardy, Meredith, Bennett, Wells, Gissing, or a dozen other men' (175).

4. See Shari Benstock, 'Expatriate Modernism: Writing on the Cultural Rim', in *Women's Writing in Exile*, ed. Mary Lynn Broe and Angela Ingram (Chapel Hill: University of North Carolina Press, 1989) 19–40; and Celeste M. Schenck, 'Exiled by Genre: Modernism, Canonicity, and the Politics of Exclusion', in the same collection, 225–50. See also Marianne DeKoven, 'Gendered Doubleness and the "Origins" of Modernist Form', *Tulsa Studies in Women's Literature* 8 (1989): 19–42.

5. Henry James, 'The Future of the Novel' (1900), reprinted in *The Future of the Novel: Essays on the Art of Fiction*, ed. Leon Edel (New York: Vintage, 1956) 40.

6. Frederic Taber Cooper, 'Feminine Unrest and Some Recent Novels', *Bookman*, December 1909: 382.

7. H.G. Wells, *The Wife of Sir Isaac Harman* (1914; London: Hogarth, 1986) 259.

8. Rachel Blau DuPlessis, *Writing Beyond the Ending: Narrative Strategies of Twentieth-Century Women Writers* (Bloomington: Indiana University Press, 1985) 2.

9. Joseph Allen Boone, *Tradition Counter Tradition: Love and the Form of Fiction* (Chicago: University of Chicago Press, 1987).

10. Hunter, *Edwardian Fiction* viii.

11. Frank Kermode, 'The English Novel, *circa* 1907', in *The Art of Telling: Essays on Fiction* (Cambridge, MA: Harvard University Press, 1983) 39, 41.

12. For example, see Schenck, 'Exiled by Genre'.

13. Certainly there were other pressures on the form of the novel that contributed to the emergence of literary modernism, but I suggest that those pressures produced by feminism, shifts in gender definitions and challenges to the institution of marriage were particularly important and meaningful ones because of the centrality of women, romance and marriage to the novel.

14. Tony Tanner, *Adultery and the Novel: Contract and Transgression* (Baltimore, MD: Johns Hopkins University Press, 1979) 15.

15. Virginia Woolf, 'Mr. Bennett and Mrs. Brown', in *The Captain's Death Bed and Other Essays* (New York: Harcourt, Brace, 1950) 110.

16. ibid. 114.

CHAPTER ONE

Epigraphs: George Moore, *Literature at Nurse, or Circulating Morals*, ed. Pierre Coustillas (1885; Atlantic Highlands, NJ: Humanities Press, 1976) 22; Alfred, Lord Tennyson, 'Locksley Hall Sixty Years After', rpt. in *The Works of Alfred Lord Tennyson*, vol. 8 (1886; New York: Macmillan, 1893) 83–108.

1. The term 'naturalism' refers to the specific school of fiction founded by Émile Zola, which was based in part on post-Darwinian biology and attempted to document, in an objective, scientific and meticulously detailed fashion, the social, economic

and biological forces which determine the course of people's lives; in general, the focus of naturalistic fiction was on urban life and the lives of the middle and lower classes. The term 'realism' can apply to several related tendencies in literature, and its use is particularly confusing in the late nineteenth century, when English critics and novelists used the terms 'realism' and 'naturalism' interchangeably. But for these writers, 'realism' did not imply the general novelistic tradition of depicting characters and events in such a manner as to give an accurate and convincing imitation of life. Instead, for them, 'realism' referred to the current British adaptations of naturalism, exemplified by the novels of George Gissing and George Moore. Like naturalism, British realism sought to depict the middle and lower classes with authenticity instead of sentiment; it scrutinized codes of morality and social institutions, and attempted graphic depictions of poverty, crime and sex, but with less objectivity and pessimistic determinism, and of necessity, less sexual frankness. When I use the term 'new realism' it will be in reference to this late-nineteenth-century literary movement, which Gissing characterized as a 'revolt against insincerity in the art of fiction'.

2. W.S. Lilly, 'The New Naturalism', *Fortnightly Review*, 1 August 1885: 251.

3. It is ironic that the National Vigilance Association, the organization which was instrumental in bringing Vizetelly to trial, was largely comprised of women, many of whom were feminists who had been active in the Contagious Diseases campaign. They did not recognize the social criticism inherent in Zola's fiction, or understand how censorship enforced the very sexual reticence they had protested in the CD campaign. Instead, they saw Zola's sexual frankness as exploitive of women, and threatening to their codes of sexual purity.

4. George Moore, *Literature at Nurse, or Circulating Morals* (1885; Atlantic Highlands, NJ: Humanities Press, 1976) 18, 21, 22.

5. See Gaye Tuchman with Nina E. Fortin, *Edging Women Out: Victorian Novelists, Publishers, and Social Change* (New Haven, CT: Yale University Press, 1989) for a sociological analysis of this development.

6. See Showalter, *Literature*, esp. ch. 3, 'The Double Critical Standard and the Feminine Novel', for a discussion of stereotypes about women's writing that were manipulated by critics in the nineteenth century.

7. Moore, *Literature* 21–2.

8. Walter Besant, E. Lynn Linton and Thomas Hardy, 'Candour in English Fiction', *New Review* 2 (January 1890): 17, 14.

9. 'The Tree of Knowledge', *New Review* 10 (June 1894): 690.

10. George Gissing, 'The Place of Realism in Fiction', *Humanitarian* July 1895, rpt. in *Victorian Novelists after 1885*, Dictionary of Literary Biography 18, ed. Ira B. Nadel and William E. Fredeman (Detroit: Gale, 1983) 357–8.

11. See Richard D. Altick, *The English Common Reader: A Social History of the Mass Reading Public, 1800–1900* (Chicago: University of Chicago Press, 1957) esp. 312–17.

12. David Rubinstein, in *Before the Suffragettes: Women's Emancipation in the 1890s* (Sussex: Harvester, 1986), attributes the coining of the phrase 'New Woman' to the

novelist Sarah Grand, who used it in an article in the *North American Review* in March 1894; the phrase became extremely popular by the summer of that year (15–16). But the New Woman was mocked and caricatured so relentlessly in the popular press that most novelists stopped short of actually referring to their heroines as 'New Women'. Whether or not there were in actuality 'New Women' was a frequently debated point; the role of the press in the creation of the concept and image of the New Woman is examined in Patricia Marks, *Bicycles, Bangs, and Bloomers: The New Woman in the Popular Press* (Lexington: University Press of Kentucky, 1990).

13. See Gail Cunningham, *The New Woman and the Victorian Novel* (London: Macmillan, 1978), esp. ch. 2, 'The Fiction of Sex and the New Woman'; Rubinstein, *Before the Suffragettes* 24–37, for detailed analyses of these novels.

14. See Cunningham, *New Woman* 10–11. Some feminist critics, such as Elizabeth Chapman in *Marriage Questions in Modern Fiction* (London: John Lane, 1897) and Janet Hogarth in 'Literary Degenerates' in the *Fortnightly Review* (April 1895: 586–92), were outspoken in their disapproval of New Woman fiction; they felt that these novels gave the misleading and dangerous impression that feminists were all sex-obsessed and neurotic, rather than serious-minded social reformers.

15. See E. Lynn Linton's series of articles on the 'Wild Women': 'The Wild Women as Politicians', *Nineteenth Century* July 1891: 79–88; 'The Wild Women as Social Insurgents', *Nineteenth Century* October 1891: 596–605; and 'The Partisans of the Wild Women', *Nineteenth Century* March 1892: 454–64. See also Mona Caird's response to Mrs Linton: 'A Defence of the So-Called "Wild Women"', *Nineteenth Century* May 1892: 811–29.

16. See Kathleen Blake, *Love and the Woman Question in Victorian Literature: The Art of Self-Postponement* (Sussex: Harvester, 1983); Sheila Jeffreys, *The Spinster and Her Enemies: Feminism and Sexuality 1880–1930* (London: Pandora, 1985), for sympathetic discussions of chastity as a political strategy and psychological necessity for many feminists at the turn of the century.

17. Grand, *Beth Book* 417.

18. 'Review of *Gallia*', *Saturday Review* 23 March 1895: 383.

19. Arthur Waugh, 'Reticence in Literature', *The Yellow Book* April 1894: 212, 217, 218.

20. Hubert Crackanthorpe, 'Reticence in Literature: Some Roundabout Remarks', *The Yellow Book* July 1894: 268–9.

21. Waugh, 'Reticence' 210.

22. 'The Year in Review', *Athenaeum* January 1894: 17–18.

23. See Edmund Gosse, 'The Tyranny of the Novel', in *Questions at Issue* (London: Heinemann, 1893) 3–31; and 'The Decay of Literary Taste', *North American Review* 161 (1895): 109–18.

24. D.F. Hannigan, 'The Tyranny of the Modern Novel', *Westminster Review* 143 (January–June 1895): 304.

25. Gissing, 'The Place of Realism' 358.

26. See Sarah Grand, 'The Morals of Manner and Appearance', *Humanitarian* August 1893; and 'The Duty of Looking Nice', *Review of Reviews* August 1893.

27. Penny Boumelha, in *Thomas Hardy and Women: Sexual Ideology and Narrative Form* (Sussex: Harvester, 1982), reads these narrative interruptions as purposeful attempts to threaten and unsettle 'the circumscribing narrative voice', and credits the New Woman novelists with 'formal experimentation' (66–7). Gerd Bjørhovde, in *Rebellious Structures*, sees the 'formlessness' of New Woman novels as important efforts to go beyond the traditional 'small canvas' of women writers (170). In *New Women, New Novels*, Ann Ardis also argues that New Woman novels should be seen as conscious attempts to experiment with the form of the novel.

28. Due to the traditional expectations of retribution and resolution cultivated by the novel, the endings of many New Woman novels are ambiguous and were frequently misinterpreted. Similarly, several novels that were written specifically to criticize the New Woman – Iota's *A Yellow Aster* (1894), Mrs Humphry Ward's *Marcella* (1894) and Grant Allen's hugely successful novel *The Woman Who Did* (1895) – were received (and condemned) as New Woman novels themselves; all that readers looked for was a heroine with the requisite qualities of a New Woman. See Rubinstein, *Before the Suffragettes* 32–3 for a discussion of the reception of *Marcella*; and Boumelha, *Thomas Hardy and Women* 86–8 for an analysis of *A Yellow Aster*. Cunningham (*New Woman*) perpetuates this confusion by analyzing both *A Yellow Aster* and *The Woman Who Did* as New Woman novels. Similarly, Ardis (*New Women, New Novels*) does not distinguish between those novels which use New Woman protagonists to convey a feminist message, and those which use the New Woman to promote an anti-feminist agenda.

29. See, for example, Hugh E.M. Stutfield, 'The Psychology of Feminism', *Blackwood's* January 1897: 115–16; and 'Tommyrotics', *Blackwood's* June 1895: 835.

30. Katherine Lyon Mix, *A Study in Yellow: The Yellow Book and its Contributors* (Lawrence: University of Kansas Press, 1960) 142–7.

31. *Punch* 27 April 1895: 203; quoted in Linda Dowling, 'The Decadent and the New Woman in the 1890s', *Nineteenth-Century Fiction* 33.4 (1979): 444–5. See Dowling for an analysis of the literary relationship between and public perceptions of the decadent and the New Woman. See also Showalter, *Sexual Anarchy*, esp. ch. 9, 'Decadence, Homosexuality, and Feminism'.

32. Stutfield's 'Tommyrotics' provides an example of how critics associated decadence, homosexuality, and the New Woman with one another. There is as much homophobia as there is gynephobia in this essay: there are many derisive references to Oscar Wilde, and Stutfield calls Walt Whitman 'that obscene old American twaddler' (839).

33. George Egerton, 'A Keynote to *Keynotes*' in *Ten Contemporaries: Notes Toward Their Definitive Biography*, ed. John Gawsworth [Terence Armstrong] (London: Ernest Benn, 1932) 58.

34. By adopting a male pseudonym, Egerton was not striving to gain acceptance as a male writer but, rather, trying to protect herself from personal attacks that the sexual frankness of her fiction would inevitably prompt. This strategy was in vain, however, for knowledge of her sex became known almost immediately after the

publication of her stories, and personal attacks did indeed ensue.

35. Quoted in Terence de Vere White, ed., *A Leaf from the Yellow Book: The Correspondence of George Egerton* (London: Richards, 1958) 26.

36. The phrase is from *On the Physiological Debility of Woman* (1898) by Paul Möbius, quoted in Bram Dijkstra, *Idols of Perversity: Fantasies of Feminine Evil in Fin-de-Siècle Culture* (New York: Oxford University Press, 1986) 172.

37. W.T. Stead, 'The Novel of the Modern Woman', *Review of Reviews* 10 (1894): 68.

38. Gosse, 'Decay' 116.

39. The campaign that the humor magazine *Punch* waged against the New Woman also reached an apex of derision and mockery in 1895.

40. B.A. Crackanthorpe, 'Sex in Modern Literature', *Nineteenth Century* April 1895: 607, 611; D.F. Hannigan, 'Sex in Fiction', *Westminster Review* 143 (1895): 617, 624.

41. Stutfield, 'Tommyrotics' 843; James Ashcroft Noble, 'The Fiction of Sexuality', *Contemporary Review* April 1895: 490, 494; M.O.W.O. [Mrs Oliphant], 'The Anti-Marriage League', *Blackwood's* January 1896: 137, 140, 149; Stutfield, 'Tommy-rotics' 836, 839.

42. B.A. Crackanthorpe, 'Sex in Modern Literature' 614.

43. Stutfield, 'Tommyrotics' 833; Noble, 'The Anti-Mariage League' 498.

44. M.O.W.O. [Mrs Oliphant], 'The Anti-Marriage League' 149.

45. Stutfield, 'Tommyrotics' 844.

46. ibid. 842, 845.

47. Walter Besant's novel *The Revolt of Man* (1882) provides an illuminating example of the pervasive anxiety at the end of the century about unstable gender roles and the increasing power of women. It depicts the horrors of a twentieth-century England completely dominated by women, and the subsequent revolt of men to return women to their proper sphere. See Showalter, *Sexual Anarchy* 41–4.

48. E. Lynn Linton, 'Partisans' 463; and 'Nearing the Rapids', *New Review* 10 (1894): 302; Rubinstein, *Before the Suffragettes* 167.

49. See Rubinstein, *Before the Suffragettes* 58–63, for a fascinating account of 'the Lanchester affair', which involved Edith Lanchester, the highly educated daughter of an architect, and James Sullivan, who was from a working-class background. Their daughter, the actress Elsa Lanchester, also tells the story of her mother's rebellion and subsequent socialist and suffrage activities in *Elsa Lanchester Herself* (New York: St. Martin's, 1983) 1–19.

50. *Jude the Obscure* was first published serially in *Harper's New Monthly Magazine*, from December 1894 to November 1895. *Jude* was published in book form on 1 November 1895, although the book itself was dated 1896.

51. Quoted in Boumelha, *Thomas Hardy and Women* 133.

52. Robert Yelverton Tyrrell, '*Jude the Obscure*', *Fortnightly Review* 1 June 1896: 858.

53. Early in Hardy's career he was willing to follow the advice of his editor, Leslie Stephen, and avoid anything in his novels that might be considered 'dangerous' for family reading; thus the serial versions of his novels were not significantly different from the book editions. But by the late 1880s, as Hardy became more interested in the realistic depiction of relations between the sexes, he was forced to

write bowdlerized versions of *The Mayor of Casterbridge* (1886), *Tess of the d'Urbervilles* and *Jude the Obscure* for serial publication, which were quite different from the final (and sexually frank) book versions. See Mary Ellen Chase, *Thomas Hardy from Serial to Novel* (New York: Russell & Russell, 1964) for a detailed account of these changes.

54. Hardy was familiar with the work of several New Woman writers, such as Caird and Grand. He copied out passages from Egerton's *Keynotes* into his notebook, and wrote her a letter praising her stories. See Boumelha, *Thomas Hardy and Women* 135–6; Cunningham, *New Women* 105–6; and *The Collected Letters of Thomas Hardy*, vol. 2, 1893–1901, eds Richard Little Purdy and Michael Millgate (Oxford; Clarendon Press, 1980) 102.

55. Review of *Jude the Obscure* in *Nation* 6 February 1896: 124.

56. Gosse, 'Tyranny' 14.

57. Tyrrell, '*Jude the Obscure*' 857.

58. Richard Le Gallienne, review of *Jude the Obscure*, *Idler* February 1896: 115.

59. '"Hill-Top Novels" and the Morality of Art', *Spectator* 23 November 1895: 722–3; A. J. Butler, 'Mr. Hardy as a Decadent', *National Review* May 1896: 384–90; M.O.W.O. [Mrs Oliphant], 'The Anti-Marriage League' 138

60. Tyrrell, '*Jude the Obscure*' 858

61. *World* 13 November 1895: 113.

62. *Nation* 6 February 1896: 124

63. Quoted in Patrick Parrinder and Robert M. Philmus, eds, *H.G. Wells's Literary Criticism* (Sussex: Harvester, 1980) 79.

64. Stutfield, 'Psychology' 117.

65. Maud Churton Braby, *Modern Marriage and How to Bear It* (1909; London: T. Werner Laurie, n.d.) 6–7.

66. H.G. Wells, *The Wife of Sir Isaac Harman* (1914; London: Hogarth, 1986) 258.

67. See Hynes, *Edwardian Turn* 261–4; Patricia Stubbs 24–5.

68. Rubinstein, *Before the Suffragettes* 201.

69. Amy Cruse, *After the Victorians* (London: Allen & Unwin, 1938) 212.

70. Review of *A Lady and Her Husband*, by Amber Reeves. *Bookman* July 1914: 557.

CHAPTER TWO

Epigraphs: Maud Churton Braby, *Modern Marriage and How to Bear It* (1909; London: T. Werner Laurie, n.d.) 4; E.M. Forster, 'Pessimism in Literature' (1906), reprinted in *Albergo Empedocle and Other Writings* (New York: Liveright, 1971) 135–6; John Galsworthy, *The Man of Property* (1906; New York: Signet, 1967) 190.

1. Jane Lewis asserts, in *Women in England 1870–1950: Sexual Division and Social Change* (Bloomington: Indiana University Press, 1984), that 'for all women marriage conferred a higher status than spinsterhood . . . marriage remained the normative expectation of women of all classes' (3). For historical information on Edwardian women and marriage, see also Suzanne Buckley, 'The Family and the Role of

Women', in *The Edwardian Age: Conflict and Stability 1900–1914*, ed. Alan O'Day (Hamden, CT: Archon, 1979) 133–43; Carol Dyhouse, *Feminism and the Family in England 1880–1939* (Oxford: Basil Blackwell, 1989); Paul Thompson, *The Edwardians: The Remaking of British Society* (Bloomington: Indiana University Press, 1975); and Lewis. Duncan Crow's anecdotal study *The Edwardian Woman* (New York: St. Martin's Press, 1978) is also useful.

2. Braby, *Modern Marriage* 90.

3. See J.A. and Olive Banks, *Feminism and Family Planning in Victorian England* (New York: Schocken, 1964); Lewis, *Women in England* 5–6, 117.

4. Braby, *Modern Marriage* 8.

5. Chapman, *Marriage Questions* 10.

6. See Braby, *Modern Marriage* 14–25, 85–8.

7. Maud Churton Braby, *The Love–Seeker: A Guide to Marriage* (London: Herbert Jenkins, 1913) 42.

8. ibid. 54–5.

9. ibid. 59; Braby, *Modern Marriage* 12.

10. See Cynthia L. White, *Women's Magazines 1693–1968* (London: Michael Joseph, 1971) 77–91, for a discussion of this and other developments in periodicals for women during the Edwardian years.

11. See Andrew Rosen, *Rise Up, Women! The Militant Campaign of the Women's Social and Political Union 1903–1914* (London: Routledge & Kegan Paul, 1974), esp. ch. 17, 'The Great Scourge', 203–15.

12. Lucy Re-Bartlett, *Sex and Sanctity* (London: Longmans, 1912); quoted in Jeffreys, *The Spinster and Her Enemies* 91.

13. Lucy Re-Bartlett, *The Coming Order* (London: Longmans, 1911); quoted in Jeffreys, *The Spinster and Her Enemies* 41.

14. See Boone, *Tradition Counter Tradition*, esp. ch. 3, 'Narrative Structure in the Marriage Tradition', for an extended analysis of these basic plot structures. See also Evelyn J. Hinz, 'Hierogamy versus Wedlock: Types of Marriage Plots and Their Relationships to Genres of Prose Fiction', *Publication of the Modern Language Association of America* 91 (1976) 900–13.

15. Walter Sichel, 'Some Phases in Fiction', *Fortnightly Review* August 1902: 287.

16. Quoted in Doris Langley Moore, *E. Nesbit* (London: Ernest Benn, 1933) 179–80.

17. E.M. Forster, *Aspects of the Novel* (1927; Harmondsworth: Penguin, 1976) 50.

18. Forster, 'Pessimism' 144.

19. On New Year's Eve 1904, Forster resolved to 'get a less superficial idea of women'; by New Year's Eve 1908, he was able to report: '[i]n society, I take more than I did to young women'. But intimacy with women was extremely difficult for Forster, and in his New Year's Eve review of 1911 he mourned the fact that he was close to only one woman – Florence Barger, the wife of a friend, who also happened to be an enthusiastic supporter of women's suffrage. See P.N. Furbank, *E.M. Forster: A Life. Volume I, The Growth of the Novelist (1879–1914)* (London: Secker & Warburg, 1977) 122, 171, 204.

20. Quoted in ibid. 199.

21. Forster, 'Pessimism' 134; Forster, 'A View without a Room: Old Friends Fifty Years Later', *The New York Times Book Review* 27 July 1958: 192; quoted in Furbank, *E.M. Forster* 165.
22. Quoted in Karen Usborne, *'Elizabeth'* (London: Bodley Head, 1986) 110.
23. Katherine Mansfield noted in her journal: 'I can never be perfectly certain whether Helen was got with child by Leonard Bast or by his fatal forgotten umbrella. All things considered, I think it must have been the umbrella.' Quoted in *E.M. Forster: The Critical Heritage*, ed. Philip Gardner (London: Routledge & Kegan Paul, 1973) 162.
24. Quoted in Furbank, *E.M. Forster* 190.
25. E.M. Forster, 'Terminal Note', *Maurice* (New York: Norton, 1987) 250.
26. Ada Leverson, *The Limit* 1911 (London: Chapman & Hall, 1950) 112.
27. For a discussion of the two-suitor convention in British fiction, see Jean E. Kennard, *Victims of Convention* (Hamden, CT: Archon, 1978) 9–20.
28. Galsworthy once compiled a list of twenty-four different causes in which he was actively involved; they included divorce law reform and women's suffrage. The list is reprinted in Catherine Dupré, *John Galsworthy: A Biography* (New York: Coward, McCann & Geoghegan, 1976) 144.
29. Letter from John Galsworthy to unidentified correspondent, 20 September 1913; quoted in James Gindin, *John Galsworthy's Life and Art: An Alien's Fortress* (London: Macmillan, 1987) 325.
30. Letter from John Galsworthy to Sir Arthur Quiller Couch, 21 October 1913; quoted in ibid. 334.
31. Letter from John Galsworthy to unidentified correspondent, 20 September 1913; quoted in ibid. 325
32. Letter from John Galsworthy to Edward Garnett, 1 June 1905; quoted in ibid. 159. Galsworthy also refers to his 'negative method' in the preface to his novel *Fraternity* (1909): it 'shows what men might be, by choosing defective characters and environments and giving their defects due prominence'.
33. It is possible that Galsworthy drew some inspiration for Mrs Pendyce from his mother, who left Galsworthy's father after more than forty years of marriage and took a flat of her own in Kensington Palace Mansions. See Dupré, *John Galsworthy* 18.
34. Galsworthy refers to (and repudiates) his reputation as a revolutionary in his preface to *The Country House*. In an undated letter to Galsworthy about a review of *The Man of Property*, Joseph Conrad wrote: 'Your consecration as a dangerous man by *The Spectator* fills me with a pure and ecstatic joy.' Quoted in Gindin, *John Galsworthy's Life and Art* 173.
35. Divorce is not represented in Galsworthy's fiction until *In Chancery*, published in 1920.
36. For discussions of the Edwardian divorce reform movement, see Hynes, *Edwardian Turn* 186–92, 208–111; Lawrence Stone, *Road to Divorce: England 1530–1987* (Oxford: Oxford University Press, 1990) 390–93. See also Roderick Phillips, *Putting Asunder: A History of Divorce in Western Society* (Cambridge: Cambridge

University Press, 1988) 479–515, for a survey of the social issues related to divorce reform during the Edwardian years.

37. Review of *Whom God Hath Joined*, *Staffordshire Sentinel* 8 November 1906. Quoted in *Arnold Bennett: The Critical Heritage*, ed. James Hepburn (London: Routledge & Kegan Paul, 1981) 198.

38. Although the reviewer in the *Academy* called it 'disgusting, sordid, utterly vile', most of the reviews of *Whom God Hath Joined* were positive, though not overly enthusiastic. See Hepburn, *Arnold Bennett* 33.

39. Arnold Bennett, 'Unfinished Perusals', in *Books and Persons* (New York: Doran, 1917) 236.

40. Bennett wrote about Rhoda Broughton, Mary Cholmondeley and Sarah Grand for the *Academy*; those essays were reprinted with others on popular fiction of the 1890s in *Fame and Fiction: An Enquiry into Certain Popularities* (London: Richards, 1901). See also Katherine Lyon Mix, *A Study in Yellow: The Yellow Book and Its Contributors* (Lawrence; University of Kansas Press, 1960) 174.

41. Letter from Arnold Bennett to Lucie Simpson, 30 January 1904; quoted in Hepburn, *Arnold Bennett* 179.

42. *Spectator* 21 November 1903: 873–4.

43. Rebecca West, *Arnold Bennett Himself* (New York: John Day, 1931) 16–17.

44. See Kennard, *Victims of Convention*, for a discussion of the history of this convention and an analysis of how it functions in female *Bildungsromane*.

45. This ideology of commitment is evident in the lives of several Edwardian novelists: Ada Leverson remained married to her husband, even after he emigrated to Canada with his illegitimate daughter; Pearl Craigie (John Oliver Hobbes) suffered through a divorce from her husband, but never considered herself free to remarry; and although Elizabeth von Arnim's second marriage (to Earl Russell) proved a disaster, she never divorced him.

46. I have taken the term 'novel of awakening' from Susan J. Rosowski's essay 'The Novel of Awakening', reprinted in *The Voyage In: Fictions of Female Development*, eds. Elizabeth Abel, Marianne Hirsch and Elizabeth Langland (Hanover, NH: University Press of New England, 1983) 49–68, but I have adapted the paradigm she outlines for my own purposes. Whereas she sees the awakening of the heroines in the novels she analyzes as inevitably 'an awakening to limitations', I see the heroines in several Edwardian novels moving beyond that initial awakening into another more positive and constructive one.

47. All biographical information is from John Harwood, *Olivia Shakespear and W.B. Yeats: After Long Silence* (London: Macmillan, 1989).

48. Blanche Leppington, 'The Debrutalisation of Man', *Contemporary Review* June 1895: 742.

49. One exception to this is the unconventional marital arrangement depicted in Violet Hunt's *The Celebrity at Home* (1904) and *The Celebrity's Daughter* (1913); the young heroine's father is a famous novelist who chooses to keep his marriage a secret from his reading public. His dual existence eventually leads to his involvement in an extramarital affair.

50. The narrative of Clara Dawes in *Sons and Lovers* conforms to the dominant pattern of the Edwardian marriage problem. Clara, a feminist, leaves her husband and has a brief affair with Paul Morel, but eventually she returns to her marriage.

CHAPTER THREE

Epigraphs: Edward Garnett, preface to *Downward: A Slice of Life* by Maud Churton Braby (1910; London: T. Werner Laurie, n.d.) n. pag.; Miles Franklin, *My Brilliant Career* (1901; New York: Washington Square, 1980) 132.

1. See Lisa Tickner, *The Spectacle of Women: Imagery of the Suffrage Campaign 1907–14* (Chicago: University of Chicago Press, 1988) ch. 4, 'Representation', for an account of the development and use of some of these types.
2. Mary Findlater, *A Narrow Way* (London: Methuen, 1901) 28.
3. W.R. Greg, writing in the *National Review* in April 1862, called unmarried women 'redundant', and recommended a program of government-sponsored emigration which would distribute these women to places where they could marry and fulfill their 'natural' destinies.
4. 'The Spinster. By One', *The Freewoman* 23 November 1911: 10–11.
5. Rebecca West, letter to the editor, *The Freewoman* 1 August 1912: 213.
6. See Laura L. Doan, 'Introduction', and Judy Little, '"Endless Different Ways": Muriel Spark's Re-Visions of Spinsters', in *Old Maids to Radical Spinsters: Unmarried Women in the Twentieth-Century Novel*, ed. Laura L. Doan (Urbana: University of Illinois Press, 1991), for two recent attempts to redefine 'spinster' in a positive, feminist fashion; both writers use the term to indicate an independent woman who chooses to remain unmarried, although that was certainly not its meaning in the early twentieth century.
7. Hynes, *Edwardian Turn* 289–91.
8. Eileen Mackenzie, *The Findlater Sisters: Literature and Friendship* (London: John Murray, 1964) 24.
9. In this context, it is significant that there were few Edwardian novels which centered upon a woman's work life. It is not entirely surprising in that the actual work experience of men or women usually plays a minor role in fiction. But given the novelty of women working in business and professional situations at the time, it is of interest that their experiences did not inspire more fiction. Usually, women's work is mentioned in a peripheral and negative way: in Bennett's *Leonora*, for example, one of the daughters works in her father's office, but resents having to do so. In Reeves's *A Lady and Her Husband* and in H.G. Wells's *The Wife of Sir Isaac Harman*, upper-middle-class wives become involved in improving the working conditions of tea-shop waitresses, but the waitresses are at best minor characters. W.L. George was exceptional in his realistic portrayal of the life of a waitress in *A Bed of Roses* (1911), but the novel is transformed into a sensation novel when the heroine chooses to be a rich man's mistress rather than live in poverty. E.V. Lucas, in his novel *Mr. Ingleside* (1910), depicts the frustrations of a young

woman searching for meaningful work, but in that her need for work is spiritual rather than material, her problems are not taken very seriously. Bennett's *Hilda Lessways* and Hunt's *White Rose of Weary Leaf* (discussed in this chapter) are rare instances of novels in which the heroines' work is a significant part of their characterization.

10. See Carol Dyhouse, *Girls Growing Up in Late Victorian and Edwardian England* (London: Routledge & Kegan Paul, 1981) 72–8; Martha Vicinus, *Independent Women: Work and Community for Single Women 1850–1920* (Chicago: University of Chicago Press, 1985) 150–52, for interesting discussions of the lack of role models for young girls, and the conflict between ideals of femininity and intellectual achievement.

11. Nadine is the daughter of the first Dodo, the heroine of Benson's enormously popular novel *Dodo, A Detail of the Day*, published in 1893.

12. Lucas Malet (Mary Kingsley), 'The Threatened Re-Subjection of Woman', *Fortnightly Review* 83 (May 1905): 816. Emma Goldman, Havelock Ellis, and the Swedish feminist Ellen Key did not differ all that much from conservatives such as Eliza Lynn Linton and Walter Heape in their criticism of the feminist movement for not emphasizing love and motherhood. See Blake, *Love and the Woman Question* 116–17.

13. See, for example, the diaries and letters of Ruth Slate and Eva Slawson, two Edwardian working women, reprinted in *Dear Girl*, ed. Tierl Thompson (London: Women's Press, 1987), especially ch. 6, 'The Free Woman'.

14. *Nation* 19 October 1912; *Outlook* 29 June 1912. These reviews are quoted in *The Trespasser*, ed. Elizabeth Mansfield (Cambridge: Cambridge University Press, 1981) 25. All subsequent biographical information about Lawrence is from Mansfield's introduction, 3–28.

15. Mansfield, *The Trespasser* 9. Ford Madox Ford warned Lawrence that the eroticism of *The Trespasser* would ruin his reputation, but Lawrence's editor, Edward Garnett, disagreed, and although two scenes were slightly altered, nothing was deleted. But Ford's criticisms did worry Lawrence, for he subsequently wrote to Garnett: 'I don't want to be talked about in an *Ann Veronica* fashion', referring to the scandal which arose around the publication of H. G. Wells's novel about a young woman who runs away with a married man. Quoted in ibid. 20.

16. Rebecca West, review of *The Spinster* and *The Trespasser*, *The Freewoman* 11 July 1912: 147–8.

17. There are a few fleeting references to the jealous love that Helena's friend, Louisa, feels for her, but Lawrence never indicates that Helena feels anything other than friendship for Louisa. Lawrence deals with lesbianism more explicitly in *The Rainbow*, where his depiction of Ursula's affair with Winifred Inger (who is characterized explicitly as a feminist) is extremely negative. Although unmarried Edwardian women did have 'passionate friendships' with one another, they were not identified at the time (by themselves or others) as lesbian relationships. See Lillian Faderman, *Surpassing the Love of Men: Romantic Friendship and Love Between Women from the Renaissance to the Present* (New York: William Morrow, 1981)

147–230; and Vicinus, *Independent Women* 152–62, for discussions of the nature of these friendships. One of the few (if not the only) explicitly lesbian character in Edwardian fiction is Anne Yeo in Ada Leverson's *Love's Shadow*; she suffers from an unrequited love for the heroine, Hyacinth Verney, and is portrayed with sympathy as well as a kind of awed respect for her unconventionality.

18. Both Dyhouse and Vicinus discuss how many women educators defined their duties in explicltly maternal terms, and Vicinus points out that several prominent unmarried feminists adopted children later in life (*Independent Women* 43–4).

19. See Lewis, *Women in England* 97–100, for a discussion of these movements, and of how the ideology of motherhood functioned during the Edwardian period.

20. *Freewoman* 30 November 1911: 31.

21. Quoted in Furbank, *E.M. Forster* 189.

22. Frances Swiney, *Awakening of Women* (1899(?)) 3rd ed (London: William Reeves 1908) 95–8. Discussed in Blake, *Love and the Woman Question* 115.

23. This is corroborated by an entry in Bennett's journal, in which he noted, with discouragement, 'I didn't seem to be getting near the personality of Hilda in my novel'. Quoted in Lucas, *Arnold Bennett* 146.

24. Quoted in Marie and Robert Secor, 'Modern Love in Violet Hunt's *White Rose of Weary Leaf*', *Turn-of-the-Century Women* Summer 1985: 49.

25. See Kimberley Reynolds, *Girls Only? Gender and Popular Children's Fiction in Britain, 1880–1910* (New York: Harvester, 1990), esp. ch. 5, 'A literature of their own? Or what girls read', 91–110.

26. See Mary Cadogan and Patricia Craig, *You're a Brick, Angela!* (London: Gollancz, 1986), especially 'Introduction' and ch. 5, 'The New Woman and The New Girl', for an account of these developments in fiction for girls.

27. See, for example, Evelyn Sharp, *The Making of a Schoolgirl* (1897; New York: Oxford University Press, 1989).

28. When I use the term *Bildungsroman*, I am using it to indicate the novel genre as it has traditionally been defined – which also means as it has been defined through novels featuring male protagonists. I am aware of how feminist critics have been working to expand the definition of the *Bildungsroman* in order to accommodate uniquely female paradigms of development; see, for example, Abel, Hirsch and Langland, eds, *The Voyage In: Fictions of Female Development*. But my focus here is not on how the generic model is unsuitable for the depiction of female development in the nineteenth century, or on how women writers have revised or transformed the *Bildungsroman*, but rather on the ways in which social, cultural and economic changes in the early twentieth century made the creation of a female *Bildungsroman* possible.

CHAPTER FOUR

Epigraph: Elizabeth Robins, *Way Stations* (New York: Dodd, Mead, 1913) 250–51.

1. For the historical information in this and subsequent summaries of the suffrage

movement, I have relied upon the following sources: W. Lyon Blease, *The Emancipation of English Women* (1910; New York: Arno, 1977); Les Garner, *Stepping Stones to Women's Liberty: Feminist Ideas in the Women's Suffrage Movement 1900–1918* (Rutherford, NJ: Fairleigh Dickinson University Press, 1984); Brian H. Harrison, *Separate Spheres: The Opposition to Women's Suffrage in Britain* (New York: Holmes & Meier, 1978); Robins, *Way Stations*; Rosen, *Rise Up, Women!*; and Vicinus, 'Male Space and Women's Bodies: The Suffragette Movement', in *Independent Women*.

2. See Tickner, *The Spectacle of Women*, for a visual history of the suffrage demonstrations.

3. Rosen, *Rise Up, Women!* 53.

4. Evelyn Sharp, *Unfinished Adventure: Selected Reminiscences from an Englishwoman's Life* (London: John Lane, 1933) 133.

5. The communities for single women that Vicinus discusses in *Independent Women*, such as sisterhoods, women's colleges and settlement houses, are not evident in the Edwardian fiction I have studied; occasionally, a female character's college education is referred to, but it is not depicted. The only exceptions I know of are Maud Churton Braby's *Downward* (1910), in which the heroine's nursing career is briefly described; Margaret L. Woods's *The Invader* (1907), which devotes a few chapters to its heroine's career at Oxford; and H.G. Wells's *Ann Veronica*. See Nina Auerbach, *Communities of Women: An Idea in Fiction* (Cambridge, MA: Harvard University Press, 1978); and Boone, *Tradition Counter Tradition* 278–318, for analyses of the rare instances in British fiction in which communities of women are represented.

6. See Katherine Stern, 'The War of the Sexes in British Fantasy Literature of the Suffragette Era', *Critical Matrix* 3.3 (1987): 78–109.

7. Quoted in Robins, *Way Stations* 112–13.

8. Tickner, *The Spectacle of Women* 84–5. In its account of the large NUWSS demonstration in June 1908, the *Sunday Times* noted that the WWSL was 'a very merry lot'.'

9. Dupré, *John Galsworthy* 136; Violet Hunt, *I Have This to Say: The Story of My Flurried Years* (New York: Boni & Liveright, 1926) 52. Hunt also recalled that she was unable to convert her good friend Henry James to the cause, but insists that his resistance had nothing to do with the subsequent slashing of his portrait in the Royal Academy by a suffragette.

10. This pamphlet was published by the WFL, probably in 1913. Ford also apparently contributed anonymous articles on women's suffrage for Christabel Pankhurst to publish. See David Dow Harvey, *Ford Madox Ford 1873–1939: A Bibliography of Works and Criticism* (Princeton: Princeton University Press, 1962) 38. Ford later wrote sympathetically about the suffrage movement in his four-part novel *Parade's End* (1924–8).

11. Sharp notes that during her prison hunger strike, officials tried to appease her not only through elegant meals but by giving her *Multitude and Solitude* to read instead of the previously offered bound volumes of *Little Folks*. However, she 'was soon too giddy to read'. See *Unfinished Adventure* 147.

12. *Way Stations* 6.
13. ibid. 5, 14.
14. ibid. 246, 251.
15. See Julie Holledge, *Innocent Flowers: Women in the Edwardian Theater* (London: Virago, 1981); and Lis Whitelaw, *The Life and Rebellious Times of Cicely Hamilton: Actress, Writer, Suffragist* (London: Women's Press, 1990) for detailed accounts of these developments.
16. A.J.R., ed., *The Suffrage Annual and Women's Who's Who* (London: Stanley Paul, 1913) 10–11.
17. Whitelaw, *Cicely Hamilton* 82.
18. See Hynes, *Edwardian Turn* 201–4 for a discussion of *Votes for Women!*
19. See Showalter, *Literature* 220–24 for a discussion of the sexual politics of *The Convert*.
20. Garner, *Stepping Stones* 2–3.
21. Quoted in Lewis, *Women in England* 95; Garner, *Stepping Stones* 31.
22. Cicely Hamilton, *Marriage as a Trade* (1909; London: Women's Press, 1981) 147.
23. De Pratz wrote for *La Fronde*, a Paris daily managed and written entirely by women.
24. For a fascinating view of the lives of two such average women, see Thompson, ed., *Dear Girl*.
25. Garner, *Stepping Stones* 46.
26. In this chapter, I use the term 'suffrage writers' to refer to writers who supported the suffrage movement through their fiction.
27. Rosen, *Rise Up, Women!* 138–9.
28. Both novels also feature curiously similar scenes in which one of the characters has a quasi-religious encounter with Mrs Despard, leader of the WFL.
29. See *Prisons and Prisoners* (1914; London: Virago, 1988) for Constance Lytton's own moving account of her ordeal.
30. Sylvia Pankhurst, however, briskly notes under recreations that she 'has no time for any'.
31. Ironically, the WSPU was the suffrage organization that placed the most emphasis on traditional ideals of femininity. But their veneration of motherhood and the home eventually gave way to virulent expressions of man-hatred, best exemplified by Christabel's WSPU pamphlet *The Great Scourge and How to End It* (London, 1913), in which she claims that 75 to 80 per cent of British men had venereal disease. To the cry 'Votes for Women!' Christabel added 'and Chastity for Men!'.
32. An exception is A.C. Fox Davies's novel *The Sex Triumphant* (London: Routledge, 1909), discussed in Stern, 'The War of the Sexes' 103–6.
33. Quoted in George Bullock, *Marie Corelli: The Life and Death of a Best-Seller* (London: Constable, 1940) 223.
34. See Showalter, *Literature* 227–32, for an analysis of several of Ward's novels and of her attitudes towards the suffrage movement.
35. Maids play an interesting role in at least three Edwardian novels about the suffrage movement. Delia's maid is used not only to reveal her essential femininity but also

to remind her of her proper class role as protector of the lower classes. Conversely, Gertrude's callous treatment of the servants confirms her lack of feminine virtues, and exposes her working-class origins. In *Margaret Holroyd*, the function of Margaret's maid is similar to that of Delia's: she reminds Margaret that her rightful place is back at her country home, where she can benevolently educate the working women in her village. But in *The Convert*, Robins uses Vida's maid to represent the narrow perspective of the working classes, for the maid abandons Vida when she becomes a suffragette.

36. See Annie Kenney, *Memories of a Militant* (London: Edward Arnold, 1924); Christabel Pankhurst, *Unshackled: The Story of How We Won the Vote* (London: Hutchinson, 1959); E. Sylvia Pankhurst, *The Suffragette Movement* (London: Longmans, Green, 1931); Emmeline Pethick-Lawrence, *My Part in a Changing World* (London: Gollancz, 1938); and Lord F.W. Pethick-Lawrence, *Fate Has Been Kind* (London: Hutchinson, 1942).

37. Some notable exceptions to this are Sinclair's *The Tree of Heaven* (1917), Woolf's *Night and Day* (1919), Rebecca West's *The Judge* (1922), and Ford's tetralogy *Parade's End* (1924–8). In all these novels the suffrage movement is presented seriously as an important factor in understanding pre-war England.

CHAPTER FIVE

Epigraphs: H.G. Wells, 'The Contemporary Novel' (1914), reprinted in Leon Edel and Gordon N. Ray, eds, *Henry James and H.G. Wells* (Urbana: University of Illinois Press, 1958) 134; May Sinclair, 'The Novels of Dorothy Richardson', *Egoist* 5 (April 1918) 57.

1. H.G. Wells, 'The Contemporary Novel' (1914), rpt. in Edel and Ray 148, 138.

2. Jane Marcus, for example, praises Sinclair as 'by far the most talented of the feminist novelists', but concludes that 'we do not think of her as an artist of genius but as a technically clever imitator of the innovators of form', 'Elizabeth Robins', Dissertation, Northwestern University, 1973, 344–5.

3. See *H.G. Wells: The Critical Heritage*, ed. Patrick Parrinder (London: Routledge & Kegan Paul, 1972) 21, 157–74.

4. Quoted in ibid. 169–70. The fact that Wells depicts Ann Veronica's father as constantly complaining about the influence of 'rubbishy novels' and 'Woman-who-Diddery' upon young women clearly indicates that he expected *Ann Veronica* to be greeted with negative criticism, and to be compared to 1890s fiction.

5. The similarities between Ann Veronica and Wells's second wife, Catherine Wells, are rarely noted, although she was a former science student of his with whom he ran away, in 1894, while still married to his first wife. With that in mind, the novel can be read as a fantasy about a sexually fulfilling marriage with Catherine, as well as a retelling of his affair with Reeves.

6. Quoted in Parrinder, *H.G. Wells* 165.

7. This attitude is evident throughout Wells's fiction and non-fiction. For example, neither feminism nor the British nor American suffrage movements are discussed

in his expansive *Outline of History* (1920; New York: Macmillan, 1930). And *In the Days of the Comet* (1906), his controversial novel about a 'Great Change', instigated by a comet, which transforms the world into a utopia, the only appreciable effect on the lives of women is that they are allowed complete sexual freedom.

8. Letter from Wells to Henry James, 19 October 1912; rpt. in Edel and Ray, *Henry James and H.G. Wells* 169.

9. It is significant in this context that the novel was written under the close supervision of Catherine Wells and was a conscious attempt by H.G. to appease the reading public who had been alienated by *Ann Veronica* and *The New Machiavelli*.

10. Letter from Wells to Henry James, 19 October 1912; rpt. in Edel and Ray, *Henry James and H.G. Wells* 169.

11. *A Lady and Her Husband* was reviewed in *Bookman* in July 1914; *The Wife of Sir Isaac Harman* was published in October 1914. In his 'Postscript' to *Experiment in Autobiography*, Wells indicates that he and Reeves had occasional contact from the time of the birth of their child until the war, after which they did not see each other for several years. See G.P. Wells, ed., *H.G. Wells in Love: Postscript to* An Experiment in Autobiography (Boston, MA: Little, Brown, 1984) 83.

12. See von Arnim's autobiography *All the Dogs of My Life* (London: Heinemann, 1936) 89–97; and Karen Usborne, *'Elizabeth': The Author of* Elizabeth and Her German Garden (London: Bodley Head, 1986) 55, 156–70.

13. It is interesting that both titles – *The Pastor's Wife* and *The Wife of Sir Isaac Harman* – emphasize the heroine's position as a possession rather than an individual with her own name, whereas Reeves's *A Lady and Her Husband* gives the heroine precedence, and ranks the husband as a possession.

14. In general, very little interest has been shown in Wells's affair with von Arnim, even though it lasted several years, and he devotes an entire chapter to it in 'Postscript' to *Experiment in Autobiography*. As is the case with Dorothy Richardson and Violet Hunt, two other mature women who had affairs with Wells, it seems that von Arnim's age makes her less appealing to biographers than the young virgins, Amber Reeves and Rebecca West. The exception to this is David G. Smith, *H.G. Wells: Desperately Mortal* (New Haved, CT: Yale University Press, 1986); he spends several pages discussing von Arnim and *The Pastor's Wife*, although he looks at the latter strictly in terms of how it relates to Wells's life, not his fiction.

15. Wells also praised von Arnim in his essay 'The Contemporary Novel': 'And in some cases the whole art and delight of a novel may lie in the author's personal interventions; let such novels as *Elizabeth and Her German Garden* and the same writer's *Elizabeth in Rügen*, bear witness' (141–2).

16. The phrase 'novel of awakening' is taken from Susan J. Rosowski's essay, 'The Novel of Awakening', in *The Voyage In: Fictions of Female Development*.

17. Hrisey Zegger notes this connection, especially in terms of the character of Wyndham in *Audrey Craven*, whom she sees as a figure for Moore. See her study *May Sinclair* (Boston, MA: Twayne, 1976) 156 n. 18.

18. Letter from May Sinclair to H.G. Wells, 16 October 1915; quoted in ibid. 55.

19. This recalls Wells's response to Rebecca West when she insisted that they get married: '. . . you could never be a wife. You want a wife yourself – you want sanity and care and courage and patience behind you just as much as I do', Wells, ed., *H.G. Wells in Love* 99.

20. Virginia Woolf's important essay 'Modern Fiction' (1925), in which she discusses this shift in the focus of fiction, is clearly indebted to Sinclair's influential review 'The Novels of Dorothy Richardson', 51–9.

21. May Sinclair, introduction, *Villette*, by Charlotte Brontë (London: Dent, 1909) xiv–xv.

22. See Zegger, *May Sinclair* 57 and 143–7, for a corresponding assessment of the role of *The Three Sisters* and Sinclair in general in the development of the modern novel.

23. Elaine Showalter is one of the few critics who has examined the connections between the feminist fiction of the Edwardian period and that of the following decades; see ch. 9, 'The Female Aesthetic', in *A Literature of Their Own* 240–62. For an analysis of this line of development in terms of representation of female consciousness, see Sydney Janet Kaplan, *Feminine Consciousness in the Modern British Novel* (Urbana: University of Illinois Press, 1975); she looks at the novels of Sinclair, Richardson and Woolf, among others. See also Gillian Hanscombe and Virginia L. Smyers, *Writing for Their Lives: The Modernist Women 1910–1940* (Boston, MA: Northeastern University Press, 1987) 188.

24. See Zegger, *May Sinclair* 73–78.

25. Sinclair and Lawrence were frequently bracketed together by literary critics in the first four decades of the century due to their common interests in psychology and sexuality. See Curtis Brown, *Contacts* (London: Cassell, 1935) 69; Frierson, *The English Novel in Transition* 223–5; Frank Swinnerton, *The Georgian Literary Scene 1910–1935* (1935; London: Hutchinson, 1969) 295–327; and William York Tindall, *Forces in Modern British Literature* (New York: Knopf, 1947) 318–59. Rebecca West's comment, made late in her life, that Sinclair 'was at once La Princess de Clèves, and the Brontës – and wished to be D.H. Lawrence', is typical of how Sinclair's innovations were reinterpreted as imitation in the latter half of the century. Quoted in T.E.M. Boll, *Miss May Sinclair: Novelist* (Rutherford, NJ: Fairleigh Dickinson University Press, 1973) 159.

26. I am indebted to Showalter's analysis of the drawbacks of the turn toward consciousness in women's fiction, although I think that her arguments could also be usefully extended to modernist fiction written by men. See *A Literature of Their Own* 240–43.

27. Several of these essays have been reprinted in *The Gender of Modernism: A Critical Anthology*, ed. Bonnie Kime Scott (Bloomington: Indiana University Press, 1990) 436–78.

28. See Virginia Woolf, 'Mr. Bennett and Mrs. Brown' (1924) rpt. in *The Captain's Death Bed and Other Essays* (New York: Harcourt, Brace, 1950); and 'Modern Fiction', in *The Common Reader* (1925; New York: Harcourt Brace, 1948) 207–18; Rebecca West, 'Uncle Bennett', in *The Strange Necessity* (1928; London: Virago, 1987) 199–214.

SELECT BIBLIOGRAPHY

PRIMARY SOURCES: WORKS BY NOVELISTS

Allen, Grant. *The Woman Who Did*. Boston, MA: Roberts, 1895.

[Arnim, Elizabeth von]. *Elizabeth and Her German Garden*. London: Macmillan, 1898.

——. *The Pastor's Wife*. By the author of *Elizabeth and Her German Garden*. 1914. New York: Penguin–Virago, 1987.

—— *All the Dogs of My Life*. Garden City, NY: Doubleday, Doran, 1936.

Bennett, Arnold. *Fame and Fiction: An Enquiry into Certain Popularities*. London: Richards, 1901.

——. *Leonora*. 1903. New York: Doran, n.d.

——. *Sacred and Profane Love*. London: Chatto & Windus, 1905.

——. *Whom God Hath Joined*. 1906. New York: Doran, n.d.

——. *The Old Wives' Tale*. London: Chapman & Hall, 1908.

——. *Hilda Lessways*. New York: Dutton, 1911.

——. 'Unfinished Persuals.' *Books and Persons*. New York: Doran, 1917. 235–8.

Benson, E.F. *Dodo the Second*. 1914. Rpt. in *Dodo: An Omnibus*. London: Hogarth, 1986.

Braby, Maud Churton. *Modern Marriage and How to Bear It*. 1909. London: T. Werner Laurie, n.d.

——. *Downward: A Slice of Life*. 1910. London: T. Werner Laurie, n.d.

——. *The Love-Seeker: A Guide to Marriage*. London: Herbert Jenkins, 1913.

Brooke, Emma Frances. *A Superfluous Woman*. London: Heinemann, 1894.

Broughton, Rhoda. *Between Two Stools*. 1912. London: Stanley Paul, n.d.

Caird, Mona. 'A Defence of the So-Called "Wild Women".' *Nineteenth Century* May 1892: 811–29.

——. *The Daughters of Danaus*. 1894. Afterword Margaret Morganroth Gullette. New York: Feminist Press, 1989.

Colmore, Gertrude. *Suffragette Sally*. 1911. Rpt. as *Suffragettes: A Story of Three Women*. London: Pandora, 1984.

Cross, Victoria [Vivian Cory]. 'Theodora: A Fragment.' *The Yellow Book* January 1895: 156–88.

Danby, Frank [Julia Frankau]. *Joseph in Jeopardy*. London: Methuen, 1912.

De Pratz, Claire. *Elisabeth Davenay*. London: Mills & Boon, 1909.

Dixon, Ella Hepworth. *The Story of a Modern Woman*. London: Heinemann, 1894.

Dodge, Janet. *Tony Unregenerate*. London: Duckworth, 1912.

Dowie, Ménie Muriel. *Gallia*. London: Methuen, 1895.

Dudeney, Mrs Henry. *Rachel Lorian*. New York: Duffield, 1909.

——. *A Runaway Ring*. London: Heinemann, 1913.

Egerton, George [Mary Chavelita Dunne Bright]. *Keynotes*. 1893. Introd. Martha Vicinus. London: Virago, 1983.

——. *Discords*. 1894. Introd. Martha Vicinus. London: Virago, 1983.

——. 'A Keynote to *Keynotes*.' In *Ten Contemporaries: Notes Toward their Definitive Bibliography*. Ed. John Gawsworth [Terence Armstrong]. London: Ernest Benn, 1932. 57–65.

Farr, Florence. *Modern Woman: Her Intentions*. London: Frank Palmer, 1910.

——. *The Solemnization of Jacklin: Some Adventures on the Search for Reality*. London: A.C. Fifield, 1912.

Findlater, Jane and Mary. *Crossriggs*. 1908. New York: Penguin–Virago, 1986.

Findlater, Mary. *A Narrow Way*. London: Methuen, 1901.

——. *The Rose of Joy*. London: Methuen, 1903.

——. *Tents of a Night*. London: Smith, Elder, 1914.

Ford, Ford Madox. *The Good Soldier*. 1915. New York: Vintage, 1983.

Ford, Isabella O. *On the Threshold*. London: Arnold, 1895.

Forster, E.M. *Where Angels Fear to Tread*. 1905. New York: Vintage, n.d.

——. 'Pessimism in Literature.' Paper read to Working Men's College Old Students' Club, 1 December 1906. Rpt. in *Albergo Empedocle and other writings*. Ed. George H. Thomson. New York: Liveright, 1971. 135–6.

——. *The Longest Journey*. 1907. New York: Vintage, 1962.

——. *A Room with a View*. 1908. New York: Bantam, 1988.

——. *Howards End*. 1910. New York: Vintage, n.d.

——. *Maurice* [1913–14]. 1971. New York: Norton, 1987.

——. *Aspects of the Novel*. 1927. Harmondsworth: Penguin, 1976.

——. *The Lucy Novels: Early Sketches for A Room with a View*. Ed. Oliver Stallybrass. Abinger Edition. London: Edward Arnold, 1977.

Franklin, Miles. *My Brilliant Career*. 1901. Introd. Carmen Callil. New York: Washington Square, 1980.

——. *My Career Goes Bung* [1902]. 1946. London: Virago, 1980.

Galsworthy, John. *Jocelyn*. 1898. Afterword Catherine Dupré. New York: Holt, Rinehart, 1976.

——. *The Man of Property*. 1906. New York: NAL, 1967.

——. *The Country House*. 1907. New York: Scribner's, 1926.

——. *Fraternity*. 1909. New York: Scribner's, 1930.

George, W.L. *A Bed of Roses*. 1911. New York: Boni & Liveright, 1919.

Gissing, George. *The Unclassed*. London: Chapman & Hall, 1884.

——. *The Odd Women*. 1893. Introd. Elaine Showalter. New York: NAL, 1983.

——. 'The Place of Realism in Fiction.' *Humanitarian* July 1895. Rpt. in *Victorian Novelists after 1885*. Dictionary of Literary Biography 18. Ed. Ira B. Nadel and William E. Fredeman. Detroit: Gale, 1983 357–8.

Glyn, Elinor. *Three Weeks*. New York: Duffield, 1907.

Grand, Sarah [Frances McFall]. *The Heavenly Twins*. New York: Cassell, 1893.

——. *The Beth Book: Being a Study of the Life of Elizabeth Caldwell Maclure, A Woman of Genius*. 1897. Introd. Elaine Showalter. New York: Dial, 1980.

Hamilton, Cicely. *Diana of Dobson's*. New York: Grosset & Dunlap, 1908.

——. *Marriage as a Trade*. 1909. Introd. Jane Lewis. London: Women's Press, 1981.

——. *Just to Get Married: A Comedy in Three Acts*. New York: Samuel French, 1914.

Hardy, Thomas. *The Woodlanders*. London: Macmillan, 1887.

——. *Jude the Obscure*. 1895. London: Osgood, McIlvaine, 1896.

——. *Tess of the d'Urbervilles*. 1891. London: Penguin, 1978.

Harrison, Marie. *The Woman Alone*. London: Holden & Hardingham, 1914.

Hill, Ethel. *The Unloved*. London: Greening, 1909.

Hobbes, John Oliver [Pearl Craigie]. *The Dream and the Business*. London: Unwin, 1906.

Hope, Anthony [A.H. Hawkins]. *The Great Miss Driver*. 1908. New York: Doubleday, 1909.

Hunt, Violet. *The Celebrity at Home*. London: Chapman & Hall, 1904.

——. *White Rose of Weary Leaf*. London: Heinemann, 1908.

——. *The Celebrity's Daughter*. London: Stanley Paul, 1913.

——. *I Have This to Say: The Story of My Flurried Years*. New York: Boni & Liveright, 1926.

Iota [Kathleen Mannington Caffyn]. *A Yellow Aster*. London: Hutchinson, 1894.

James, Henry. 'The Future of the Novel.' 1900. Rpt. in *The Future of the Novel: Essays on the Art of Fiction*. Ed. Leon Edel. New York: Vintage, 1956. 30–42.

——. 'The Death of a Lion.' Rpt. in *The Yellow Book: A Selection*. Ed. Norman Denny. London: Bodley Head, 1950. 17–62.

Lawrence, D.H. *The White Peacock*. London: Heinemann, 1911.

——. *The Trespasser*. 1912. Ed. Elizabeth Mansfield. Cambridge: Cambridge University Press, 1981.

——. *Sons and Lovers*. London: Duckworth, 1913.

—— 'Daughters of the Vicar.' 1914. In *The Complete Short Stories*. Vol. 1. New York: Viking, 1973. 136–86.

——. *The Rainbow*. London: Methuen, 1915.

Legge, Margaret. *A Semi-Detached Marriage*. London: Alston Rivers, 1912.

——. *The Rebellion of Esther*. London: Alston Rivers, 1914.

Leverson, Ada. *Love's Shadow*. 1908. Rpt. in *The Little Ottleys*. Introd. Sally Beauman. London: Virago. 1982.

——. *The Limit*. 1911. London: Chapman & Hall, 1950.

——. *Tenterhooks*. 1912. Rpt. in *The Little Ottleys*. Introd. Sally Beauman. London: Virago, 1982.

——. *Love at Second Sight*. 1916. Rpt. in *The Little Ottleys*. Introd. Sally Beauman. London: Virago, 1982.

Lowndes, Marie Belloc. *Studies in Wives*. London: Heinemann, 1909.

Lucas, E.V. *Mr. Ingleside*. New York: Macmillan, 1910.

Mackenzie, Compton. *Carnival*. 1912. New York: Appleton, 1921.

Masefield, John. *Multitude and Solitude*. 1909. New York: Macmillan, 1916.

Maud, Constance Elizabeth. *No Surrender*. 1911. London: Duckworth, 1912.

Mayor, F.M. *The Third Miss Symons*. 1913. Pref. John Masefield. Introd. Susan Hill. London: Virago, 1980.

Moore, George. *A Mummer's Wife*. London: Vizetelly, 1885.

——. *Literature at Nurse, or Circulating Morals*. 1885. Ed. Pierre Coustillas. Atlantic Highlands, NJ: Humanities Press, 1976.

——. *A Drama in Muslin: A Realistic Novel*. London: Vizetelly, 1886.

——. *Esther Waters*. London: Walter Scott, 1894.

——. 'Mildred Lawson.' In *Celibates*. 1895. New York: Brentano's, 1915. 1–254.

Nesbit, E. [Edith Bland]. *The Red House*. London: Methuen, 1902.

Reeves, Amber. *The Reward of Virtue*. London: Heinemann, 1911.

——. *A Lady and Her Husband*. New York: Putnam's, 1914.

Richardson, Henry Handel [Ethel Florence Lindesay Richardson]. *The Getting of Wisdom*. 1910. Introd. Germaine Greer. London: Virago, 1981.

Robins, Elizabeth. *The Convert*. 1907. Introd. Jane Marcus. Old Westbury, NY: Feminist Press, 1980.

——. *Votes for Women!* Rpt. in *How the Vote Was Won and other suffragette plays*. Ed. Dale Spender and Carole Hayman. London and New York: Methuen, 1985.

——. *Way Stations*. New York: Dodd, Mead, 1913.

Saki [H.H. Munro]. 'The Gala Programme: An Unrecorded Episode in Roman History.' Rpt. in *The Short Stories of Saki*. Introd. Christopher Morley. New York: Modern Library, 1958. 617–20.

Schreiner, Olive. *The Story of an African Farm*. 1883. Harmondsworth: Penguin, 1987.

Sedgwick, Anne Douglas. *Amabel Channice*. New York: Century, 1908.

Shakespear, Olivia. *Uncle Hilary*. London: Methuen, 1910.

Sharp, Evelyn. *The Making of a Schoolgirl*. 1897. New York: Oxford University Press, 1989.

——. *Rebel Women*. London: A.C. Fifield, 1910.

——. *Unfinished Adventure: Selected Reminiscences from an Englishwoman's Life*. London: John Lane, 1933.

Sinclair, May. *Audrey Craven*. Edinburgh and London: Blackwood, 1897.

——. *Superseded*. 1901. New York: Henry Holt, 1906.

——. *The Divine Fire*. London: Constable, 1904.

——. *The Helpmate*. London: Constable, 1907.

——. *The Judgment of Eve*. 1907. New York: Harper, 1908.

——. *Kitty Tailleur*. London: Constable, 1908.

——. *The Creators*. New York: Century, 1910.

——. *The Flaw in the Crystal*. New York: Dutton, 1912.

——. *The Three Brontës*. London: Hutchinson, 1912.

——. *The Combined Maze*. London: Hutchinson, 1913.

——. *The Three Sisters*. 1914. Introd. Jean Radford. London: Virago, 1982.

——. 'The Novels of Dorothy Richardson.' *Egoist* 5 (April 1918): 57–9.

Swan, Annie S. *Margaret Holroyd, or The Pioneers*. London: Hodder & Stoughton, 1910.

Syrett, Netta. *Nobody's Fault*. London: John Lane, 1896.

Thurston, Katherine Cecil. *Max*. New York: Harper, 1910.

Truscott, L. Perry [Katharine Spicer-Jay Hargrave]. *Motherhood*. London: Unwin, 1904.

Wales, Hubert [John Pigott]. *The Yoke*. London: John Long, 1907.

——. *The Spinster*. London: John Long, 1912.

Ward, Mrs Humphry. *Marcella*. New York and London: Macmillan, 1894.

——. *Daphne or 'Marriage à la Mode'*. London: Cassell, 1909.

——. *Delia Blanchflower*. 1914. London: Ward, Lock, 1915.

Wells, H.G. *A Modern Utopia*. London: Chapman & Hall, 1905.

——. *In the Days of the Comet*. 1906. Introd. Brian Aldiss. London: Hogarth, 1985.

——. *Ann Veronica*. 1909. Introd. Jeanne MacKenzie. London: Virago, 1980.

——. *Tono-Bungay*. 1909. Lincoln: University of Nebraska Press, 1978.

——. *The New Machiavelli*. New York: Duffield, 1910.

——. *The Passionate Friends*. 1913. Introd. Victoria Glendinning. London: Hogarth, 1986.

——. *Marriage*. New York: Duffield, 1912.

——. 'The Contemporary Novel [1914]. Rpt. in *Henry James and H.G. Wells*. Ed. Leon Edel and Gordon N. Ray. Urbana: University of Illinois Press, 1958. 131–56.

——. *The Wife of Sir Isaac Harman*. 1914. Introd. Victoria Glendinning. London: Hogarth, 1986.

——. *The Outline of History: Being a Plain History of Life and Mankind*. London: G. Newnes, 1920.

——. *An Experiment in Autobiography: Discoveries and Conclusions of a Very Ordinary Brain (Since 1866)*. 1934. Boston, MA: Little, Brown, 1962.

——. *H.G. Wells in Love: Postscript to an* Experiment in Autobiography. Ed. G.P. Wells. Boston, MA: Little, Brown, 1984.

West, Rebecca. 'Indissoluble Matrimony.' *Blast*, 20 June 1914. Rpt. in *The Young Rebecca: Writings of Rebecca West 1911–1917*. Ed. Jane Marcus. New York: Viking, 1982. 267–89.

Willcocks, M.P. *The Wingless Victory*. London: John Lane, 1907.

——. *Wings of Desire*. London: John Lane, 1912.

Woods, Margaret L. *The Invader*. New York: Harper, 1907.

PRIMARY SOURCES: SELECTED BOOKS, ARTICLES, AND REVIEW ESSAYS

A.J.R., ed. *The Suffrage Annual and Women's Who's Who*. London: Stanley Paul, 1913.

Besant, Walter, E. Lynn Linton and Thomas Hardy. 'Candour in English Fiction.' *New Review* 2 (January 1890): 6–21.

——. et al. 'Tree of Knowledge.' *New Review* 10 (1894): 675–90.

Blease, W. Lyon. *The Emancipation of English Women*. 1910. New York: Arno, 1977.

Butler, A.J. 'Mr. Hardy as a Decadent.' *National Review* May 1896: 384–90.

Chapman, Elizabeth R[achel]. *Marriage Questions in Modern Fiction, and Other Essays on Kindred Subiects*. London: John Lane, 1897.

Cooper, Frederic Taber. 'Feminine Unrest and Some Recent Novels.' *Bookman* December 1909: 382–8.

Courtney, W.L. *The Feminine Note in Fiction*. London: Chapman & Hall, 1904.

Crackanthorpe, B.A. 'Sex in Modern Literature.' *Nineteenth Century* April 1895: 607–16.

Crackanthorpe, Hubert. 'Reticence in Literature: Some Roundabout Remarks.' *The Yellow Book* July 1894: 259–69.

Douglas, Sir George. 'On Some Critics of *Jude the Obscure*.' *Bookman* January 1896: 120–22.

Fawcett, Millicent Garrett. 'The Woman Who Did.' *Contemporary Review* May 1895: 625–31.

The Freewoman and *The New Freewoman*. London, November 1911–December 1913.

'Gallia.' *Saturday Review* 23 March 1895: 383–4.

Gosse, Edmund. 'The Tyranny of the Novel.' 1892. Rpt. in *Questions at Issue*. London: Heinemann, 1893. 3–31.

——. 'The Limits of Realism in Fiction.' In *Questions at Issue*. London: Heinemann, 1893. 137–54.

——. 'The Decay of Literary Taste.' *North American Review* 161 (1895): 109–18.

Hannigan, D.F. 'Sex in Fiction.' *Westminster Review* 143 (1895): 616–25.

——. 'The Tyranny of the Modern Novel.' *Westminster Review* 143 (1895): 303–6.

'"Hill-Top Novels" and the Morality of Art.' *Spectator* 23 November 1895: 722–4.

Hogarth, Janet E. 'Literary Degenerates.' *Fortnightly Review* April 1895: 586–92.

Kenton, Edna. 'A Study of the Old "New Women".' Part I *Bookman* April 1913: 154–8; Part II *Bookman* May 1913: 261–4.

Le Gallienne, Richard. Review of *Jude the Obscure*. *Idler* February 1896: 114–15.

Leppington, Blanche. 'The Debrutalisation of Man.' *Contemporary Review* June 1895: 725–43.

Lilly, W.S. 'The New Naturalism.' *Fortnightly Review* 1 August 1885: 240–56.

Linton, E. Lynn. 'The Wild Women as Politicians.' *Nineteenth Century* July 1891: 79–88.

——. 'The Wild Women as Social Insurgents.' *Nineteenth Century* October 1891: 596–605.

——. 'The Partisans of the Wild Women.' *Nineteenth Century* March 1892: 455–64.

——. 'Nearing the Rapids.' *New Review* 10 (1894): 302–10.

Malet, Lucas [Mary Kingsley]. 'The Threatened Re-Subjection of Woman.' *Fortnightly Review* May 1905: 806–19.

M.O.W.O. [Mrs Oliphant]. 'The Anti-Marriage League.' *Blackwood's* January 1896: 135–49.

Noble, James Ashcroft. 'The Fiction of Sexuality.' *Contemporary Review* April 1895: 490–98.

Nordau, Max. *Degeneration* [1895]. Trans. from the second edition of

German. Introd. George L. Mosse. New York: Howard Fortig, 1968.

Review of *Jude the Obscure*, by Thomas Hardy. *Nation* 6 February 1896: 123–35.

Review of *Jude the Obscure*, by Thomas Hardy. *World* 13 November 1895: 113.

Sichel, Walter. 'Some Phases in Fiction.' *Fortnightly Review* August 1902: 285–300.

'Socio-Literary Portents.' *Speaker* 22 December 1894: 683–5.

[Stead. W.T.] 'The Novel of the Modern Woman.' *Review of Reviews* 10 (1894): 64–74.

Stutfield, Hugh E.M. 'Tommyrotics.' *Blackwood's* June 1895: 833–45.

——. 'The Psychology of Feminism.' *Blackwood's* January 1897: 104–17.

Tyrrell, Robert Yelverton. 'Jude the Obscure.' *Fortnightly Review* 1 June 1896: 857–64.

Waugh, Arthur. 'Reticence in Literature.' *The Yellow Book* April 1894: 201–19.

'The Year in Review.' *Athenaeum* 6 January 1894: 17–18.

SECONDARY SOURCES

Abel, Elizabeth, Marianne Hirsch and Elizabeth Langland, eds. *The Voyage In: Fictions of Female Development*. Hanover, NH: University Press of New England, 1983.

Altick, Richard. *The English Common Reader: A Social History of the Mass Reading Public, 1800–1900*. Chicago: University of Chicago Press, 1957.

Ardis, Ann. *New Women, New Novels: Feminism and Early Modernism*. New Brunswick, NJ: Rutgers University Press, 1990.

Banks, J.A. and Olive. *Feminism and Family Planning in Victorian England*. New York: Schocken, 1964.

Batchelor, John. *The Edwardian Novelists*. New York: St. Martin's, 1982.

Batho, Edith C. and Bonamy Dobrée. *The Victorians and After 1830–1914*. Introductions to English Literature, vol. IV. Rev. edn. London: Cresset, 1950.

Beauman, Nicola. *A Very Great Profession: The Woman's Novel 1914–39*. London: Virago, 1984.

Benstock, Shari. 'Expatriate Modernism: Writing on the Cultural Rim.' *Women's Writing in Exile*. Eds Mary Lynn Broe and Angela Ingram. Chapel Hill, NC: University of North Carolina Press, 1989. 19–40.

Bjørhovde, Gerd. *Rebellious Structures: Women Writers and the Crisis of the Novel 1880–1900*. Oslo: Norwegian University Press, 1987.

Blain, Virginia, Isobel Grundy and Patricia Clements, eds. *The Feminist Companion to Literature in English: Women Writers from the Middle Ages to the Present*. New Haven, CT: Yale University Press, 1990.

Blake, Kathleen. *Love and the Woman Question in Victorian Literature: The Art of Self-Postponement*. Sussex: Harvester, 1983.

Boll, Theophilus E.M. *Miss May Sinclair: Novelist*. Rutherford, NJ: Fairleigh Dickinson University Press, 1973.

Boone, Joseph Allen. *Tradition Counter Tradition: Love and the Form of Fiction*. Chicago: University of Chicago Press, 1987.

Boulton, James T., ed. *The Letters of D.H. Lawrence*. Vol. 1. Cambridge: Cambridge University Press, 1979.

Boumelha, Penny. *Thomas Hardy and Women: Sexual Ideology and Narrative Form*. Sussex: Harvester, 1982.

Brooks, Peter. *Reading for the Plot: Design and Intention in Narrative*. New York: Random House, 1985.

Buckley, Jerome. *Season of Youth: The Bildungsroman from Dickens to Golding*. Cambridge, MA: Harvard University Press, 1974.

Buckley, Suzanne. 'The Family and the Role of Women.' In *The Edwardian Age: Conflict and Stability 1900–1914*. Ed. Alan O'Day. Hamden, CT: Archon, 1979. 133–43.

Bullock, George. *Marie Corelli: The Life and Death of a Best-Seller*. London: Constable, 1940.

Burkhart, Charles. *Ada Leverson*. New York: Twayne, 1973.

Cadogan, Mary and Patricia Craig. *You're a Brick, Angela!: The Girls' Story 1839–1985*. London: Gollancz, 1986.

Calder, Jenni. *Women and Marriage in Victorian Fiction*. New York: Oxford University Press, 1976.

Charms, Leslie de. *Elizabeth of the German Garden*. Garden City, NY: Doubleday, 1959.

Colby, Vineta. *The Singular Anomaly: Women Novelists of the Nineteenth Century*. New York: New York University Press, 1970.

Crosland, Margaret. *Beyond the Lighthouse: English Women Novelists in the Twentieth Century*. New York: Taplinger, 1981.

Crow, Duncan. *The Edwardian Woman*. New York: St. Martin's, 1978.

Cruse, Amy. *After the Victorians*. London: Allen & Unwin, 1938.

Cunningham, Gail. 'The "New Woman Fiction" of the 1890s.' *Victorian Studies* 18 (1973): 177–86.

———. *The New Woman and the Victorian Novel*. London: Macmillan, 1978.

Daims, Diva and Janet Grimes, eds. Asst. ed. Doris Robinson. *Toward A Feminist Tradition: An Annotated Bibliography of Novels in English by Women 1891–1920*. New York: Garland, 1982.

Dangerfield, George. *The Strange Death of Liberal England*. 1935. London: MacGibbon & Kee, 1966.

DeKoven, Marianne. 'Gendered Doubleness and the "Origins" of

Modernist Form.' *Tulsa Studies in Women's Literature* 8.1 (1989): 19–42.

Dowling, Linda. 'The Decadent and the New Woman in the 1890s.' *Nineteenth-Century Fiction* 33.4 (1979): 434–53.

Drabble, Margaret. *Arnold Bennett*. New York: Knopf, 1974.

DuPlessis, Rachel Blau. *Writing Beyond the Ending: Narrative Strategies of Twentieth-Century Women Writers*. Bloomington: Indiana University Press, 1985.

Dupré, Catherine. *John Galsworthy: A Biography*. New York: Coward, McCann, & Geoghegan, 1976.

Dyhouse, Carol. *Girls Growing Up in Late Victorian and Edwardian England*. London: Routledge & Kegan Paul, 1981.

——. *Feminism and the Family in England 1880–1939*. Oxford: Basil Blackwell, 1989.

Edel, Leon and Gordon N. Ray, eds. *Henry James and H.G. Wells: A Record of their Friendship, their Debate on the Art of Fiction, and their Quarrel*. Urbana: University of Illinois Press, 1958.

Ellmann, Richard. 'Two Faces of Edward.' In *Edwardians and Late Victorians*. English Institute Essays, 1959. Ed. Richard Ellmann. New York: Columbia University Press, 1960.

Felski, Rita. *Beyond Feminist Aesthetics: Feminist Literature and Social Change*. Cambridge, MA: Harvard University Press, 1989.

Fernando, Lloyd. *'New Women' in the Late Victorian Novel*. University Park: Pennsylvania State University Press, 1977.

Frierson, William C. *The English Novel in Transition 1885–1940*. Norman: University of Oklahoma Press, 1942.

Furbank, P.N. *E.M. Forster: A Life. Volume I. The Growth of the Novelist (1879–1914)*. London: Secker & Warburg, 1977.

Gardner, Philip, ed. *E.M. Forster: The Critical Heritage*. London: Routledge & Kegan Paul, 1973.

Garner, Les. *Stepping Stones to Women's Liberty: Feminist Ideas in the Women's Suffrage Movement 1900–1918*. Rutherford, NJ: Fairleigh Dickinson University Press, 1984.

Gilmour, Robin. *The Novel in the Victorian Age: A Modern Introduction*. London: Edward Arnold, 1986.

Gindin, James. *John Galsworthy's Life and Art: An Alien's Fortress*. London: Macmillan, 1987.

Glyn, Anthony. *Elinor Glyn*. Rev. edn. London: Hutchinson, 1968.

Hanscombe, Gillian, and Virginia L. Smyers. *Writing for Their Lives: The Modernist Women 1910–1940*. Boston, MA: Northeastern University Press, 1987.

Harris, Wendell V. 'Egerton: Forgotten Realist.' *Victorian Newsletter* 33 (1968): 31–5.

——. 'John Lane's Keynotes Series and the Fiction of the 1890s.' *PMLA* 83 (1968): 1407–13.

Harrison, Brian. *Separate Spheres: The Opposition to Women's Suffrage in Britain*. New York: Holmes & Meier, 1978.

Harwood, John. *Olivia Shakespear and W.B. Yeats: After Long Silence*. London: Macmillan, 1989.

Heilbrun, Carolyn G. *Writing a Woman's Life*. 1988. New York: Ballantine, 1989.

Hepburn, James, ed. *Arnold Bennett: The Critical Heritage*. London: Routledge & Kegan Paul, 1981.

Hewitt, Douglas. *English Fiction of the Early Modern Period 1890–1940*. London and New York: Longman, 1988.

Hite, Molly. *The Other Side of the Story: Structures and Strategies of Contemporary Feminist Narrative*. Ithaca, NY: Cornell University Press, 1989.

Houghton, Walter E. *The Victorian Frame of Mind. 1830–1870*. New Haven, CT: Yale University Press, 1957.

Hunter, Jefferson. *Edwardian Fiction*. Cambridge, MA: Harvard University Press, 1982.

Hynes, Samuel. *The Edwardian Turn of Mind*. Princeton, NJ: Princeton University Press, 1968.

——. *Edwardian Occasions: Essays on English Writing in the Early Twentieth Century*. New York: Oxford University Press, 1972.

Jackson, Holbrook. *The Eighteen Nineties: A Review of Art and Ideas at the Close of the Nineteenth Century*. New York: Knopf, 1922.

Jeffreys, Sheila. *The Spinster and Her Enemies: Feminism and Sexuality 1880–1930*. London: Pandora, 1985.

Johnson, R. Brimley. *Some Contemporary Novelists (Women)*. London: Leonard Parsons, 1920.

Kaplan, Sydney Janet. *Feminine Consciousness in the Modern British Novel*. Urbana: University of Illinois Press, 1975.

Kennard, Jean E. *Victims of Convention*. Hamden, CT: Archon, 1978.

Kent, Susan. *Sex and Suffrage in Britain, 1860–1914*. Princeton, NJ: Princeton University Press, 1987.

Kermode, Frank. 'The English Novel, *circa* 1907.' In *The Art of Telling: Essays on Fiction*. Cambridge, MA: Harvard University Press, 1983.

Kersley, Gillian. *Darling Madame: Sarah Grand and Devoted Friend*. London: Virago, 1983.

Lago, Mary and P.N. Furbank, eds. *Selected Letters of E.M. Forster. Volume One 1879–1920*. Cambridge, MA: Harvard University Press, 1983.

Lanser, Susan Sniader. *Fictions of Authority: Women Writers and Narrative Voice*. Ithaca, NY and London: Cornell University Press, 1992.

Lester, John A. *Journey Through Despair: Transformations in British Literary Culture 1880–1914*. Princeton, NJ: Princeton University Press, 1968.

Lewis, Jane. *Women in England 1870–1950: Sexual Division and Social Change*. Bloomington: Indiana University Press, 1984.

Lovell, Terry. *Consuming Fiction*. London: Verso, 1987.

Lucas, John. *Arnold Bennett: A Study of His Fiction*. London: Methuen, 1974.

MacInnes, Colin. 'The Heart of a Legend: The Writings of Ada Leverson.' *Encounter* 92 (May 1961): 46–56.

Mackenzie, Eileen. *The Findlater Sisters: Literature and Friendship*. London: John Murray, 1964.

MacKenzie, Norman and Jeanne MacKenzie. *H.G. Wells: A Biography*. New York: Simon & Schuster, 1973.

Marcus, Jane. 'Elizabeth Robins.' Dissertation. Northwestern University, 1973.

———, ed. *The Young Rebecca: Writings of Rebecca West 1911–1917*. New York: Viking, 1982.

May, J. Lewis. *John Lane and the Nineties*. London: John Lane, 1936.

Miller, Nancy K. 'Emphasis Added: Plots and Plausibilities in Women's Fiction.' Rpt. in *The New Feminist Criticism: Essays on Women, Literature, and Theory*. Ed. Elaine Showalter. New York: Pantheon, 1985.

Mix, Katherine Lyon. *A Study in Yellow: The Yellow Book and its Contributors*. Lawrence: University of Kansas Press, 1960.

Moore, Doris Langley. *E. Nesbit, A Biography*. London: Ernest Benn, 1933.

Muir, Edwin. *The Present Age from 1914*. Introductions to English Literature, vol. V. London: Cresset, 1939.

Mulford, Wendy. 'Socialist-Feminist Criticism: A Case Study, Women's Suffrage and Literature, 1906–14.' In *Re-Reading English*. Ed. Peter Widdowson. London: Methuen, 1982.

Oldfield, Sybil. *Spinsters of this Parish: The Life and Times of F.M. Mayor and Mary Sheepshanks*. London: Virago, 1984.

Parrinder, Patrick, ed. *H.G. Wells: The Critical Heritage*. London: Routledge & Kegan Paul, 1972.

———, and Robert Philmus, eds. *H.G. Wells's Literary Criticism*. Sussex: Harvester, 1980.

Pratt, Annis, with Barbara White, Andrea Loewenstein and Mary Wyer. *Archetypal Patterns in Women's Fiction*. Bloomington: Indiana University Press, 1981.

Pritchett, V.S. 'Knightsbridge Kennels.' In *The Living Novel and Later Appreciations*. Rev. edn. New York: Random House, 1964. 263–9.

Purdy, Richard Lttle and Michael Millgate, eds. *The Collected Letters of Thomas Hardy*. Vol. 2, 1893–1901. Oxford: Clarendon Press, 1980.

Reynolds, Kimberley. *Girls Only? Gender and Popular Children's Fiction in Britain. 1880–1910*. New York: Harvester, 1990.

Rose, Jonathan. *The Edwardian Temperament 1895–1919*. Athens, OH: Ohio University Press, 1986.

Rosen, Andrew. *Rise Up, Women! The Militant Campaign of the Women's*

Social and Political Union 1903–1914. London: Routledge & Kegan Paul, 1974.

Rover, Constance. *The Punch Book of Women's Rights*. South Brunswick, NJ: A.S. Barnes, 1970.

Rubinstein, David. *Before the Suffragettes: Women's Emancipation in the 1890s*. Sussex: Harvester, 1986.

Scanlon, Leone. 'The New Woman in the Literature of 1883–1909.' *University of Michigan Papers in Women's Studies* 2.2 (1976): 133–59.

Schenck, Celeste M. 'Exiled by Genre: Modernism, Canonicity, and the Politics of Exclusion.' *Women's Writing in Exile*. Ed. Mary Lynn Broe and Angela Ingram. Chapel Hill: University of North Carolina Press, 1989. 226–50.

Scott, Bonnie Kime, ed. *The Gender of Modernism: A Critical Anthology*. Bloomington: Indiana University Press, 1990.

Secor, Marie. 'Violet Hunt, Novelist: A Reintroduction.' *English Literature in Transition* 19.1 (1976): 25–34.

——, and Robert Secor. 'Modern Love in Violet Hunt's *White Rose of Weary Leaf*.' *Turn-of-the-Century Women* Summer 1985: 43–50.

Showalter, Elaine. *A Literature of Their Own: British Women Novelists from Brontë to Lessing*. Princeton, NJ: Princeton University Press, 1977.

——. *Sexual Anarchy: Gender and Culture at the Fin de Siècle*. New York: Viking, 1990.

Smith, David C. *H.G. Wells: Desperately Mortal*. New Haven, CT: Yale University Press, 1986.

Stubbs, Patricia. *Women and Fiction: Feminism and the Novel 1880–1920*. Sussex: Harvester, 1979.

Swinnerton, Frank. *The Georgian Literary Scene 1910–1935*. 1935. London: Hutchinson, 1969.

Tanner, Tony. *Adultery and the Novel: Contract and Transgression*. Baltimore, MD: Johns Hopkins University Press, 1979.

Thompson, Paul. *The Edwardians: The Remaking of British Society*. Bloomington: Indiana University Press, 1975.

Thompson, Tierl, ed. *Dear Girl: The Diaries and Letters of Two Working Women 1897–1917*. London: Women's Press, 1987.

Thomson, David. *England in the Nineteenth Century (1815–1914)*. Harmondsworth: Penguin, 1987.

Tickner, Lisa. *The Spectacle of Women: Imagery of the Suffrage Campaign 1907–14*. Chicago: University of Chicago Press, 1988.

Todd, Janet, ed. *British Women Writers: A Critical Reference Guide*. New York: Continuum, 1989.

Torgovnick, Marianne. *Closure in the Novel*. Princeton, NJ: Princeton University Press, 1981.

Trotter, David. 'Edwardian Sex Novels.' *Critical Quarterly* 31.1 (1989): 92–106.

Tuchman, Gaye with Nina E. Fortin. *Edging Women Out: Victorian Novelists, Publishers, and Social Change.* New Haven, CT: Yale University Press, 1989.

Usborne, Karen. *'Elizabeth': The Author of* Elizabeth and Her German Garden. London: Bodley Head, 1986.

Vicinus, Martha, ed. *Suffer and Be Still: Women in the Victorian Age.* Bloomington: Indiana University Press, 1972.

——. *Independent Women: Work and Community for Single Women 1850–1920.* Chicago: University of Chicago Press, 1985.

Watt, Ian. *The Rise of the Novel: Studies in Defoe, Richardson, and Fielding.* Berkeley: University of California Press, 1957.

Wellington, Amy. *Women Have Told: Studies in the Feminist Tradition.* Boston, MA: Little, Brown, 1930.

West, Rebecca. *Arnold Bennett Himself.* New York: John Day, 1931.

——. 'Uncle Bennett.' In *The Strange Necessity: Essays and Reviews.* 1928. London: Virago, 1987. 199–214.

White, Cynthia. *Women's Magazines 1693–1968.* London: Michael Joseph, 1971.

White, Terence de Vere, ed. *A Leaf from the Yellow Book: The Correspondence of George Egerton.* London: Richards, 1958.

Whitelaw, Lis. *The Life and Rebellious Times of Cicely Hamilton: Actress, Writer, Suffragist.* London: Women's Press, 1990.

Woolf, Virginia. 'Mr. Bennett and Mrs. Brown.' 1924. Rept. in *The Captain's Death Bed and Other Essays.* New York: Harcourt, Brace, 1950. 94–119.

——. 'Modern Fiction.' In *The Common Reader.* 1925. New York: Harcourt Brace, 1948. 207–18.

Wyndham, Violet. *The Sphinx and Her Circle: A Biographical Sketch of Ada Leverson 1862–1933.* London: André Deutsch, 1963.

Zegger, Hrisey Dimitrakis. *May Sinclair.* Boston, MA: Twayne, 1976.

Zytaruk, George J., and James T. Boulton, eds. *The Letters of D.H. Lawrence.* Vol. II. Cambridge: Cambridge University Press, 1981.

INDEX

235

Index

Index

White, Amber Blanco, *See* Reeves, Amber
White, Cynthia, 210n.10
Whitelaw, Lis, 217n.15
Wilde, Oscar, 26, 31, 32, 36, 58, 207n.32
Willcocks, M. P., 70, 72, 81, 82
  The Wingless Victory, 71
  Wings of Desire, 72–3
Woman Question, 3, 13–14, 87
Women's Freedom League (WFL), 126,
  134–5, 138, 146, 216n.10, 217n.28
Women's Social and Political Union
  (WSPU), 125, 126, 133, 134, 138, 142,
  144, 146, 154–5, 159, 217n.31
women's suffrage movement, 32, 37, 38,
  40, 43, 49, 86, 125–7, 143–6, 154–5,
  216n.11
Women Writers' Suffrage League
  (WWSL), 128, 129, 130, 188, 216n.8
Woods, Margaret, 128, 129
  The Invader, 216n.5

Woolff, Virginia, 8–9, 27, 59, 195, 198–200,
  201, 220n.20
  Night and Day, 123, 218n.37
  The Voyage Out, 123
work, for women, 27–8, 40, 80, 81, 85–6,
  88–90, 92, 95, 98, 99, 104, 214n.13
  in *The Creators* (Sinclair), 189–93
  depicted in fiction, 91, 111, 113, 145,
  213–14n.9
  in Wells' novels, 172, 182, 183
working class women, 138–40, 144–5,
  150–1, 152
Wyllarde, Dolph, 71

The Yellow Book, 25–6, 58

Zangwill, Israel, 13, 14, 128
Zegger, Hrisey, 219n.17, 220nn. 22 and 24
Zola, Émile, 10, 11, 13, 23, 31, 33, 204–5n.1,
  205n.3